Kelly Nicole Banneyer
Editor

Separation Anxiety

Presentation and Intervention

nova
Medicine & Health
New York

DOI: https://doi.org/10.52305/GQJD3574

NOTICE TO THE READER

Library of Congress Cataloging-in-Publication Data

ISBN: 979-8-89530-386-3 (Softcover)
ISBN: 979-8-89530-476-1 (eBook)

Published by Nova Science Publishers, Inc. † New York

Contents

Chapter 1

Separation Anxiety Disorder: An Introduction

**Karin L. Price*
and Lindsay T. Ives**
Department of Pediatrics, Division of Psychology, Baylor College of Medicine, Houston, TX, USA

Abstract

This chapter provides a comprehensive introduction to Separation Anxiety Disorder (SAD), beginning with an overview of its diagnostic criteria according to the DSM-5. It differentiates normative separation anxiety, often seen in early childhood, from the clinical presentation of SAD, which involves excessive and developmentally inappropriate fear or distress regarding separation from attachment figures. The chapter reviews the prevalence of SAD in addition to an overview of common co-occurring conditions, such as other anxiety disorders and autism spectrum disorder. The chapter provides an overview of several common parent- and self-report questionnaires to measure symptoms and severity of SAD in youth. Finally, the chapter concludes with an overview of evidence-based treatment, with a particular focus on family-focused and exposure-based cognitive behavioral therapy (CBT).

Keywords: separation anxiety disorder (SAD), SAD prevalence, SAD assessment, SAD treatment

* Corresponding Author's Email: klprice@bcm.edu.

In: Separation Anxiety: Presentation and Intervention
Editor: Kelly Nicole Banneyer
ISBN: 979-8-89530-386-3

Diagnostic Criteria of Separation Anxiety Disorder

Separation anxiety disorder (SAD) is classified under Anxiety Disorders in the DSM-5-TR (American Psychiatric Association [APA], 2022). It is characterized by anxiety about leaving the home or separating from attachment figures that exceeds developmentally appropriate expectations (APA, 2022, p. 217). To meet diagnostic criteria, individuals must exhibit at least three of eight potential symptoms listed in Table 1.

To be diagnosed with SAD, symptoms should be present for at least four weeks in children and adolescents and for at least six months in adults. They must cause significant distress or impairment socially, academically, occupationally, or in another important domain. Symptoms should not be better explained by another mental disorder, such as resistance to change in autism spectrum disorder, delusions or hallucinations in psychotic disorders, refusal to leave home without a trusted individual in agoraphobia, concern about harm in generalized anxiety disorder, or worry about disease in illness anxiety disorder (APA, 2022, p. 217). The DSM-5 has removed a specific age of onset allowing for SAD to be diagnosed in adulthood, whereas it was previously thought to be a childhood disorder (2022). More information about SAD in adults can be found in Chapter 10 of this text.

Table 1. DSM-5 Diagnostic Symptoms of Separation Anxiety Disorder

1	Clinically significant distress upon anticipating or leaving the home or separating from major attachment figures
2	Excessive worry about attachment figures being lost or harmed (e.g., illness, injury, natural disaster, death)
3	Worry about oneself experiencing an event that causes separation from an attachment figure, such as being lost or kidnapped, becoming ill, or experiencing an accident
4	Reluctance or refusal to leave home or go to school or work because of worry about separation
5	Fear to be away from attachment figures while at home or outside the home
6	Significant distress or refusal to sleep away from home or without an attachment figure nearby
7	Recurrent nightmares about separation
8	Somatic symptoms such as headaches, stomachaches, nausea, or vomiting in anticipation of or after separating from attachment figures

Note: Three of the 8 symptoms are necessary for a diagnosis and must be present for at least 4 weeks

Normative Separation Anxiety and Separation Anxiety Disorder

Separation anxiety is a universal phase of human development that typically manifests between six and 12 months of age and usually remains observable until approximately three years of age. Evolutionarily, normative separation anxiety likely provided survival benefits given relatively significant and prolonged helplessness in human infancy and early childhood (Faust et al., 2020). Developmentally appropriate separation anxiety typically abates as a child develops a greater sense of autonomy, cognitive ability, and an understanding that a separated attachment figure will return (Battaglia, 2015). The re-emergence of transient separation anxiety is common in children when they enter school for the first time, and a child's physical separation from attachment figures to participate in academic settings is the most common precipitator for identifying SAD.

More significant than expected duration or intensity of separation anxiety symptoms may result in a diagnosis of SAD. SAD is an exaggeration of otherwise developmentally normal anxiety and manifests as excessive concerns, worry, and even dread of the actual or anticipated separation from an attachment figure or home. SAD has a significant impact on the child's quality of life and functioning across several areas, including school, social interactions, and close relationships.

As compared to developmentally typical separation anxiety, children with SAD often demonstrate prolonged school refusal behaviors that do not improve within a typical timeframe for "getting used to" a new environment. Behaviors reflective of SAD may include refusal to enter a school building, physically clinging to a caregiver, vocalizing somatic symptoms such as a headache or stomachache, and emotional/behavioral outbursts when separation or attempted separation occurs. Outbursts may include severe temper tantrums or aggression in young children, in addition to crying and clinging. These difficulties lead to impaired school functioning, including both acquisition of new learning and development of typical peer relationships (Ehrenreich et al., 2008).

In addition, children with SAD often display developmentally atypical separation concerns in the home environment that go beyond typical preferences for being with caregivers. For example, children with SAD may be afraid to be in a room alone, refuse to sleep alone, or shadow their parent, even in their comfortable home environment (Ehrenreich, et al, 2008).

Prevalence

SAD is one of the most frequently occurring disorders in children and adolescents (Beesdo et al., 2009). According to the DSM-5, approximately 4% of children meet criteria for SAD within a given 6- to 12-month period (APA, 2022, p. 218). The longitudinal Great Smoky Mountains Study found cumulative prevalence rates for SAD to be 4.8% in males and 5.2% in females (Copeland et al., 2014). Within pediatric clinical samples, 7.6% of children met diagnostic criteria for SAD in a large, multi-site study in the United States (Ginsburg et al., 2014). SAD has been found to peak during early childhood, with rates decreasing significantly by adolescence. Prevalence is equivalent between toddler-aged boys and girls but higher among school-aged girls than boys. Approximately 1.6% of adolescents meet criteria for SAD (APA, 2022, p. 218). SAD prevalence rates based on child reports have been found to be higher than parent reports (Choudhury et al., 2003).

The 12-month prevalence rate of SAD in adults is estimated to be between 0.9% and 1.9% (APA, 2022, p. 219). In an international study that included 18 countries, the 12-month prevalence of adult SAD ranged from <0.1% to 2.7%, and SAD was more commonly found in women than men (Silove et al., 2015).

Age of Onset

SAD can be diagnosed at any point in development. Its onset ranges from preschool age to adulthood (APA, 2022, p. 219). One study estimated the average age of onset for childhood SAD to be 6 years old (Shear et al., 2006). Of all the anxiety disorders, SAD has been found to have one of the earliest ages of onset (Beesdo et al., 2009).

SAD can also onset during adulthood. The National Comorbidity Survey Replication found that adult SAD generally begins in the late teens or early 20s (Shear et al., 2006). Among adults with SAD in 18 countries, individuals in high- and upper-middle-income countries reported that symptoms began during late adolescence on average (Silove et al., 2015). Adults in low and lower-middle-income countries identified median age of onset in their mid-20s (Silove et al., 2015).

In children with SAD, difficulty or refusal to separate from caregivers to go to school is common (APA, 2022, p. 219). School-aged children often voice worries about potential dangers, such as kidnapping, accidents, or death. Adults with SAD tend to experience challenges with significant life changes, such as moving or getting married, as well as excessive worry about their children, spouses, romantic partners, parents, or pets. Across ages, excessively checking on important family members and loved ones is a common safety behavior.

Co-Occurring Conditions

Overall, high rates of comorbidity have been documented in children suffering from anxiety disorders, with the most common being co-occurring anxiety disorders (Verduin & Kendall, 2003). However, there tend to be differences in comorbidity patterns for different anxiety disorders and in different age groups. Because SAD is among the earliest anxiety disorders to be identified in youth, young children (ages 4-11 years) with a primary diagnosis of SAD are less likely to meet criteria for a concurrent anxiety disorder than young children diagnosed with generalized anxiety disorder or social anxiety disorder. For older youth with SAD, comorbidity rates are similar to those for other anxiety disorders. Possibly, anxiety problems are more specific earlier in childhood, with symptoms becoming more generalized with increasing age, resulting in greater co-occurrence with other disorders (Spence et al., 2018).

There is evidence to suggest that a diagnosis of SAD in childhood may serve as an early indicator of anxiety risk in adulthood. A childhood diagnosis of separation anxiety disorder significantly increases the risk of panic disorder and any anxiety disorder in adulthood. Studies investigating SAD as a predictor for depression are mixed. There is no known association between a childhood diagnosis of SAD and the development of substance use disorders in adulthood (Kossowsky, et al., 2013; Lewinsohn, et al., 2008).

Finally, children diagnosed with an autism spectrum disorder (ASD) exhibit higher rates of anxiety symptoms compared to typically developing children and those with other neurodevelopmental disorders (Vasa et al.,2020; White et al., 2009). Data suggest that, for children diagnosed with ASD, elevated rates of anxiety are present in the first three years of life and may include separation worries. In older children with ASD, specific, social, and generalized fears were most common across studies. Chapter 9 of this book provides more information about the presentation of SAD in individuals with autism spectrum disorder.

Assessment

Completing a comprehensive diagnostic interview that assesses a child's development, symptoms, behavior, environment, and overall functioning is often sufficient to diagnose SAD and develop a treatment plan. For those desiring a more structured diagnostic interview, the Anxiety Disorder Interview Schedule for DSM-5 (ADIS-5; Silverman et al., 2024) is a well-validated diagnostic interview suitable for measuring all anxiety disorders, mood disorders, and attention-deficit/hyperactivity disorder in children. The ADIS-5 is a semi-structured diagnostic interview that primarily assesses child anxiety disorders through interviews between the child and the parent. The interviews cover the range of anxiety-related disorders outlined in the DSM-5, with each diagnosis assigned a clinician severity rating (CSR), a symptoms severity rating, and a functional impairment rating. The ADIS-5's parent and child versions possess high inter-rater and test-retest reliability. The ADIS-5 is considered the gold-standard diagnostic evaluation for anxiety disorders.

Validated screening tools can be helpful when there is difficulty in obtaining full diagnostic criteria from an interview, in identifying possible comorbid conditions, and in monitoring treatment effectiveness. There are several well-validated screening tools available for anxiety disorders in children, and a few of them are discussed here. It is recommended that an evaluator consider multiple sources of information where possible, particularly the caregiver and the child.

Screen for Child Anxiety-Related Emotional Disorders

The Screen for Child Anxiety-Related Emotional Disorders (SCARED; Birmaher, et al., 1997) is one of the most commonly used tools for assessing anxiety in children. It can be used free of charge with an acceptable time burden on clinicians and families, making it an excellent tool for diagnosing and managing anxiety disorders in children. The SCARED is a 41-item tool that has been validated for use with children ages 8-18 years and includes both child and parent report measures. The total score is based on five subscale scores that assess the most common pediatric anxiety disorders: generalized anxiety, social anxiety, separation anxiety, somatic symptoms/panic, and school phobia.

The SCARED has been validated in numerous settings worldwide. It is sensitive to change, and reductions of 55% on the SCARED-Parent and 50% on the SCARED-Youth optimally predict treatment response (Caporino, et al., 2017). The SCARED has shown some discordance in the information provided by the child and parent. However, it is considered a stable, reliable, valid, and sensitive measure of anxiety, and has shown strict measurement invariance and solid test-retest reliability (Behrens et al., 2019).

Spence Children's Anxiety Scale

Similar to the SCARED, the Spence Children's Anxiety Scale (SCAS; Spence, 1997) is a 38 (parent) to 44 (child) item measure that assesses six domains of anxiety including generalized anxiety, panic/agoraphobia, social phobia, separation anxiety, obsessive-compulsive disorder and physical injury fears. The SCAS includes both child self-report and parent-report versions and is designed for use with children ages 8-15 years. Strong internal reliability, test-retest reliability, convergent/divergent validity, discriminant validity and construct validity have been consistently demonstrated (Nauta, et al., 2004).

Spence Preschool Anxiety Scale

The Spence Preschool Anxiety Scale (PAS; Edwards et al., 2001; Spence et al., 2010) is a 28-item parent report tool that assesses a wide range of anxiety symptoms in preschool-aged children (2.5-6.5 years). The scale provides an overall measure of anxiety, in addition to scores on five subscales assessing a specific aspect of child anxiety: generalized anxiety, social anxiety, obsessive-compulsive disorder, physical injury fears, and separation anxiety. The PAS is sensitive to change and can be used to assess response to treatment. The PAS is better used to independently identify social anxiety, obsessive-compulsive disorder and fears of physical injury; however, it is not clear whether separation anxiety and generalized anxiety represent clearly distinct factors on this measure. On the revised version of the PAS, the total scale and four subscales showed strong internal consistency, 12-month stability, and maternal-paternal agreement. Scores on the scale also showed expected correlations with a measure of emotional distress, diagnosed anxiety disorders, and behavioral indicators of anxiety (Edwards et al., 2010).

Separation Anxiety Avoidance Inventory

The Separation Anxiety Avoidance Inventory (SAAI; In-Albon et al., 2013) is an SAD-specific tool designed to assess the avoidance of seven separation situations for youth ages 4-15 years. The SAAI includes both child (SAAI-C) and parent (SAAI-P) versions, both of which have demonstrated good internal consistency, test-retest reliability, and construct and discriminant validity (2013). The SAAI is sensitive to treatment change and has solid parent-child agreement. The SAAI should be used in combination with other tools that assess specific SAD symptoms, frequency, and duration, as well more subjective aspects of worry and distress, which are core features of SAD.

Treatment

The recommended first-line treatment for Separation Anxiety Disorder is cognitive behavioral therapy (CBT). Similar to CBT for other anxiety disorders, CBT for SAD includes child and caregiver psychoeducation, gradual exposure to anxiety-provoking situations, and changing caregiver responses (accommodations) to child anxiety. Exposure therapy focuses on an individually tailored, collaboratively developed set of exposure practices, starting with easier tasks and progressing to more anxiety-provoking situations. For a child with SAD, exposures might start with the child going to sleep in her own bed with the bedroom door open, hallway light on, and parent sitting in the room. Treatment would gradually progress through removing each of these accommodations until the child is able to go into her own bed with the bedroom door closed, the hallway light off, and the parent elsewhere in the home. Through the exposure process, the child learns that her worst fears (e.g., that she will be kidnapped if she sleeps in her own bed instead of with her parents) are disconfirmed, and that she is brave enough to sleep alone. Effective CBT typically requires 10 to 15 outpatient sessions with exposure practices occurring at home and in the community between visits. For children with SAD-related school refusal, engagement with school-based collaborators to facilitate exposures at school is often helpful. Chapter 3 of this book provides more information concerning parent-focused treatment for SAD in young children and Chapter 4 provides information about exposure-based CBT. Chapters 6-10 provide information about treatment in sub-specialty populations of individuals with SAD.

For children with mild SAD symptoms (e.g., with recent symptom onset or impairment limited to one setting), patient and caregiver psychoeducation and coaching alone can be an effective intervention. For those with significant co-occurring conditions, significant impairment (e.g., school refusal that results in absenteeism), or prolonged symptoms that are not responsive to CBT, referral to a psychiatrist for medication may be necessary. Chapter 5 of this text provides more information about medication management of SAD symptoms.

Conclusion

SAD is one of the most frequently occurring anxiety disorders in children and adolescents and has one of the earliest ages of onset among anxiety disorders that occur in childhood. SAD can be viewed as an extension of developmentally typical separation anxiety, which usually appears between six and 12 months of age, abates around three years of age, and manifests as excessive concerns, worry, and dread of the actual or anticipated separation from an attachment figure or home. While younger children with SAD have lower rates of co-occurring anxiety disorders, older children with SAD have comorbidity rates similar to those in children with social anxiety disorder and generalized anxiety disorder. There are several well-validated assessment instruments to assist with diagnosis of SAD, including semi-structured interviews, broadband anxiety scales, and narrow-band measures of SAD symptoms that are sensitive to symptom improvement during treatment. The recommended first-line treatment for childhood onset SAD is family-based CBT that includes child and caregiver psychoeducation, gradual exposure to anxiety-provoking situations, and changing caregiver responses (accommodations) to child anxiety. For those with significant co-occurring conditions, significant impairment, or prolonged symptoms that are not responsive to CBT, referral to a psychiatrist for medication may be necessary.

References

American Psychiatric Association. (2022). Anxiety Disorders. In *Diagnostic and statistical manual of mental disorders* (5th ed., text rev.). https://doi.org/10.1176/appi.books.9780890425787.

Battaglia M. (2015). Separation anxiety: At the neurobiological crossroads of adaptation and illness. *Dialogues in Clinical Neuroscience, 17(3)*, 277-85.

Beesdo, K., Knappe, S., & Pine, D. S. (2009). Anxiety and anxiety disorders in children and adolescents: Developmental issues and implications for DSM-V. Psychiatric Clinics of North America, 32(3), 483–524. https://doi.org/10.1016/j.psc.2009.06.002.

Behrens B., Swetlitz C., Pine D. S., & Pagliaccio D. (2019). The Screen for Child Anxiety Related Emotional Disorders (SCARED): Informant discrepancy, measurement invariance, and test-retest reliability. *Child Psychiatry and Human Development, 50(3),* 473-482.

Birmaher B., Khetarpal S., Brent D., Cully M., Balach L., Kaufman J., & Neer S. M. (1997). The Screen for Child Anxiety Related Emotional Disorders (SCARED): Scale construction and psychometric characteristics. *Journal of the American Academy of Child & Adolescent Psychiatry, 36,* 545–553. https://doi.org/10.1097/00004583-199704000-00018.

Caporino, N. E., Sakolsky, D., Brodman, D. M., McGuire, J. F., Piacentini, J., Peris, T. S., Ginsburg, G. S., Walkup, J. T., Iyengar, S., Kendall, P. C., & Birmaher, B. (2017). Establishing clinical cutoffs for response and remission on the Screen for Child Anxiety-Related Emotional Disorders (SCARED). *Journal of the American Academy of Child and Adolescent Psychiatry, 56(8)*, 696–702. https://doi.org/10.1016/j.jaac.2017.05.018.

Choudhury, M. S., Pimentel, S. S., & Kendall, P. C. (2003). Childhood Anxiety Disorders: Parent–Child (Dis) Agreement Using a Structured Interview for the DSM-IV. *Journal of the American Academy of Child & Adolescent Psychiatry,* 42(8), 957–964. https://doi.org/10.1097/01.CHI.0000046898.27264.A2.

Copeland, W. E., Angold, A., Shanahan, L., & Costello, E. J. (2014). Longitudinal Patterns of Anxiety From Childhood to Adulthood: The Great Smoky Mountains Study. *Journal of the American Academy of Child & Adolescent Psychiatry*, 53(1), 21–33. https://doi.org/10.1016/j.jaac.2013.09.017.

Edwards, S. L., Rapee, R. M., Kennedy, S. J., & Spence, S. H. (2010). The assessment of anxiety symptoms in preschool-aged children: The Revised Preschool Anxiety Scale. *Journal of Clinical Child and Adolescent Psychology, 39(3)*, 400–409. https://doi.org/10.1080/15374411003691701.

Ehrenreich, J. T., Santucci, L. C., & Weiner, C. L. (2008). Separation anxiety disorder in youth: Phenomenology, assessment, and treatment. *Behavioral Psychology, 16(3)*, 389-412. doi: 10.1901/jaba.2008.16-389.

Faust, K. M., Carouso-Peck, S., Elson, M. R., & Goldstein, M. H. (2020). The origins of social knowledge in altricial species. *Annual Review of Developmental Psychology, 2*, 225-246.

Ginsburg, G. S., Becker, E. M., Keeton, C. P., Sakolsky, D., Piacentini, J., Albano, A. M., Compton, S. N., Iyengar, S., Sullivan, K., Caporino, N., Peris, T., Birmaher, B., Rynn, M., March, J., & Kendall, P. C. (2014). Naturalistic Follow-up of Youths Treated for Pediatric Anxiety Disorders. *JAMA Psychiatry*, 71(3), 310–318. https://doi.org/10.1001/jamapsychiatry.2013.4186.

In-Albon, T., Meyer, A. H., & Schneider, S. (2013). Separation anxiety avoidance inventory-child and parent version: psychometric properties and clinical utility in a clinical and school sample. *Child Psychiatry and Human Development, 44(6)*, 689-97.

Kossowsky, J., Pfaltz, M. C., Schneider, S., Taeymans, J., Locher, C., & Gaab, J. (2013). The separation anxiety hypothesis of panic disorder revisited: A meta-analysis. *American Journal of Psychiatry, 170(7)*, 768–781. https://doi.org/10.1176/appi.ajp.2012.12070893.

Lewinsohn, P. M., Holm-Denoma, J. M., Small, J. W, Seeley, J. R., & Joiner, T. E. (2008). Separation anxiety disorder in childhood as a risk factor for future mental illness (2008). *Journal of the American Academy of Child & Adolescent Psychiatry, 47(5),* 548-555. https://doi.org/10.1097/CHI.0b013e31816765e7.

Nauta, M. H., Scholing, A., Rapee, R. M., Abbott, M., Spence, S. H., & Waters, A. (2004). A parent-report measure of children's anxiety: psychometric properties and comparison with child-report in a clinic and normal sample. *Behaviour Research and Therapy, 42 (7)*, 813-839. doi: 10.1016/S0005-7967(03)00200-6. PMID: 15149901.

Shear, K., Jin, R., Ruscio, A. M., Walters, E. E., & Kessler, R. C. (2006). Prevalence and Correlates of Estimated DSM-IV Child and Adult Separation Anxiety Disorder in the National Comorbidity Survey Replication (NCS-R). The American Journal of Psychiatry, 163(6), 1074–1083. https://doi.org/10.1176/appi.ajp.163.6.1074.

Silove, D., Alonso, J., Bromet, E., Gruber, M., Sampson, N., Scott, K., Andrade, L., Benjet, C., Caldas De Almeida, J. M., De Girolamo, G., De Jonge, P., Demyttenaere, K., Fiestas, F., Florescu, S., Gureje, O., He, Y., Karam, E., Lepine, J.-P., Murphy, S., … Kessler, R. C. (2015). Pediatric-Onset and Adult-Onset Separation Anxiety Disorder Across Countries in the World Mental Health Survey. American Journal of Psychiatry, 172(7), 647–656. https://doi.org/10.1176/appi.ajp.2015.14091185.

Silverman, W. K., Albano, A. M, & Kerns, C. M. *Anxiety and Related Disorders Interview Schedule for DSM-5, Child and Parent Version: Clinician Manual* (New York, 2024; online edn, Oxford Academic, 1 Mar. 2024), https://doi.org/10.1093/med-psych/9780199348343.001.0001, accessed 10 July 2024.

Spence, S. H., Zubrick, S. R., & Lawrence, D. (2018). A profile of social, separation and generalized anxiety disorders in an Australian nationally representative sample of children and adolescents: prevalence, comorbidity and correlates. *Australian and New Zealand Journal of Psychiatry, 52(5)*,446–60.

Spence, S. H., Rapee, R., McDonald, C., & Ingram, M. (2001). The structure of anxiety symptoms among preschoolers. *Behaviour Research and Therapy, 39*, 1293 - 1316.

Spence, S. H. (1997). Structure of anxiety symptoms among children: A confirmatory factor-analytic study. *Journal of Abnormal Psychology, 106(2),* 280-297.

Vasa, R. A., Keefer, A., McDonald, R. G., Hunsche, M. C. and Kerns, C. M. (2020), A scoping review of anxiety in young children with autism spectrum disorder. *Autism Research, 13,* 2038-2057. https://doi.org/10.1002/aur.2395.

Verduin, T. L. & Kendall, P. C. (2003). Differential occurrence of comorbidity within childhood anxiety disorders. *Journal of Clinical Child & Adolescent Psychology* 32, 290-295. https://doi.org/10.1207/S15374424JCCP3202_15.

White, S. W., Oswald, D., Ollendick, T., & Scahill, L. (2009). Anxiety in children and adolescents with autism spectrum disorders. *Clinical Psychology Review, 29(3),* 216–229. https://doi.org/10.1016/j.cpr.2009.01.003.

Chapter 2

Separation Anxiety Across Cultures

Aditi Sabhlok[1,*]
My-Linh Luu[2]
Joon Lee[3]
and Jinu Kim[1,2]
[1]Department of Pediatrics, Baylor College of Medicine, Houston, TX, USA
[2]Department of Psychology, University of Houston, Houston, TX, USA
[3]Department of Psychological Sciences, Rice University, Houston, TX, USA

Abstract

This chapter explores the presentation of separation anxiety across different cultural contexts. It begins by reviewing the prevalence of separation anxiety, highlighting cross-cultural variations. Central to understanding these differences are the roles of cultural values and attitudes toward child rearing, attachment, and parenting styles, which influence how children and caregivers experience and respond to separation. Particular attention is given to the practice of co-sleeping, a practice that varies across cultures and may or may not be associated with separation anxiety. Finally, case vignettes from diverse cultural backgrounds illustrate how separation anxiety presents and develops, offering practical insights for clinicians and educators. Through these examples, the chapter emphasizes the need for culturally sensitive approaches to diagnosing and treating separation anxiety disorder.

Keywords: separation anxiety, parenting styles, co-sleeping, cross-cultural psychology, cultural values

---

* Corresponding Author's Email: aditi.sabhlok@utexas.edu.

In: Separation Anxiety: Presentation and Intervention
Editor: Kelly Nicole Banneyer
ISBN: 979-8-89530-386-3

Prevalence

Separation anxiety disorder (SAD) is a common childhood anxiety disorder (Feriante et al., 2023), with prevalence rates estimated to be between 5% and 25% worldwide (Ehrenreich et al., 2008) and between 4% and 7.6% among children in the United States (Copeland et al., 2013; Ginsburg et al., 2014; Kessler et al., 2005). In a global survey across 18 countries, the prevalence rate of SAD was 4.8% for both pediatric and adult cases, with a 9.2% rate in the United States (Silove et al., 2015). Differences in these rates may be attributable to cultural norms, social attitudes, mental health literacy, and socio-environmental factors.

Rates of SAD vary across other countries. For example, in Europe, a cross-national study identified a prevalence of 13% in Belgium, France, Germany, Italy, the Netherlands, and Spain (Alonso et al., 2007), while a more recent study found rates ranging from 0.9% to 6.4% (Silove et al., 2015). In the Middle East, anxiety and SAD rates vary significantly; Iranian studies report prevalence rates from 0.7% to 15.7% based on region (Alavi et al., 2010; Essau et al., 2012; Khaleghi et al., 2018; Mohammadi et al., 2020; Zarafshan et al., 2015). Other countries, including Saudi Arabia and the United Arab Emirates, report much higher rates of 70.7% (Alfakeh et al., 2021) and 45.5%, respectively (Al-Yateem et al., 2020).

In Latin America, SAD is prevalent but under-researched. For example, Chile reported a 4.8% prevalence among children and adolescents aged 4 to 18 (De la Barra et al., 2014), with adult rates including 9.8% in Colombia, 6.1% in Peru, and 4.5% in Mexico (Silove et al., 2015). In communities in Brazil, 3.2% of 6-year-olds met diagnostic criteria for SAD (Petresco et al., 2014), while combined pediatric and adult data indicate a rate of 7.7% (Silove et al., 2015). The lack of empirical data from middle-income countries in Central and South America highlights a significant existing gap in representation of diverse ethnic and racial groups within SAD prevalence statistics, particularly given global trends of high rates of anxiety-related disorders among children and adolescents.

Studies in China indicate a low rate of SAD among school-aged children and adolescents, as low as 0.6% in some regions (Silove et al., 2015). However, mental health discussions are often stigmatized in many Asian cultures (Kramer et al., 2002; Lee & Turney, 2012), suggesting this lower rate may not accurately reflect the true prevalence of SAD, as children and adults may underreport symptoms due to societal expectations to control emotions.

Societal factors, poverty, and traumatic events in such contexts can exacerbate anxiety symptoms and lead to SAD (Allen et al., 2008; Merikangas, 2005; Patel & Kleinman, 2003). For instance, in northeastern Uganda, a study found a prevalence rate of 5.8%, higher than in many Western countries, attributed to political unrest and poverty (Abbo et al., 2013). Refer to Chapter 6 of this book for additional information about the impact that trauma has on separation anxiety symptoms.

While available literature provides a starting point for understanding how and to what extent prevalence of SAD varies, there is still a notable paucity of research on the prevalence and presentation of SAD across diverse cultures and ethnic groups. To date, prevalence and intervention research on SAD often focuses on predominantly White populations in Western, urban areas. This can overlook how cultural factors and societal norms influence the expression and reporting of SAD, potentially leading to misdiagnosis or under-diagnosis. By recognizing these variations, mental health professionals can better support individuals and families managing SAD across diverse communities globally, including various ethnic and racial groups within the United States.

Cultural Factors That Influence Separation Anxiety

Cultural factors, including family values, parenting, and parent-child attachment styles, significantly influence the prevalence and manifestation of SAD across various racial and ethnic groups (Bögels et al., 2012). Understanding these cultural differences is important for developing effective prevention strategies and interventions tailored to the unique needs and experiences of diverse families.

Cultural Values and Attitudes

Cultural values vary markedly between Western and Eastern societies. Individualism in Western cultures emphasizes autonomy and independence, while collectivism in Eastern cultures prioritizes relationship-oriented goals and interdependence (Tamis-LeMonda et al., 2007). Children raised in individualistic cultures may feel more comfortable separating from their caregivers, whereas children from collectivistic cultures may experience greater attachment to and discomfort from separation from family members, due to an emphasis on group belonging. In many collectivistic cultures, the focus on interconnectedness can lead to separation anxiety being viewed as a typical response to the significance of group belonging (Varela & Hensley-Maloney, 2009). Parental perceptions of separation anxiety symptoms can lead to under-diagnosis, as some parents may interpret these behaviors as cultural norms rather than issues requiring attention or intervention (Nguyen & McAloon, 2018). For example, in some Asian families, separation anxiety may be considered a natural and acceptable part of childhood development, prompting parents to downplay its significance or interference in daily routines or social functioning (2018).

Research suggests that collectivism may increase the likelihood of separation anxiety when children feel disconnected from their cultural norms (Calzada et al., 2017). For example, Latino adolescents from Central and South American backgrounds exhibit higher levels of worry and separation anxiety compared to their White peers (Varela & Hensley-Maloney, 2009). In contrast, individualistic cultures emphasize autonomy, encouraging children to develop independence at a younger age, which may result in fewer symptoms of separation anxiety (Lutz & Hock, 1995). Compton and colleagues (2000) found that African American parents often adopt a more collectivistic approach to parenting, while White parents may favor an individualistic approach that emphasizes independence.

Attachment

Cultural attitudes and beliefs about parent-child attachment styles significantly influence the presentation of separation anxiety across diverse groups. Children with secure attachment typically show distress when their mothers leave but are easily comforted upon return (Nguyen & McAloon, 2018). In contrast, children with insecure attachment styles may experience heightened distress and exhibit angry or aggressive behavior toward their mothers upon her return (2018). Insecure attachment has been linked to childhood anxiety disorders, including specific phobias and separation anxiety disorder (Colonnesi et al., 2011; Dallaire & Weinraub, 2005; Warren et al., 1997). Research by Calzada and colleagues (2017) highlights that fostering independence is often associated with authoritative parenting practices, which balance responsiveness with clear boundaries, helping children develop autonomy and coping skills for separation. However, it is important to recognize that the concept of "secure attachment" is typically conceptualized as rooted in Western cultural values, which emphasize child independence (Nguyen & McAloon, 2018), and these research findings may not generalize in the same way to other cultural groups.

Parenting Styles

Higher levels of perceived parental control are associated with increased separation anxiety symptoms (Ballash et al., 2006). When children perceive their parents as highly controlling, they may feel pressure to meet expectations, which can lead to heightened attachment and difficulty with separation (Nguyen & McAloon, 2018). At the same time, for some cultural groups, including Hispanic/Latino and African American communities, higher levels of parental control are often viewed as normative and adaptive in promoting order and safety (Halgunseth et al., 2006; Hill & Craft, 2003; Varela et al., 2009). This approach aligns with cultural values that prioritize respect, order, and social hierarchy, illustrating the diversity of parenting practices and their implications for children's emotional development in response to opportunities for independence and separation.

Co-Sleeping Practices Across Cultures

Sleep disturbances and challenges with bedtime routines are commonly associated with separation anxiety, making family sleep practices—particularly co-sleeping—a significant focus of attention, most prominently in Western communities. Co-sleeping, the practice of a caregiver and child sharing a sleeping space, varies widely across cultures. Co-sleeping can manifest as room-sharing (i.e., using the same room with separate sleeping surfaces) or bed-sharing (i.e., using the same sleeping surface) (Goldberg & Keller, 2007; McKenna et al., 2007). Bed-sharing rates are notably higher in Asian and African countries compared to European and North American nations (Mileva-Seitz et al., 2017). Cultural norms, socioeconomic factors, individual parental beliefs, and developmental concerns influence these differences. In the context of separation anxiety, co-sleeping can serve as a comfort for children struggling with the distress of being apart from their caregivers, but this behavior could also maintain the separation anxiety. Attitudes toward co-sleeping vary widely; while some cultures view it as essential for family bonding, others see it as a barrier to fostering independence. Understanding these varying perspectives across developmental stages can illuminate how co-sleeping practices impact children's emotional well-being and their experiences of separation anxiety.

In certain Western countries, particularly the United States and Canada, co-sleeping is often discouraged to promote child independence. Public health agencies, including the American Academy of Pediatrics, advise against many co-sleeping practices to reduce the risk of sleep-related infant deaths (Moon et al., 2022). Despite these warnings, co-sleeping during and beyond infancy is practiced more frequently among non-White families in the U.S. compared to White families (Bombard et al., 2018; Joyner et al., 2010; Milan et al., 2007; Salm Ward et al., 2016). For example, the incidence of all-night co-sleeping with children up to four years of age was significantly higher in Hispanic-American families (21%) than in White-American urban children (8%) (Schachter et al., 1989). For room-sharing sleeping practices, this difference was further pronounced: 80% of Hispanic-American children slept in their parents' bedroom versus 10% of White children (1989). These practices have been linked to both cultural values, such as the role of communal living in intergenerational transmission of the importance of family (Milan et al., 2007) as well as socioeconomic factors, including family income and home size, parent work schedules, and convenience of room or bedsharing to accommodate delays to meal and/or bedtimes (Blanco et al., 2024). Certain European countries, such as Denmark and Sweden, have higher rates of bed- and room-sharing, reflecting different cultural norms even within predominantly White societies (Mileva-Seitz et al., 2017; Nelson et al., 2001; Welles-Nystrom, 2005).

In many non-Western countries, particularly in Asia, co-sleeping is common and generally encouraged. In South Korea, co-sleeping is seen as a natural practice that promotes "emotional stability," and fosters familial bonds and security, aligned with collectivistic cultural norms (Chung & An, 2014). This practice is also prevalent in Japan (Latz et al., 1999) and China (Huang et al., 2010), as well as in South and Southeast Asian countries, highlighting a shared cultural emphasis on family interdependence (Mindell et al., 2010). Duration of normative co-sleeping practices is often longer in Asian countries than in Western countries. In Korea, parent-reported "optimal" length of co-sleeping ranged from three to six years of age (Chung & An, 2014). In Japan, the reported prevalence of co-sleeping rates across age groups is higher: up to 91% for children under the age of five years, 79% between the ages of six to

10 years, 50% for children between 11 to 15 years old, and 17% between the ages of 16 to 20 years (Moriki, 2012).

Co-sleeping is also observed in various African nations. A study in southeastern Nigeria found that about two-thirds of mothers bed-share with their infants, often citing breastfeeding as a primary reason (Ibeziako et al., 2009). Factors such as having multiple children and parental education level, which correlate with wealth and larger living spaces, also influence bed-sharing practices (Klonoff-Cohen & Edelstein, 1995). A comparison between the Aka, a hunter-gatherer group, and the Ngandu, an agrarian society in Central Africa, revealed that over three-quarters of infants and children bed-share in both groups (Hewlett & Roulette, 2014). Co-sleeping behaviors in these societies are often seen as protective measures for children, particularly given high child mortality rates due to environmental risks. Even within similarly located communities, differences in parental attitudes regarding co-sleeping emerge, which researchers attribute to variation in living conditions, societal organization, and cultural norms (2014). For example, Aka homes are smaller and prioritize egalitarianism and child autonomy, particularly for older children, in choosing their sleeping arrangements, whereas Ngandu parents exert more control and stop co-sleeping earlier, and have greater economic resources for independent sleeping.

Overall, co-sleeping practices vary significantly across, and even within, cultures, influenced by cultural norms, socioeconomic factors, societal organization, environmental risks and safety considerations, and parental beliefs about child-rearing that shape co-sleeping norms. While co-sleeping is often encouraged in many Asian and African countries and communities due to values emphasizing familial bonds and child protection, it is generally discouraged in Western countries such as the U.S. due to sleep-related infant mortality concerns. These findings highlight the nuanced interaction of cultural, economic, and social factors that shape co-sleeping practices worldwide, as well as how these practices and behaviors are interpreted in the context of anxiety.

Case Vignettes

The following vignettes illustrate presentations of separation anxiety across various cultural backgrounds at different stages of development, focusing on parental attitudes and perceptions, associated behaviors, and cultural factors that exacerbate separation challenges. These vignettes also highlight cultural considerations for treatment.

"Hana"

Hana is a 4-year-old Korean-American girl who presented with significant separation anxiety and sleep difficulties. She lives with her parents, who are well-educated and value high achievement, as well as her infant brother. Hana's sleep problems began in infancy, characterized by excessive nighttime crying and difficulty with self-soothing, and were exacerbated by several unsuccessful attempts at sleep training. Due to familial distress related to sleep, which her mother described as "traumatic," Hana's parents began co-sleeping with her. While this initially provided some relief, it has since interfered with Hana's sleep independence.

At age 3, several stressors—including a family move, the birth of her brother, changes in her parents' work schedules, and starting daycare—exacerbated Hana's anxiety. She exhibited intense emotional responses when separated from her parents, particularly from her mother, manifesting as sustained crying episodes, especially in crowds and during drop-offs at daycare. Hana also engaged in checking behaviors, sought constant reassurance from her mother, required her physical proximity across settings, and showed significant reluctance to engage in self-play. At home, Hana continued to struggle with sleep; her nighttime routine often extended beyond two hours, reducing her sleep duration below the recommended amount for her age. She frequently woke up at night and required her mother's physical contact to fall back asleep.

While family mental health history may have predisposed Hana to difficulties with self-regulation, parental factors and cultural background contributed to the maintenance of her separation anxiety. This was further compounded by the stress and pressure related to achievement and success emphasized in Korean families, which her parents communicated to the therapist in treatment. Hana's parents noted that the Korean cultural context often stigmatizes mental health issues, leaving Hana's mother with limited support and knowledge from her parents and community, impacting her ability to support Hana during infancy and with her current anxiety.

The family's Asian collectivist background emphasized strong parental guidance and achievement, contributing to both parental over-accommodation of reassurance-seeking behavior and delayed nighttime routines, as well as increased pressure on Hana to meet developmental expectations related to sleep, school, and behavior. This pressure also resulted in overt parental distress when Hana failed to meet those expectations. These inconsistent parental responses likely perpetuated patterns of behavior related to Hana's anxiety.

Given Hana's age and the behavioral manifestations of her anxiety, initial treatment centered on providing her parents with effective behavior management strategies. This approach aimed to reduce over-attention to her distress and related non-compliance in the context of daytime separation goals. These strategies also focused on enhancing consistency in parental responses with the application of these skills to address sleep and nighttime separation challenges.

"Tatiana"

Tatiana is an 8-year-old bicultural girl. Her mother is from Russia and her father is from the United States. Upon presenting for treatment for anxiety, her parents raised concerns regarding sleep routines and practices. Tatiana had been co-sleeping with her parents since infancy, which her mother noted is a common cultural practice in Russia. However, Tatiana's father preferred that she sleep independently and transition to her own room. Although the family acknowledged the importance of independent sleep and noted occasions when Tatiana reacted negatively to attempts at separation at night, it was not identified as a priority for treatment at intake.

From her Russian cultural perspective, Tatiana's mother viewed co-sleeping as important to foster close physical and emotional bonding. This belief continued to support the practice of co-sleeping in their home despite Tatiana's father's preference for independent sleep. Transitioning to independent sleep was more challenging for Tatiana as she was accustomed to the closeness and security of co-sleeping since infancy, which further reinforced symptoms of separation anxiety at night, including seeking reassurance and physical proximity from her parents. Although her parents recognized the potential benefits of independent sleep, they prioritized other treatment goals, which delayed an active focus on changing her bedtime routine and further maintained existing patterns of reinforcement related to sleep.

When addressing co-sleeping in families with differing personal or cultural attitudes, it is important to consider cultural context and each caregiver's perceptions of distress and interference. In Tatiana's case, her father stated that co-sleeping interfered with his relationship with her mother, while Tatiana's mother believed it was a customary practice rooted in her Russian cultural background. These differences highlight the need to understand and respect both parents' perspectives, as co-sleeping was considered normative to her mother but not to her father. Treatment considerations included open communication between parents about their expectations regarding sleep arrangements, psychoeducation regarding parental accommodation and disentangling this from cultural sleep practices, as well as exploring interventions that balance cultural values with relationship needs.

"Elena"

Elena is a 14-year-old Hispanic girl who presented with significant separation anxiety characterized by panic attacks and difficulty separating from her mother, particularly in crowds and public spaces. She experienced overwhelming anxiety when her mother attempted to leave the home or when she was out of sight in public, often resulting in somatic symptoms, such as rapid heartbeat and shortness of breath. This anxiety led to school avoidance, social withdrawal, and decreased independence, in addition to negatively impacting daily routines and family functioning.

Cultural factors played a role in the maintenance of Elena's anxiety. Her family valued strong connections and engaged in most activities together, with Elena often acting as a caregiver to her younger siblings as well. While this fostered interconnectedness with immediate and extended family members, it heightened feelings of responsibility, attention to family safety, and discomfort with separation. As Elena's cultural background emphasized familial bonds, discomfort with separation felt normative. Family outings and gatherings were common, while individual activities often were financially and logistically challenging, reinforcing the notion that being apart from family is undesirable, unmanageable, or daunting.

Elena's anxiety was also intertwined with concerns about health, security, and social evaluation, rooted in her medical and family history, such as her parents' divorce and safety issues in her neighborhood. Additionally, her mother, who self-reported a history of anxiety, frequently monitored her children's whereabouts, described her own discomfort with separating from her children in public spaces, and often provided reassurance. This, in part, reinforced Elena's worry thoughts, checking behaviors, as well as Elena's reliance on her mother's presence for feelings of security. Consequently, Elena's panic attacks frequently occurred when she was expected to engage in activities without her family, leading to school avoidance and social withdrawal. The interplay of her mother's anxiety, cultural values surrounding family cohesion, and her emotional responses perpetuated symptoms of separation anxiety.

A core component of intervention with Elena and her family focused on psychoeducation and the rationale for exposure-based approaches. Elena's mother expressed concern that Elena might "get used to" or "tolerate" discomfort, given her own long-standing experiences with anxiety. Thus, exposure goals were framed as exercises to build confidence and bravery. Involving both her mother and brothers in the therapeutic process was essential to help Elena develop strategies for managing her anxiety while challenging and addressing her mother's own discomfort with separation during exposure practice. This helped to foster Elena's independence and confidence in public spaces, and her motivation to return to school, in a way that integrated family goals and values regarding responsibility, education, and connectedness.

Conclusion

The prevalence and manifestation of separation anxiety vary significantly across racial and ethnic groups, underscoring the importance of incorporating cultural factors into assessment and treatment approaches. By recognizing and respecting the unique experiences of diverse families, mental health professionals can continue to develop culturally sensitive and effective diagnostic tools and interventions. Further research is essential to understand the complex interplay between cultural values, parenting styles, and child outcomes, as well as to identify effective strategies for promoting healthy attachment and separation skills in children from various backgrounds.

References

Abbo, C., Kinyanda, E., Kizza, R. B., Levin, J., Ndyanabangi, S., & Stein, D. J. (2013). Prevalence, comorbidity and predictors of anxiety disorders in children and adolescents in rural north-eastern Uganda. *Child and Adolescent Psychiatry and Mental Health, 7*(1), 21. https://doi.org/10.1186/1753-2000-7-21.

Alavi, A., Mohammadi, M. R., Joshaghani, N., & Mahmoudi-Gharaei, J. (2010). Frequency of psychological disorders among children in urban areas of Tehran. *Iranian Journal of Psychiatry, 5*(2), 55–59.

Alfakeh, S. A., Gadah, A. A., Alharbi, K. A., Jan, F. M., Hejazi, M. S., Addas, O. K., Alamoudi, M. K., & Al Taifi, A. I. (2021). Childhood anxiety disorders prevalence in Saudi Arabia. *Saudi Medical Journal, 42*(1), 91–94. https://doi.org/10.15537/smj.2021.1.25624.

Allen, J. L., Rapee, R. M., & Sandberg, S. (2008). Severe life events and chronic adversities as antecedents to anxiety in children: A matched control study. *Journal of Abnormal Child Psychology, 36*(7), 1047–1056. https://doi.org/10.1007/s10802-008-9240-x.

Alonso, J., & Lépine, J. P. (2007). Overview of key data from the European Study of the Epidemiology of Mental Disorders (ESEMeD). *Journal of Clinical Psychiatry, 68*(Suppl 2), 3–9.

Al-Yateem, N., Bani Issa, W., Rossiter, R. C., Al-Shujairi, A., Radwan, H., Awad, M., Fakhry, R., & Mahmoud, I. (2020). Anxiety related disorders in adolescents in the United Arab Emirates: A population-based cross-sectional study. *BMC Pediatrics, 20*(1), 245. https://doi.org/10.1186/s12887-020-02155-0.

Ballash, N., Leyfer, O., Buckley, A. F., & Woodruff-Borden, J. (2006). Parental control in the etiology of anxiety. *Clinical Child and Family Psychology Review, 9*, 113-133.

Blanco, E., Hyde, E. T., & Martinez, S. M. (2024). Assessing sleep behaviors in Latino children and adolescents: What is known, what are we missing, and how do we move forward? *Current Opinion in Pediatrics, 36*(1), 17–22.

Bögels, S. M., Knappe, S., & Clark, L. A. (2013). Adult separation anxiety disorder in DSM-5. *Clinical Psychology Review, 33*(5), 663–674. https://doi.org/10.1016/j.cpr.2013.03.006.

Bombard, J. M., Kortsmit, K., Warner, L., Shapiro-Mendoza, C. K., Cox, S., Kroelinger, C. D., Parks, S. E., Dee, D. L., D'Angelo, D. V., Smith, R. A., Burley, K., Morrow, B., Olson, C. K., Shulman, H. B., Harrison, L., Cottengim, C., & Barfield, W. D. (2018). Vital signs: Trends and disparities in infant safe sleep practices—United States, 2009-2015. *MMWR. Morbidity and Mortality Weekly Report, 67*(1), 39–46. https://doi.org/10.15585/mmwr.mm6701a6.

Calzada, E., Barajas-Gonzalez, R. G., Huang, K.-Y., & Brotman, L. (2017). Early childhood internalizing problems in Mexican- and Dominican-origin children: The role of cultural socialization and parenting practices. *Journal of Clinical Child and Adolescent Psychology, 46*(4), 551–562. https://doi.org/10.1080/15374416.2015.1041593.

Chung, S., & An, H. (2014). Cultural issues of co-sleeping in Korea. *Sleep Medicine Research, 5*(2), 37–42. https://doi.org/10.17241/smr.2014.5.2.37.

Colonnesi, C., Stams, G. J., & Noom, M. J. (2011). Meta-analytic review of the association between internalizing symptoms and insecure attachment in middle childhood. *Journal of Abnormal Child Psychology, 39*(2), 155–166. https://doi.org/10.1007/s10802-010-9464-z.

Compton, S. N., Nelson, A. H., & March, J. S. (2000). Social phobia and separation anxiety symptoms in community and clinical samples of children and adolescents. *Journal of the American Academy of Child and Adolescent Psychiatry, 39*(8), 1040–1046. https://doi.org/10.1097/00004583-200008000-00020.

Copeland, W. E., Shanahan, L., Erkanli, A., Costello, E. J., & Angold, A. (2013). Indirect comorbidity in childhood and adolescence. *Frontiers in Psychiatry*, *4*, 144.

Dallaire, E., & Weinraub, M. (2005). Young children's understanding of their mothers' departures: A longitudinal study from 6 to 36 months. *Child Development, 76*(5), 1050–1065.

De la Barra, F., Vicente, B., Saldivia, S., & Melipillan, R. (2014). Separation anxiety, social phobia, and generalized anxiety disorders in the Chilean epidemiological study of children and adolescents. *Journal of Child and Adolescent Behavior, 2*(3). https://doi.org/10.4172/jcalb.1000133.

Duarte, C., Hoven, C., Berganza, C., Bordin, I., Bird, H., & Miranda, C. T. (2003). Child mental health in Latin America: Present and future epidemiologic research. *The International Journal of Psychiatry in Medicine, 33*(3), 203–222. https://doi.org/10.2190/4WJB-BW16-2TGE-565W.

Ehrenreich, J. T., Santucci, L. C., & Weiner, C. L. (2008). Separation anxiety disorder in youth: Phenomenology, assessment, and treatment. *Psicologia Conductual, 16*(3), 389. https://doi.org/10.1901/jaba.2008.16-389.

Essau, C. A., Olaya, B., Pasha, G., O'Callaghan, J., & Bray, D. (2012). The structure of anxiety symptoms among adolescents in Iran: A confirmatory factor analytic study of the Spence Children's Anxiety Scale. *Journal of Anxiety Disorders, 26*(8), 871–878. https://doi.org/10.1016/j.janxdis.2012.08.001.

Feriante, J., Torrico, T. J., & Bernstein, B. (2023). Separation anxiety disorder. In *StatPearls*. StatPearls Publishing.

Ginsburg, G. S., Becker, E. M., Keeton, C. P., Sakolsky, D., Piacentini, J., Albano, A. M., Compton, S. N., Iyengar, S., Sullivan, K., Caporino, N., Peris, T., Birmaher, B., Rynn, M., March, J., & Kendall, P. C. (2014). Naturalistic follow-up of youths treated for pediatric anxiety disorders. *JAMA Psychiatry, 71*(3), 310–318. https://doi.org/10.1001/jamapsychiatry.2013.4186.

Goldberg, W. A., & Keller, M. A. (2007). Co-sleeping during infancy and early childhood: Key findings from the literature and implications for practice. *Pediatrics in Review, 28*(6), 222–229. https://doi.org/10.1542/pir.28-6-222.

Halgunseth, L. C., Ispa, J. M., & Rudy, D. (2006). Parental control in Latino families: An integrated review of the literature. *Child Development*, *77*(5), 1282-1297.

Hewlett, B. S., & Roulette, J. W. (2014). Cosleeping beyond infancy. *Ancestral Landscapes in Human Evolution: Culture, Childrearing and Social Wellbeing*, 129-163.

Hill, N. E., & Craft, S. A. (2003). Parent-school involvement and school performance: Mediated pathways among socioeconomically comparable African American and Euro-American families. *Journal of Educational Psychology*, *95*(1), 74.

Huang, X. N., Wang, H. S., Zhang, L. J., & Liu, X. C. (2010). Co-sleeping and children's sleep in China. *Biological Rhythm Research*, *41*(3), 169-181.

Ibeziako, N. S., Ibekwe, R. C., & Ibe, B. C. (2009). Infant Sleeping Environment in South-Eastern Nigeria (Sleeping Place and Sleeping Position): A Preliminary Survey. *Journal of Tropical Medicine*, *2009*(1), 283046.

Joyner, B. L., Oden, R. P., Ajao, T. I., & Moon, R. Y. (2010). Where should my baby sleep: A qualitative study of African American infant sleep location decisions. *Journal of the National Medical Association*, *102*(10), 881-889.

Kessler, R. C., Berglund, P., Demler, O., Jin, R., Merikangas, K. R., & Walters, E. E. (2005). Lifetime prevalence and age-of-onset distributions of DSM-IV disorders in the National Comorbidity Survey Replication. *Archives of General Psychiatry, 62*(6), 593–602. https://doi.org/10.1001/archpsyc.62.6.593.

Khaleghi, A., Mohammadi, M. R., Zandifar, A., Ahmadi, N., Alavi, S. S., Ahmadi, A., ... & Badrfam, R. (2018). Epidemiology of psychiatric disorders in children and adolescents; in Tehran, 2017. *Asian Journal of Psychiatry*, *37*, 146-153.

Klonoff-Cohen, H., & Edelstein, S. L. (1995). Bed sharing and the sudden infant death syndrome. *British Medical Journal*, *311*(7015), 1269-1272.

Kramer, E. J., Kwong, K., Lee, E., & Chung, H. (2002). Cultural factors influencing the mental health of Asian Americans. *Western Journal of Medicine, 176*(4), 227.

Latz, S., Wolf, A. W., & Lozoff, B. (1999). Cosleeping in context: Sleep practices and problems in young children in Japan and the United States. *Archives of Pediatrics and Adolescent Medicine*, *153*(4), 339-346.

Lee, H., & Turney, K. (2012). Investigating the relationship between perceived discrimination, social status, and mental health. *Society and Mental Health*, *2*(1), 1-20.

Lutz, W. J., & Hock, E. (1995). Maternal separation anxiety: Relations to adult attachment representations in mothers of infants. *The Journal of Genetic Psychology*, *156*(1), 57-72.

McKenna, J. J., Ball, H. L., & Gettler, L. T. (2007). Mother–infant cosleeping, breastfeeding and sudden infant death syndrome: what biological anthropology has discovered about normal infant sleep and pediatric sleep medicine. *American Journal of Physical Anthropology: The Official Publication of the American Association of Physical Anthropologists*, *134*(S45), 133-161.

Merikangas, K. R. (2005). Vulnerability factors for anxiety disorders in children and adolescents. *Child and Adolescent Psychiatric Clinics*, *14*(4), 649-679.

Milan, S., Snow, S., & Belay, S. (2007). The context of preschool children's sleep: racial/ethnic differences in sleep locations, routines, and concerns. *Journal of Family Psychology*, *21*(1), 20.

Mileva-Seitz, V. R., Bakermans-Kranenburg, M. J., Battaini, C., & Luijk, M. P. (2017). Parent-child bed-sharing: The good, the bad, and the burden of evidence. *Sleep Medicine Reviews*, *32*, 4-27.

Mindell, J. A., Sadeh, A., Kohyama, J., & How, T. H. (2010). Parental behaviors and sleep outcomes in infants and toddlers: a cross-cultural comparison. *Sleep Medicine*, *11*(4), 393-399.

Mohammadi, M. R., Pourdehghan, P., Mostafavi, S. A., Hooshyari, Z., Ahmadi, N., & Khaleghi, A. (2020). Generalized anxiety disorder: Prevalence, predictors, and comorbidity in children and adolescents. *Journal of Anxiety Disorders*, *73*, 102234.

Moon, R. Y., Carlin, R. F., Hand, I., & Task Force on Sudden Infant Death Syndrome. (2022). Sleep-related infant deaths: updated 2022 recommendations for reducing infant deaths in the sleep environment. *Pediatrics*, *150*(1).

Moreno, E., & Bravo, C. (2018). Prevalence and correlates of anxiety disorders in children and adolescents: A systematic review. *Psychological Bulletin, 144*(2), 181–203. https://doi.org/10.1037/bul0000144.

Moriki, Y. (2012). Mothering, co-sleeping, and sexless marriages: implication for the Japanese population structure. *国際基督教大学学報. II-B, 社会科学ジャーナル*, (74), 27-45.

Nelson, E. A. S., Taylor, B. J., Jenik, A., Vance, J., Walmsley, K., Pollard, K., ... & ICCPS Study Group. (2001). International child care practices study: Infant sleeping environment. *Early human Development*, *62*(1), 43-55.

Nguyen, S. A., & McAloon, J. (2018). A cross-cultural comparison of parental perceptions of childhood separation anxiety disorder symptoms and likelihood to seek help. *Journal of Cross-Cultural Psychology*, *49*(3), 453-469.

Patel, V., & Kleinman, A. (2003). Poverty and common mental disorders in developing countries. *Bulletin of the World Health Organization*, *81*, 609-615.

Petresco, S., Anselmi, L., Santos, I. S., Barros, A. J., Fleitlich-Bilyk, B., Barros, F. C., & Matijasevich, A. (2014). Prevalence and comorbidity of psychiatric disorders among 6-year-old children: 2004 Pelotas Birth Cohort. *Social Psychiatry and Psychiatric Epidemiology*, *49*, 975-983.

Salm Ward, T. C., Robb, S. W., & Kanu, F. A. (2016). Prevalence and characteristics of bed-sharing among black and white infants in Georgia. *Maternal and Child Health Journal*, *20*, 347-362.

Schachter, F. F., Fuchs, M. L., Bijur, P. E., & Stone, R. K. (1989). Cosleeping and sleep problems in Hispanic-American urban young children. *Pediatrics*, *84*(3), 522-530.

Silove, D., Alonso, J., Bromet, E., Gruber, M., Sampson, N., Scott, K., ... & Kessler, R. C. (2015). Pediatric-onset and adult-onset separation anxiety disorder across countries in the World Mental Health Survey. *American Journal of Psychiatry, 172*(7), 647-656.

Tamis-LeMonda, C. S., Adolph, K. E., Dimitropoulou, K. A., & Zack, E. (2007). "No! Don't! Stop!": Mothers' words for impending danger. *Parenting: Science and Practice*, *7*(1), 1-25.

Varela, R. E., & Hensley-Maloney, L. (2009). The influence of culture on anxiety in Latino youth: A review. *Clinical Child and Family Psychology Review*, *12*, 217-233.

Varela, R. E., Sanchez-Sosa, J. J., Biggs, B. K., & Luis, T. M. (2009). Parenting strategies and socio-cultural influences in childhood anxiety: Mexican, Latin American descent, and European American families. *Journal of anxiety Disorders*, *23*(5), 609-616.

Warren, S. L., Huston, L., Egeland, B., & Sroufe, L. A. (1997). Child and adolescent anxiety disorders and early attachment. *Journal of the American Academy of Child & Adolescent Psychiatry*, *36*(5), 637-644.

Welles-Nystrom, B. (2005). Co-sleeping as a window into Swedish culture: considerations of gender and health care. *Scandinavian Journal of Caring Sciences*, *19*(4), 354-360.

Zarafshan, H., Mohammadi, M. R., & Salmanian, M. (2015). Prevalence of anxiety disorders among children and adolescents in Iran: A systematic review. *Iranian Journal of Psychiatry*, *10*(1), 1.

Chapter 3

Brief Behavioral Intervention for Anxiety in Young Children

**Kelly N. Banneyer*
and Marni Axelrad**
Department of Pediatrics, Division of Psychology, Baylor College of Medicine, Houston, TX, USA

Abstract

Separation anxiety disorder is one of the most common anxiety disorders impacting young children. Several CBT-based programs and parent management training have been shown to result in significant decreases in anxiety symptoms. One evidence-based parent management training program is The Brief Behavioral Intervention (BBI). BBI was designed as a brief 6-8 session manualized treatment to address disruptive behaviors in preschoolers. The core components of BBI involve training parents in child-directed interaction, differential attention, effective commands, and time out for aggressive behaviors. BBI is traditionally conducted with one therapist meeting with parent(s) and child together for weekly 1-hour sessions and often involves extended family members or other guardians. This chapter will discuss BBI treatment and CBT-based adaptations that have been made to adapt the program for children with separation anxiety and other anxiety disorders. These adaptations include discussing accommodation within the framework of differential attention and incorporating exposure and response prevention practice. Best practice for treating separation anxiety disorder and other anxiety disorders in young children is discussed, including assessment measures and the BBI for Anxiety protocol.

---

* Corresponding Author's Email: banneyer@bcm.edu.

In: Separation Anxiety: Presentation and Intervention
Editor: Kelly Nicole Banneyer
ISBN: 979-8-89530-386-3

Keywords: separation anxiety disorder (SAD), SAD intervention, brief behavioral intervention (BBI), parent management training (PMT), cognitive behavioral therapy (CBT), exposure and response prevention (ERP)

Introduction to Separation Anxiety Disorder in Young Children

Anxiety disorders are a common problem in preschool-age youth, with a prevalence estimated at 9.4-19.2% (see Tandon, 2017). In this age range, the most common anxiety disorders seen are specific phobias, separation anxiety, and social anxiety disorders (2017). The prevalence of separation anxiety disorder is estimated at 0.3-5.4% in preschool-age children (2017). Given the high prevalence of anxiety symptoms presenting in young children, researchers have worked to adapt cognitive behavior therapy (CBT) programs and parent management training programs (PMT) to decrease anxiety symptoms in this population. This chapter will give an overview of evidence for the use of specific assessment and intervention approaches that have been researched in young, or preschool-age, children. This chapter also provides specific treatment modules that therapists can use when adapting the Brief Behavioral Intervention (BBI) protocol for use with young children with anxiety.

Assessment Tools

In assessing anxiety disorders in young children, one should consider assessment tools for diagnosis and assessment tools for screening or progress monitoring.

Diagnosis

Several diagnostic tools are commonly employed. The best practice for diagnosis involves multiple methods and informants, including interviews with caregivers, direct observation of the child, direct interaction or interview with the child, and parent- or teacher- report measures.

Semi-Structured Diagnostic Interviews with Caregivers

One of the primary methods used in diagnosing anxiety disorders in preschool-aged children is semi-structured interviews with caregivers given limited insight from children at this age. These interviews allow clinicians to gather detailed information about the child's symptoms from the perspective of caregivers. Several diagnostic tools have been developed specifically for preschool-aged children.

- *Preschool Age Psychiatric Assessment (PAPA; Egger et al., 1999).* The PAPA interview is designed specifically for the preschool population, providing a structured format for assessing psychiatric disorders in children who are two to five years old. It focuses on a wide range of symptoms, including those related to anxiety.
- *Diagnostic Infant and Preschool Assessment (DIPA; Sheeringa & Haslett, 2010).* The DIPA is another semi-structured interview that targets psychiatric symptoms in infants and preschoolers. It covers anxiety disorders and other emotional and behavioral disorders in children from one to six years old.
- *Diagnostic Interview of Children and Adolescents for Parents of Preschool and Young Children (DICA-PPY; Ezpeleta et al., 2011).* This tool is a modification of the DICA for use with younger children, offering a framework for assessing psychiatric conditions in preschoolers through parent interviews.
- *Online Assessment of Preschool Anxiety (OAPA; Morgan et al., 2019).* Online platforms have made tools more accessible and easier for parents to complete. The OAPA tool allows parents to report on their child's anxiety symptoms through an online system, providing clinicians with a structured set of data that can aid in the diagnosis of anxiety disorders.

Child Observation System

Observational tools are also critical in diagnosing anxiety disorders in young children. Through structured observation, clinicians can directly assess anxiety-related behaviors in the child's natural or clinical environment. One such observation system is the Anxiety Dimensional Observation Scale (ANX-DOS; Mian et al., 2015). This observational tool is specifically designed to assess anxiety dimensions in young children. It focuses on the observable behaviors that indicate anxiety, providing a dimensional perspective rather than a categorical one.

Screening and Progress Monitoring

In assessing anxiety symptoms in preschool children, parent-report measures are the most common format for screening and monitoring progress. Parent-report anxiety scales provide a structured way for parents to report on their child's anxiety symptoms. One widely used tool is the Preschool Anxiety Scale (PAS; Spence et al., 2001), which has been validated for assessing anxiety in young children. This scale has been translated and validated in other languages, including Spanish and Chinese. A revised version of this scale, the Preschool Anxiety Scale Revised (PASR; Edwards et al., 2010), has also been developed to improve the precision and scope of anxiety assessment in preschoolers.

In addition to parent reports, obtaining information directly from the child is also important for a more comprehensive assessment. This information is usually obtained through child interview or informal interview with the child. However, the Berkeley Puppet Interview (Measelle & Ablow, 2017) is a structured tool used for child self-report. This interview method uses puppets to engage preschoolers in describing their emotions and experiences, allowing for a more child-friendly approach to self-reporting.

Adapting Anxiety-Focused Behavioral Intervention to Young Children

Two recent meta-analyses have demonstrated the effectiveness of cognitive behavioral interventions in reducing anxiety in young children (Fisak et al., 2023; Vallis et al., 2020). Vallis and colleagues (2020) conducted a meta-analysis of studies focused on cognitive behavioral interventions for young children with anxiety disorders, anxiety symptoms, or behavioral concerns. Their random-effects meta-analysis, which included 43 studies, revealed a significant decrease in anxiety following intervention. Children who participated in cognitive behavioral interventions experienced a greater reduction in anxiety symptoms compared to those in control conditions, with these improvements maintained over time.

Fisak and colleagues (2023) evaluated psychosocial interventions for young children with anxiety and anxiety disorders, analyzing 24 studies primarily using approaches from cognitive behavioral therapy (CBT) or Parent-Child Interaction Therapy (PCIT) frameworks. Their findings indicated that these interventions were generally effective in reducing anxiety symptoms. Targeted prevention programs produced moderate to large effect sizes for anxiety improvement, while treatment-focused studies demonstrated large effect sizes in anxiety reduction. The analysis also showed that targeted interventions led to more significant reductions in anxiety compared to universal programs. Importantly, the study found that the positive effects of these interventions persisted during follow-up.

Parent Management Training to Address Anxiety

Parent management training (PMT) is the first line behavioral intervention for young children. Because of its efficacy in the treatment of behavioral disorders in young children, researchers have examined the modification and application of different parent management training approaches for children with anxiety disorders (Carpenter et al., 2014). Parent-Child Interaction Therapy (PCIT) is one of the most well-studied versions of PMT. Numerous studies have evaluated PCIT application to children with anxiety and/or for children behavioral inhibition and have found these approaches to be successful in a variety of modalities and settings (Barstead et al., 2018; Choate et al., 2005; Chronis-Tuscano et al., 2015; Comer et al., 2012, 2021; Pincus et al., 2008). Outside of PCIT, other PMT approaches have been modified to successfully treat anxiety (e.g., Cartwright-Hatton et al., 2005) and depressive symptoms (e.g., Chapman et al., 2015).

Brief Behavioral Intervention

The Brief Behavioral Intervention (BBI; see Axelrad & Chapman, 2016) is a 6-8 session manualized behavioral intervention using PMT. This treatment has been shown to effectively reduce disruptive symptoms in preschoolers, decrease parental stress, and maintain improvement over time (Axelrad et al., 2009; 2013). Because of prior evidence for use of PMT programs to treat anxiety disorders in preschoolers, BBI was adapted for use with preschoolers presenting with primary anxiety concerns by adapting aspects of the protocol and incorporating aspects of CBT. PMT with CBT components can be helpful in order to address parental accommodation and excessive child reassurance seeking, which may maintain anxiety. PMT strategies can also help give parents strategies to use during exposure practice and can help address co-occurring disruptive behaviors or manage a strong-willed temperament.

Adapting Brief Behavioral Intervention for Anxiety

When adapting the original BBI protocol for use with children presenting with anxiety, it is best to take a modular approach to treatment, as outlined in Table 1 below. As in the original BBI protocol, Daily Routines, Differential Attention, and Effective Commands are included as part of the core modules to be completed. However, Special Time and Time Out are noted as flexible modules, indicating they can be used as needed and can be inserted into the treatment program when most helpful. After completing core and necessary flexible sessions, some families will benefit from additional exposure or problem-solving sessions to help continue progress or help to meet additional treatment goals. Additional information about exposure and response prevention is provided in Chapter 4 of this book.

Table 1. Modular Approach to BBI for Anxiety

Core Modules	Flexible Modules	Additional Sessions
Daily Routines and Psychoeducation	Special Time	Exposure and Response Prevention (ERP)
Differential Attention	Time Out	Problem-Solving
Effective Commands		

The core theory behind each PMT session remains consistent, but the language and focus are adapted to specifically address anxiety. The Daily Routines Session should include psychoeducation on anxiety, highlighting how parental accommodation contributes to its maintenance. The Differential Attention Session plays a critical role in treating anxiety in young children, as it helps parents reduce accommodation and reassurance, reinforces brave behaviors, and avoids punishing the child when anxiety prevents task completion. The Effective Commands Session equips parents with structured statements for guiding exposure practice and provides strategies for immediate positive reinforcement for acts of bravery.

Guidelines for the two flexible modules can be found in the original manual available at https://www.mededportal.org/publication/10376 (Axelrad & Chapman, 2016). A Special Time session is beneficial when there are challenges in the parent-child relationship, such as frustration in managing the child's anxiety, or when the child frequently seeks control. This activity is particularly useful in treating selective mutism, as it allows parents to create situations where the child is encouraged to speak without being questioned excessively, providing opportunities for positive reinforcement of vocalizations. A Time Out Session should be included if the child exhibits aggressive behavior. Exposure sessions, which build on the skills introduced in the Effective Commands Session, are essential for addressing specific fears or rituals tied to identifiable triggers (Refer to Chapter 5). Finally, Problem-Solving Sessions should be used to tackle any remaining concerns or to review previously discussed concepts.

Brief Behavioral Intervention for Anxiety Protocol

Providers using these modules to address anxiety concerns in young children should be well-versed in and trained on the original BBI protocol. The manual offers flexibility in its application. It can be implemented as outlined above for children presenting primarily with anxiety concerns, or it can serve as a supplement to traditional BBI treatment for children exhibiting both disruptive behaviors and anxiety. When working with a child displaying both oppositional behaviors and anxiety, it may be necessary to address the oppositionality first to ensure compliance with exposure practices. Additionally, PMT strategies can be valuable for families whose preschoolers began with traditional exposure-based CBT but encountered obstacles in treatment progress.

For specific protocols and resources, refer to the following appendices: Appendix A includes the therapist protocol for the Daily Routine and Psychoeducation Module, and Appendix B contains the associated ABC Chart Handout. The therapist protocol for the Differential Attention Module can be found in Appendix C, with parental handouts on Increasing Brave Behaviors and Reducing Attention to Anxiety in Appendices D and E. Finally, the Effective Commands for Brave Behaviors Module is detailed in Appendix F, along with its corresponding parental handouts in Appendices G and H.

Conclusion

In conclusion, Separation Anxiety Disorder (SAD) remains a prevalent issue for many young children, but effective treatments are available. Best care involves diagnostic and assessment measures normed for young children and evidence-based treatment approaches. Adaptation to cognitive behavioral programs have been found to be effective anxiety symptoms in young children. Additionally, adaptations to parent management training programs to address anxiety symptoms are also effective intervention approaches. This chapter discusses one such adaptation, Brief Behavioral Intervention (BBI) for Anxiety. By equipping parents with tools such as psychoeducation, differential attention to reduce accommodation, and effective commands for exposure tasks, BBI for Anxiety provides a framework for therapists to address anxiety symptoms in preschoolers.

Appendix A

Daily Routines and Psychoeducation Module

Session Components

I. Relevant Histories and Identification of Concerns
II. Daily Routine
III. Conceptualization and Introduction to Treatment
IV. Psychoeducation about Anxiety and Accommodation
V. ABC Charting
VI. Closing and Handouts

I. Relevant Histories and Identification of Concerns

1. Identify family's primary concerns, goals, and possible services/interventions they may be seeking in addition to BBI for Anxiety.
2. Review information previously gathered in the diagnostic intake (e.g., developmental milestones, health history, family mental health history, psychosocial history).
3. Review results of pre-treatment parent measures with the family.

II. Daily Routine

1. During this interview, obtain details of the day from start to finish, including times when anxiety interferes with the child's functioning. Look for specific anxious and accommodating behaviors in the structure of the daily routine. Before beginning, ask the family what word they usually use to describe the child's worries to be able to match the language the family already uses (e.g., "has anxiety," "is afraid," "shows worries," "acts upset"). Be sure to ask about the morning routine, school functioning, the afternoon routine, and the bedtime routine. To gauge accommodation, the provider should ask if the family has changed any routines or avoided any triggers because of the child's anxiety.

Example Narrative: *I'd like to start by getting an idea of your daily routine, to help identify where some of the problems occur.*

Listen for Several Key Areas

- Anxiety-provoking triggers
- Typical parent and child responses to anxiety-provoking situations
- Disruptive behaviors related to anxiety and related to non-compliance/oppositionality
- Problem routines and repetitive rituals
- Inappropriate caregiver expectations
- Current reactions to anxiety that illustrate family values and patterns
- Current rewards and motivators that can be used when discussing reinforcements later in the program
- Sleep amount and independence

III. Conceptualization and Introduction to Treatment

1. Explain which types of intervention are evidence-based (i.e., cognitive behavioral therapy with exposure and response prevention, parent management training) to address anxiety and behavioral problems in young children.

Example Narrative: *This program uses a combination of Cognitive Behavioral Therapy and Parent Management Training techniques, which are the recommended treatments for anxiety and behavior change in preschoolers. It is important to include parents in anxiety treatment for young children because parents will be implementing changes in the home. Having young children talk about their feelings or play individually with a therapist is not helpful in reducing avoidance or increasing brave behaviors across settings.. By helping parents learn the strategies, parents can become coaches in the home to address anxious reactions when they naturally occur.*

IV. Psychoeducation About Anxiety and Accommodation

1. The therapist should first normalize the experience of anxiety and identify that the goal is not to remove anxiety but to reduce the control anxiety has and for the child to be able to tolerate feeling (a little) uncomfortable at times. Explain the cycle of anxiety, including the negative reinforcement cycle that occurs when a child is reassured or accommodated. Explain how avoidance also feeds this cycle. Be sure to include the reason for targeting parent behavioral change in the intervention.

Example Narrative: *For all emotions, there is a relation between thoughts, feelings, and behaviors. For example, if a child sees a dog, the child may think, "I like dogs. My dog is really nice and likes to play." After having this thought, the child may have positive feelings and act by smiling at the dog or asking to approach and pet it. In the same situation, another child may think, "Dogs are scary. That dog may bark or bite me." That child may then experience physiological arousal associated with anxiety, such as increased heart rate, sweaty palms, or an upset stomach. In response, the child will act by avoiding the dog or asking a parent to make the dog go away. When trying to change a situation, starting by trying to change feelings and thoughts is difficult, especially because these reactions happen automatically and young children have little insight into the relation between thoughts and feelings. What is most effective is working to change anxious behaviors. If we change anxious behaviors, anxious thoughts and feelings will also change. Many times, anxious behaviors in children take the form of avoidance or seeking reassurance and accommodation. Accommodation is any behavior that a parent or other individual does to try and lessen a child's anxiety. However, accommodating behaviors usually help the child to avoid a situation. When a* *child's fears are accommodated, the child never learns that they can be brave and tolerate different situations. Similarly, when a child asks numerous questions about an anxiety-provoking situation (such as "When are you picking me up from school? Are you sure? Am I sick? Is it okay?"), parental reassurance does not help the child to achieve new learning. Instead, answering these questions may reinforce the idea that the situation is scary and a "big deal" and something the child should worry about. In this program, we will talk about gradually reducing the amount of accommodation that the child receives. We will also externalize your child's anxiety. Anxious behaviors can be frustrating, but it is important to distinguish between being frustrated at your child and being frustrated at the anxiety.*

2. It can also be beneficial to help parents externalize the child's anxiety. This helps to align the parents with the child and the therapist and gives the parents a more adaptive place to direct frustration that may be present. For example, the parents can discuss how they are frustrated with the anxiety instead of being frustrated with the child. Older or advanced preschoolers may also like to externalize the anxiety by giving it a nickname.

Example Narrative: *I'd like you to think of the anxiety outside of your child. Anxiety is like a bully, making your child do things they wouldn't want to or avoid situations that they might enjoy. We are all coming together here to help learn strategies to "boss back" the bully so that it is no longer in charge.*

V. ABC Charting

1. Review the purpose of an Antecedent-Behavior-Consequence (ABC) chart to get a better idea of specific triggers, behaviors, and responses. The clinician should ensure that parents understand they should be documenting both the child and parental behaviors.
2. Provide the ABC chart (see Appendix B) and explain antecedents/behaviors/consequences to be recorded. If the child attends a childcare or preschool, provide additional forms if there are problems at school. It can be helpful to go over the sample handout with the parent.

Example Narrative: *I'd like you to take this behavior chart home with you and over the next week document exactly what is happening when your child is confronted with an anxiety-provoking situation. I want to know what happens if a difficulty arises, but I also want to know about situations that went well or times when your child was brave.*

VI. Closing

1. Remember to give the child a 5-minute warning before the end of the session and reward them appropriately at the end for following instructions to clean up and prepare to leave. We want to start to reinforce hard work in this setting for the child and to model reinforcement for the family.

Example Narrative: *You did so well following the rules and letting me talk to you and your parents today. You earned a sticker for following the rules. Thank you for helping to clean up.*

1. Schedule next session. Sessions ideally occur on a weekly basis.

Handouts

1. Information pertaining to any other recommended treatments (e.g., medications, school intervention, speech and language services).
2. ABC Chart (See Appendix B)

Appendix B

ABC Chart

Day & Time	What Happened Before	What Happened During (Describe Each Person's Behavior)	What Happened After
Example: Monday 2 pm	I told Lila I had to go to the store, and she was going to stay home with her grandmother.	Lila started to cry, grabbed onto my leg, and asked me not to go. I rubbed her back and told her that she would be okay for 20 minutes.	After 20 minutes, I tried to leave again, and Lila kept crying. I asked her grandmother to go to the store instead.

Appendix C

Differential Attention for Anxiety

Session Components

I. Review Child-Directed Play with Family
II. Collect and Review ABC Chart
III. Differential Attention for Anxiety
IV. Plan for Implementation of Special Time Play and Differential Attention
V. Closing and Handouts

I. (If Special Time Completed Prior to this Session) Review Child-Directed Play with Family

1. Observe parent(s) and child engaged in child-directed play (Special Time) for several minutes.
2. Provide labeled praise to parent(s) for adherence with guidelines (i.e., no questions, commands, or teaching) as well as provide constructive feedback as needed.
3. Problem solve any reported concerns. If parent did not have time to complete child-directed play since it was introduced, problem solve the difficulties that arose (e.g., identify a specific time and set an alarm, identify activities for other children in the household during that time) and review its importance.

II. Collect and Review ABC Chart

1. Praise child for positive and brave behaviors reported since previous session.
2. You will use current chart and any previously collected charts to demonstrate use of differential attention in order to refer to specific examples of anxious and/or attention-seeking behaviors.

III. Introduce Differential Attention for Anxiety

1. Introduce the concept. The use of differential attention involves positively reinforcing brave behaviors and reducing attention to anxious behaviors (such as seeking reassurance).

Example Narrative: *Children often seek accommodation to avoid doing something that makes them feel uncomfortable or anxious. Children quickly learn that behaving in a certain way or saying certain things will result in getting out of a feared situation. These behaviors may take the form of tantrums, frequent question-asking, crying, or even refusing to move. Sometimes families get stuck in a cycle where a child gains most attention from anxious behaviors instead of brave or other positive behaviors. Today we are going to discuss ways to manage these behaviors more effectively by using YOUR attention to reinforce or praise your child for being brave. Differential attention is a combination of using positive attention to reinforce or increase positive and brave behaviors with purposeful ignoring of anxious behaviors. This will help reinforce your child's brave and independent behaviors, which will in turn help your child to achieve new learning. This strategy is not used to manage or decrease aggressive behaviors or any behaviors that may place your child or another person at-risk of being harmed. It is also not used to manage noncompliance. We will talk more about those behaviors in the coming weeks, for now keep on doing what you have been doing to manage these behaviors.*

Teaching Points: Benefits of Differential Attention

- Powerful way to teach children how to gain attention adaptively
- Helps children learn to be independent
- Sets clear expectations
- Increases brave behaviors
- Extinguishes anxious behaviors
- Helps children feel good about themselves

1. Increasing Positive Attention.
    a. Start by introducing labeled praise to reinforce brave behaviors. If the family struggles with praise or with this concept, differential attention can be explained over two different

sessions, focusing on positive attention for brave behaviors one week and reducing attention to anxiety the following week.

Example Narrative: *We know that you praise your child and have positive interactions with them, but we are going to discuss how we can make positive attention even more powerful to help reduce anxiety by paying attention and reinforcing brave and independent behaviors. The average child receives much more attention for positive behaviors than for negative or anxious behaviors. However, children who struggle with anxiety may receive the same amount of attention for themselves as they receive for their anxiety. So, the first thing we want to do is increase the amount of positive attention your child receives for engaging in brave and independent behaviors. You want to give positive attention to your child instead of "feeding" their anxiety.*

Teaching Points: Increasing Positive Attention

- Make positive attention specific by providing examples from the ABC chart.
- Praise immediately.
- Avoid criticism. (Don't say – You are playing by yourself right now, I don't understand why you can't keep playing while Mom cooks dinner).
- Catch your child being brave.
- Praise frequently – a good rule is 3 pieces of positive attention for every 1 command or criticism

2. Identify target behaviors for Positive Attention. Ask the parent: *What behaviors can you praise your child for right now? What brave behaviors can you praise your child for at home?* Tell the parent to take over the role of praising in the session. If parents do not believe in the utility of praising behaviors a child "should" be doing, discuss the transition from extrinsic to intrinsic motivation.

Reducing Attention to Anxiety

a. Provide description. If the child also displays disruptive behaviors outside of anxiety, the therapist will need to discuss the best way to ignore in multiple situations. For example, an attention-seeking disruptive behavior should be ignored consistently and completely each time. However, in anxiety-provoking situations accommodation may need to be faded out gradually.

Example Narrative: *Positive attention is made more powerful by gradually reducing attention to anxious behavior or compulsions. Anxiety is reinforced when it is given attention. By giving reassurance and paying attention to anxiety, we are making anxiety more likely to repeat and increase over time. Therefore, we are going to gradually remove attention from reassurance seeking and decrease the amount of accommodation. With continued use, the brave behavior will overcome the anxious behavior. For example, f you spend 15 minutes talking to your child about how they are safe at night and you have an alarm in your house, the words you are saying are meant to be positive, but the child will interpret how much time you spent talking about the situation and may think that there is a risk or the situation is a "big deal" because you spent so much time discussing it.*

b. Identify target behaviors to progressively ignore. Create a hierarchy of accommodating behaviors and choose two or three behaviors low on the hierarchy for the parent to start to decrease or remove. For example, if their child repeatedly asks what time they will be picked up from school, a first step may be to answer the question the first time it is asked every day and then to respond with, "I already answered that," or "You know the answer. You tell me," when the child asks again. Other children may like caregivers to respond with a silly word or with anxiety's nickname rather than directly respond to the reassurance-seeking question. Over time, the parent can progress to ignoring follow-up questions and can eventually ignore all reassurance-seeking questions.

Teaching Points: Reducing Attention to Anxiety

- Ignore immediately and briefly.
- Ignore consistently. Discuss intermittent reinforcement (i.e., the principle that if a child is occasionally reinforced for a behavior, we can inadvertently train the behavior to occur at high frequencies).

- Make ignoring obvious. For some children, you may include a ***brief*** statement prior to ignoring: *"I will talk to you when you use your big girl voice."* Do not provide lengthy rationale or multiple reminders.
- Make ignoring powerful by making rest of the day about high quality attention, this is particularly important the moment the behavior you are ignoring stops. Find something very quickly to enthusiastically praise or comment on.
- When ignoring a target behavior, attend to the child immediately when he or she begins behaving appropriately.
- Discuss extinction bursts with families before the end of session. (e.g., *Your child may start to ask more questions at first or become upset because they are used to having their questions answered. Be prepared and be consistent.*).
- Highlight that ignoring inappropriate behavior is actively doing something to modify the behavior.

Example Narrative: *It may feel like you are not doing anything about the behavior because you are not verbally correcting it, but remember that you* ***are*** *doing something by ignoring it. You are teaching your child that anxiety is not a big deal and they are able to tolerate uncomfortable feelings on their own.*

IV. Plan for Implementation of Special Time Play and Differential Attention

1. Encourage family to continue daily Special Time (if already introduced). Additionally, summarize behaviors identified during the session for the family to focus on praising and ignoring over the next week.

V. Closing

1. Remember to give the child a 5-minute warning before the end of the session.

Example Narrative: *You did so well following the rules and letting mommy/daddy talk today. You earned a sticker for following the rules. Thank you for helping to clean up.*

1. Schedule next appointment.

Handouts

1. Increasing Positive Attention to Brave Behaviors (see Appendix D)
2. Reducing Attention to Anxiety (see Appendix E)
3. ABC Chart (see Appendix B)

Appendix D

Increasing Positive Attention to Brave Behaviors

Children behave in ways to get attention from others, and when they are scared they often learn that they are only safe if their caregivers respond to them in certain ways. They often seek accommodation from caregivers in the forms of reassuring statements or changes to the routine ("safety behaviors"). Responding to these behaviors actually keeps the anxiety from going away because your child never learns he or she will be safe without the presence of the safety behaviors. Instead of giving attention to anxious behaviors, providing lots of positive attention for brave and on-task behavior is a powerful way to teach children how to behave (and to let your child know that you enjoy when they behave well). Praising children when they are brave and when they act appropriately is also an important way to help children feel good about themselves.

Steps to Giving Positive Attention

1. Make positive attention specific. Tell your child exactly what you liked and what you would like him or her to do again.
   Example 1: Sara, great job being brave and sitting by yourself!
   Example 2: Julian, you picked up your toys right away when I asked you. I'm proud of you for following instructions right away.
2. Give positive attention right away. Give your child positive attention while the good behavior is happening and/or immediately after a brave behavior occurs.
3. Avoid Criticism. When your child learns something new or does something differently, he or she needs lots of praise to be able to do

it again. First, praise what went well. Then, help your child with any part that was difficult for them.

4. Catch your child being brave or on-task. Watch for times when your child is being brave or acting appropriately and praise them immediately.
5. Praise frequently. You want to pay more attention to brave behaviors than to the anxiety. Praising small behaviors frequently also allows your child to recognize what you sound like when you are proud of them and will cause the positive and brave behaviors to increase quickly.

Appendix E

Reducing Attention to Anxiety

Positive attention is made more powerful by gradually reducing attention to anxious or safety behaviors. Anxiety is made stronger when it is given attention. By giving reassurance and paying attention to anxiety, we are making anxiety more likely to repeat and increase over time. Therefore, it is important to gradually remove attention from reassurance seeking and to decrease the amount of accommodation. With continued use, the brave behavior will overcome the anxious behavior.

Ignoring is also appropriate for minor and attention-seeking disruptive behaviors.

Steps to Effective Ignoring

1. *Ignore immediately.* As soon as your child starts to behave in a maladaptive way, immediately stop giving attention. If this is too hard at first, try to decrease your attention over time. For example, answer your child's question the first time and then ignore if your child asks the same question again. You could also respond by saying, "I don't know," or by asking your child to wait a certain amount of time before the question is answered.
2. *Ignore briefly.* If behavior continues or escalates, then give appropriate consequences. Anxiety is not an excuse for disruptive behavior.

3. *Ignore consistently.* To teach your child that anxiety-provoking events are not serious or dangerous, ignore the anxious behavior whenever it occurs. You may need to practice ignoring only one behavior at a time.
4. *Make ignoring obvious.* Make sure your child understands that you are ignoring the anxiety. Some children like for you to use a silly word or code word (such as the name for the anxiety) as a signal that you are not allowed to answer certain questions. You can also redirect your child's behavior by showing interest in another activity.
5. *Make ignoring powerful.* Removing your attention from anxiety is effective only if most of the attention you give your child is positive and focused on brave behaviors.

Appendix F

Effective Commands for Brave Behaviors

Session Components

I. Collect and Review ABC Chart
II. Problem Solve Strategies Previously Introduced
III. Introduce Effective Commands
IV. Steps to Effective Commands
V. Effective Commands in Public Places
VI. Closing and Handouts

I. Collect and Review ABC Chart

1. Praise child for positive and brave behaviors reported since previous session.
2. You will use this chart in session today to demonstrate effective commands. It will be helpful if you also bring old charts with some examples of when the caregiver could have addressed a problem on the with the use of an effective command.

II. Problem Solve Strategies Previously Introduced (i.e., Special Time, Differential Attention)

A. Review any problems that parents might be experiencing and brainstorm solutions.

III. Introduce Effective Commands

Teaching Points – Benefits of Effective Commands

- State what TO DO (e.g., *Go turn on the light.*), instead of what NOT TO DO (e.g., *Stop standing next to Mommy*).
- Encourage children to respond immediately.
- Help improve parent/child relationship (decreases parent frustration, increases child's opportunity to receive praise).
- Make bravery practice (i.e., exposure practice) more effective.

Example Narrative: *Often when we want a child to do something, we present it as a favor. Now, I know when you say, "Are you ready to go to school?" what you really mean is that it is time to start walking out the door. But, your child may believe they have a choice. When you present a command as a question or a favor, you are giving your child the chance to say no. If your child is feeling anxious, they are even more likely to say no or try to avoid the situation in some way. The solution is to give a simple, concrete statement as a command. "Julian, please come to the door." It is also helpful if your child has had a transitional warning prior to a command coming. Think about your life. When you are at work, you know when things are scheduled. If your boss came to you and said, "I need you to come to this meeting right now" you would feel frazzled. You know when you have meetings, and you have time to finish what you are doing prior to a meeting beginning. We often don't give children this courtesy and we ask them to do something they may not be expecting. Understandably, children may get upset and this can lead to a spike in anxiety and a tantrum. To make transitions easier we give transitional warnings 5 minutes ahead of the time when we need them to start cleaning up or moving on to the next task. For instance, in here you will always hear me tell your child when there is 5 minutes left, so they can finish playing before it is time to clean up. If your child becomes anxious and asks follow-up questions* *with transitional warnings, apply differential attention strategies to minimize attention given to this reassurance seeking.*

Another mistake we sometimes make is to give a command and then not follow through. If we do this, children learn they don't always have to listen. Or we give a command many times before our faces turn red, our voices get louder, and our children realize now is the time to listen. Again, we have taught children they don't have to listen until you ask repeatedly and become upset. Our goal is to have children listen the first time we calmly ask. I'm going to ask you to think carefully about the commands you give during the day, and only give a command you are serious about and willing to see through.

An additional mistake is asking a child to do many things at once. Many children cannot keep more than one task in mind at a time. Now, if you asked me to go upstairs and get my backpack, and then when I came downstairs with the backpack you asked me to go back up to get my jacket, I would probably be annoyed you didn't tell me to do everything at once. However, children often do not feel that way – they are usually pretty happy to run back and forth as many times as you tell them. So, we give one command at a time. "Julian,, bring your backpack here." When we think about asking our children to do things that make them nervous, you are much more likely to have success if you break up the command and give them small individual commands to gradually work toward the overall goal. When your child comes back having successfully completed the command, make sure you give them enthusiastic labeled praise. "Julian, thank you for getting your backpack all by yourself!"

After you give the specific command, count to five in your head. If your child is not moving in the direction of following the command, then follow up with an if-then statement. "Julian, ***if*** *you get your backpack now,* ***then*** *you will be able to bring your toy in the car." Count to five in your head, if your child is not complying then he has lost the privilege. It helps if the privilege is occurring immediately after completion of the command or is something that that your child enjoys and usually occurs at that time of day. The contingency you use can be to keep a privilege that your child usually has. For commands to engage in anxiety-provoking situations, providing a small, tangible reward, such as a sticker or small treat, could also be helpful.*

Teaching Points: Guidelines of Effective Commands

- If you give a command, make certain you are willing to follow through with the contingency you have set– this will likely greatly reduce number of commands you give in a day.
- Make certain child is paying attention by making eye contact and eliminating any competing distractions such as a tablet or other screen.
- Give commands in a neutral tone. We do not want to train children only to listen when we raise our voices.
- Do not present the command in the form of a question or a favor. Here some examples of what NOT to say: Are you ready to go in by yourself?, It's time to go to the bathroom by yourself, OK? It would make Mommy so happy if you would walk to the car right now.
- Only give one command at a time. (e.g., Go get your socks.) If you give two commands, they must be closely related (e.g., Go get your socks and shoes.)
- Make commands specific. This also makes it easier to determine if the child has complied with the command. (e.g., Julian, get ready for bed by yourself." For some children, this command involves many steps and you will have to be even more specific. Example: "Julian, please go pick out pajamas." You can then do the same with the other tasks he should complete by himself.)
- Make sure you give specific labeled praise for following through with commands.

IV. Steps to Effective Commands

A. Walk the family through the step-by-step algorithm to effective commands.
   a. Offer an effective command. Here's an example of your child wanting you to come with them into the bathroom at home. *Example: Please go to the bathroom by yourself.*
   b. Provide specific labeled praise if child complies with request. *Example: Thank you for going by yourself. Good job being brave!*
   c. If not, count to five in your head to give them a chance to comply and then offer a warning using an if-then statement. *Example: If*

you go to the bathroom by yourself, then you may earn a bedtime story when you are done.

d. Count to five again in your head; and then follow-through with the if-then statement. If your child does not enter independently, you can say something like, "Looks like no story today but we can try again tomorrow." If you think the practice was too difficult, then the next time you can give a command for an easier step, such as having the child enter the bathroom by themselves for five seconds before the parent enters.

B. Discuss the importance of identifying meaningful, logical consequences for daily tasks. Consequences that are immediate and meaningful are more powerful and effective in promoting compliance. This can be difficult to do "on the fly." Problem-solve possible options with the family using information from the ABC Chart. Also discuss a reward system for commands that are given for the child to engage in situations that are still anxiety-provoking. These rewards could be small things such as stickers, trading cards, or individual candies. Older children sometimes may like earning tickets or tokens to save up for a larger prize.

C. Time permitting, complete several practices in session of giving the child specific commands to complete a low anxiety-provoking task. You can refer to the accommodation hierarchy previously made or create a new hierarchy based on specific fears. For example, with separation anxiety, you may prompt the child to sit and stay in the room while the parent steps out for five seconds. If the child runs to the door, you can offer a contingency, such as a sticker. Even if the child whines or says "no," the provider should demonstrate differential attention strategies by ignoring the anxious behavior and praising the child for being brave. This practice should be completed several times, and the time could be gradually increased if the child seems to tolerate the practice well. This sets the stage for exposure practice to be continued during the next session.

V. Effective Commands in Public Places (If Needed)

1. This is a good time to use an example from the ABC chart if they have an example of anxious or disruptive behaviors in public.

Teaching Points: Steps to Effective Commands in Public

- Do not try and "battle" too many anxiety-provoking situations in one day or put too many unnecessary demands on your child when they are already distressed. Life always brings about unexpected situations, but anxiety practice is best done gradually and regularly.
- Remind the child of the rules before entering a store/restaurant or remind them of the plan for the bravery practice. Get down so you are eye level with the child and say something like "I'm going to walk you to the door of your classroom and then you will go in by yourself. If you can walk by yourself, then you will earn a sticker."
- You do not have to buy something every time you go in public. Often you can give a child the option they would have had anyway (e.g., picking out cereal) but you need be willing to remove the privilege if the child is unsuccessful.
- Give frequent praise for following the rule and for every step toward bravery.
- Give gentle reminders when the child starts to not follow the rule. However, don't reassure your child. Say something like, "You are so brave, you can do it!" instead of, "You will be okay. Mommy will be right here."
- If child clearly breaks the rule or is unsuccessful with the practice, say something like "We will try again next time for the sticker." Ignore tantrum that may follow.

VI. Closing

1. Remember to give the child a 5-minute warning before the end of the session. When it is time to give the command to clean up, prompt the parent to do so and to use an if-then statement with the contingency.

Example Narrative: *Let's practice. Go ahead and tell Johnny to clean up using a simple instruction. If he does not start to do so after 5 seconds, use the if-then statement with a sticker as a reward.*

Schedule next appointment. Follow-up appointments will be spent problem-solving the above strategies and continuing to practice exposure tasks.

Handouts

1. Engaging Your Child in Brave Behaviors with Effective Commands (see Appendix G)
2. If-Then Statements and Rewards for Brave Behavior (see Appendix H)
3. ABC Chart (see Appendix B)

Appendix G

Engaging Your Child in Brave Behaviors with Effective Commands

Praising brave behaviors and removing attention from anxious behaviors will help your child start to learn to be brave. However, if your child is repeatedly afraid of a certain situation, oftentimes this specific situations needs to be practiced. For this practice to be effective, your child will need to follow the instructions you give.

Guidelines for Effective Commands

- *Make sure your child is paying attention to you.* Make eye contact. Reduce all distractions and chances for avoidance by turning off all screens.
- *Make sure you mean it*! Never give a command you will not see to completion or threaten a consequence you will not give. When instructing your child to engage in a new behavior, choose one that will not be too difficult.
- *Do not ask as a question or favor*. Instructions should be statements. Example: Say "Turn off the light," instead of, "Will you turn off the light for Mom?"
- *Only give one command at a time*. Do not overwhelm your child.
- *Tell your child what to do.* Be specific. Avoid unclear or limited statements (such as, "Please behave," or "Stop it.")
- *Use transitional warnings when appropriate*. Some commands may be more effective when a transitional warning comes first. Example: "In five minutes it will be time to get ready for bed."

Steps for Effective Commands

1. State the instruction. Then pause for a short period. Example: "Please go to the bathroom by yourself."
2. Give a contingency with an "If…then" statement. Then pause. Example: "If you go to the bathroom by yourself, then you may earn a bedtime story when you are finished."
3. Praise. Give praise as soon as you child moves to follow the instruction and once your child is successful.
4. Follow through with the contingency. Those that are *immediate* and *meaningful* are more likely to be effective.

Appendix H

"If…Then" Statements and Rewards for Brave Behavior

"If…then" statements provide a contingency for children who need a reward for engaging in a difficult, brave behavior or who may need a warning before complying with effective commands. Due to the stress and frustration that may occur throughout a child's demonstration of reassurance-seeking behavior, it may be helpful for caregivers to have some statements prepared ahead of time.

Strategy

1. Provide Effective Command
2. Wait 5-10 seconds
3. If the child complies within 5-10 seconds, provide ample labeled praise
4. If the child does not comply within 5-10 seconds, provide an "If…then" statement.
5. The "If...then" statement can be phrased positively or negatively, but it will be more effective if phrased positively.

    Positively: "If you [insert command], then you can / get / earn…"

    Negatively: "If you don't [insert command], then you can't / lose…"

At Home Example Privileges/Rewards

- Can play video games or watch videos for ___ minutes (specify amount of time)
- Can play outside for ___ minutes (specify amount of time)
- Can help mom or dad ___ (specify activity and time)
- Can play with art supplies for ___ minutes (specify amount of time)
- Can eat treat, cookie, or snack (specify amount)
- Can have extra play time with parent or grandparent (specify amount of time)

In Public/Stores Example Privileges/Rewards

- Can be special helper
- Can earn a toy for $___ or less (specify value)
- Can pick out a special cereal or treat
- Can pick a song to listen to in car
- Can push the cart at the store
- Can push elevator button

At School Example Privileges/Rewards

- Can be special helper (e.g., pass out papers, pick up supplies)
- Can continue sitting with friends
- Can read a book for X minutes
- Can engage in fun activity for X minutes or at certain time
- Can sit next to teacher (if desired)

References

Axelrad, M. E., Butler, A. M., Dempsey, J., & Chapman, S. G. (2013). Treatment effectiveness of a brief behavioral intervention for preschool disruptive behavior. *Journal of Clinical Psychology in Medical Settings*, *20*(3), 323-332.

Axelrad, M. E., & Chapman, S. (2016). The Brief Behavioral Intervention for Preschoolers With Disruptive Behaviors: A Clinical Program Guide for Clinicians. *MedEdPORTAL Publications*, *12*, 10376. Available from: https://www.mededportal.org/publication/10376.

Axelrad, M. E., Garland, B. H., & Love, K. B. (2009). Brief behavioral intervention for young children with disruptive behaviors. *Journal of Clinical Psychology in Medical Settings, 16*(3), 263-269.

Barstead, M. G., Danko, C. M., Chronis-Tuscano, A., O'Brien, K. A., Coplan, R. J. & Rubin, K. H. (2018). Generalization of an early intervention for inhibited preschoolers to the classroom setting. Journal of Child and Family Studies, 27(9), 2943–2953. https://doi.org/10.1007/s10826-018-1142-0.

Carpenter, A. L., Puliafico, A. C., Kurtz, S. M., Pincus, D. B., & Comer, J. S. (2014). Extending parent–child interaction therapy for early childhood internalizing problems: New advances for an overlooked population. *Clinical child and family psychology review, 17*(4), 340-356.

Cartwright-Hatton, S., McNally, D., White, C., & Verduyn, C. (2005). Parenting skills training: an effective intervention for internalizing symptoms in younger children? *Journal of Child and Adolescent Psychiatric Nursing, 18*(2), 45-52.

Chapman, S., Barna, A. T., Axelrad, M. (2015). Treatment of Preschool Depression with Parent Management Training: A Case Study. *Journal of Depression and Anxiety, 4*(171). doi:10.4172/2167-1044.1000171.

Choate, M. L., Pincus, D. B., Eyberg, S. M., & Barlow, D. H. (2005). Parent-child interaction therapy for treatment of separation anxiety disorder in young children: A pilot study. *Cognitive and Behavioral Practice, 12*(1), 126-135.

Chronis-Tuscano, A., Rubin, K. H., O'Brien, K. A., Coplan, R. J., Thomas, S. R., Dougherty, L. R., Cheah, C. S. L., Watts, K., Heverly-Fitt, S., Huggins, S. L., Menzer, M., Begle, A. S. & Wimsatt, M. (2015). Preliminary evaluation of a multimodal early intervention program for behaviorally inhibited preschoolers. *Journal of Consulting and Clinical Psychology, 83*(3), 534–540. https://doi.org/10.1037/a0039043.

Comer, J. S., Furr, J. M., del Busto, C., Silva, K., Hong, N., Poznanski, B., Sanchez, A., Cornacchio, D., Herrera, A., Coxe, S., Miguel, E., Georgiadis, C., Conroy, K. & Puliafico, A. (2021). Therapistled, Internet-delivered treatment for early child social anxiety: A waitlist-controlled evaluation of the iCALM telehealth program. *Behavior Therapy, 52*(5), 1171–1187. https://doi.org/10.1016/j.beth.2021.01.004.

Comer, J. S., Puliafico, A. C., Aschenbrand, S. G., McKnight, K., Robin, J. A., Goldfine, M. E., & Albano, A. M. (2012). A pilot feasibility evaluation of the CALM Program for anxiety disorders in early childhood. *Journal of anxiety disorders, 26*(1), 40-49.

Danko, C. M., O'Brien, K. A., Rubin, K. H., & Chronis-Tuscano, A. (2018). The Turtle Program: PCIT for young children displaying behavioral inhibition. In *Handbook of Parent -Child Interaction Therapy* (pp. 85-98). Springer, Cham.

Edwards, S. L., Rapee, R. M., Kennedy, S. J., & Spence, S. H. (2010). The assessment of anxiety symptoms in preschool-aged children: the revised Preschool Anxiety Scale. *Journal of Clinical Child & Adolescent Psychology, 39*(3), 400-409.

Egger, H. L., Ascher, B. H., & Angold, A. (1999). Preschool age psychiatric assessment (PAPA). *Durham (North Carolina): Duke University Medical Center.*

Ezpeleta, L., de la Osa, N., Granero, R., Domènech, J. M., & Reich, W. (2011). The diagnostic interview of children and adolescents for parents of preschool and young children: Psychometric properties in the general population. *Psychiatry Research, 190*(1), 137-144.

Fisak, B., Penna, A., Mian, N. D., Lamoli, L., Margaris, A., & Cruz, S. A. M. F. D. (2023). The effectiveness of anxiety interventions for young children: a Meta-analytic review. *Journal of Child and Family Studies*, *32*(8), 2546-2557.

Measelle, J., & Ablow, J. C. (2017). The Berkeley Puppet Interview for Child Assessment. In *Puppet Play Therapy* (pp. 29-47). Routledge.

Mian, N. D., Carter, A. S., Pine, D. S., Wakschlag, L. S., & Briggs-Gowan, M. J. (2015). Development of a novel observational measure for anxiety in young children: The Anxiety Dimensional Observation Scale. *Journal of Child Psychology and Psychiatry*, *56*(9), 1017-1025.

Morgan, A. J., Tamir, E., Rapee, R. M., Lyneham, H. J., McLellan, L. F., & Bayer, J. K. (2019). Online Assessment of Preschool Anxiety: description and initial validation of a new diagnostic tool. *Child and Adolescent Mental Health*, *24*(3), 259-265.

Pincus, D. B., Eyberg, S. M., & Choate, M. L. (2005). Adapting parent-child interaction therapy for young children with separation anxiety disorder. *Education and treatment of children*, 163-181.

Scheeringa, M. S., & Haslett, N. (2010). The reliability and criterion validity of the Diagnostic Infant and Preschool Assessment: a new diagnostic instrument for young children. *Child Psychiatry & Human Development*, *41*, 299-312.

Spence, S. H., Rapee, R., McDonald, C., & Ingram, M. (2001). The structure of anxiety symptoms among preschoolers. *Behaviour Research and Therapy*, 39, 1293–1316.

Tandon, M. (2017). Early Childhood Mental Health: Empirical Assessment and Intervention from Conception through Preschool. *Child and Adolescent Psychiatric Clinics of North America, 26*(3), xiii-xiv.

Vallis, E. H., Zwicker, A., Uher, R., & Pavlova, B. (2020). Cognitive-behavioural interventions for prevention and treatment of anxiety in young children: A systematic review and meta-analysis. *Clinical Psychology Review*, *81*, 101904.

Chapter 4

Exposure and Response Prevention for Separation Anxiety Disorder

Kelly N. Banneyer*

Department of Pediatrics, Division of Psychology, Baylor College of Medicine, Houston, TX, USA

Abstract

Cognitive Behavioral Therapy (CBT) with Exposure and Response Prevention (ERP) is the strongest evidence-based behavioral intervention for treating separation anxiety disorder (SAD). This family-centered approach integrates several core components: measurement-based care, psychoeducation, and the externalization of anxiety. Therapists employ a team-based strategy, engaging both individuals with SAD and their families to identify specific anxiety triggers and set personalized treatment goals. Key elements of the intervention include developing a rating system to track anxiety, implementing response prevention to reduce maladaptive safety behaviors, and gradually reducing family accommodation of the individual's anxiety-driven behaviors. Central to the treatment is exposure practice, where patients gradually face feared situations to learn resilience and bravery. Targeting independent sleep may be an additional goal as part of this intervention that warrants specific considerations. By focusing on collaboration with families and tailoring treatment to the individual's needs, this approach effectively supports long-term management of separation anxiety disorder. This chapter provides specific examples for each of the components of CBT with ERP intervention.

---

* Corresponding Author's Email: banneyer@bcm.edu.

In: Separation Anxiety: Presentation and Intervention
Editor: Kelly Nicole Banneyer
ISBN: 979-8-89530-386-3

Keywords: separation anxiety disorder (SAD), SAD treatment, SAD intervention, exposure and response prevention, exposure therapy, ERP

Exposure and Response Prevention

The Child and Adolescent Anxiety Multi-modal Study (CAMS; Walkup et al., 2008) demonstrated behavioral intervention is superior to placebo control and just as effective as medication management in the treatment of childhood anxiety disorders, including separation anxiety disorder (SAD). Cognitive Behavioral Therapy (CBT) incorporating Exposure and Response Prevention (ERP) is the gold standard behavioral treatment for anxiety disorders (Higa-McMillan et al., 2016). This intervention has several shortened names, including CBT with ERP, exposure-based CBT, ERP, or Exposure Therapy. Note that all of these terms refer to the same intervention.

The goals of ERP are to establish new learning in anxiety provoking situations. The "Exposure" part of ERP means exposing individuals to feared situations, and the "Response Prevention" part means eliminating safety behaviors, or anxious responses, when the feared situation is present. This chapter will focus on the ERP components of intervention for separation anxiety disorder. Note that this intervention should follow a diagnostic assessment to create an accurate conceptualization and to determine that presenting concerns are in fact caused by separation anxiety. This chapter will focus on approaches for standard separation anxiety symptoms, but you should refer to chapters 5-10 of this text for nuances of specific populations where separation anxiety symptoms may arise. It is also important to recognize that this intervention should always be individualized to each individual or family, and in the case of treating separation anxiety, family involvement is necessary.

Components of CBT with ERP

Measurement-Based Care

Even after the diagnostic intake, treatment should begin with measurement-based care, which is a core component of evidence-based practice (Beck, 2020). Measurement–based care includes outcome measurement and progress-monitoring, and these practices benefit the patient, the clinician, and the organization. Patient benefits of measurement-based care include increased symptom reduction; improvement in interpersonal problems, social functioning, quality of life; and faster treatment recovery (Scott & Lewis, 2015). It also allows patients to have an active role in treatment, which further contributes to these benefits (2015). For clinicians, measurement-based care assists with diagnosis and differential diagnosis, establishing targets for intervention, treatment planning, and enhancing collaborative care (2015). Furthermore, the use of measurement-based care provides evaluative data for organizations and encourages providers to maintain the use of evidence-based care (2015). Refer to Chapter 1 for assessment methods in school-age children and Chapter 3 for assessment methods in preschool-age children.

Psychoeducation

According to the tenets of CBT, there is a relation between thoughts, feelings, and actions (Beck, 2020). As the definition of separation anxiety disorder states, [American Psychiatric Association (APA), 2022], thoughts experienced in SAD may involve "attachment figures being lost or harmed" or thoughts about "oneself experiencing an event that causes separation from an attachment figure" (2022, p. 217). These thoughts trigger emotional feelings, such as fear and distress to be away from attachment figures, and somatic feelings, such as "headaches, stomachaches, nausea, or vomiting in anticipation of or after separating from attachment figures" (2022, p. 217). Actions typically involve avoidance of separation, such as "reluctance or refusal to leave home or go to school or work" or "refusal to sleep away from home or without an attachment figure nearby" (2022, p. 217).

Especially when working with children, new learning occurs through actions. Family members and individuals themselves have very little control over the thoughts and feelings experienced. The aspect of the cycle that individuals have the most control over is their actions. However, if individuals with SAD learn that safety or avoidance behaviors results in reduced distress, then the anxious behaviors are negatively reinforced. ERP helps to change this cycle. ERP is effective because it helps the individual change and replace anxious actions with more brave and adaptive behaviors, which will lead to positive changes in thoughts and feelings. In other words, we want individuals with SAD to learn that they can tolerate uncomfortable feelings associated with separation and ultimately that the feared situations are not likely to occur, even when the individual with SAD is separated from an attachment figure.

Externalization of Anxiety

It can be helpful for individuals with SAD to identify their anxious thoughts to be able to identify targets for ERP. It can also be helpful to externalize anxiety to help individuals differentiate the anxiety and be able to work against "it" as opposed to working against themselves. Some individuals may refer to SAD symptoms as "Anxiety" or as "Worry." Sometimes young children may like to give the anxiety a nickname.

Establishment of a Team-Based Approach

The mental health provider should work to establish rapport with their patient and caregivers (when applicable). Introducing this dynamic using a team metaphor can be helpful. In a behavioral approach, the therapist can be conceptualized as the coach. The "coach" knows lots of strategies and approaches to use to help address anxiety. The patient is the "star player." In ERP, it can be helpful to let the patient know that they are in control. While the therapist will make lots of suggestions for strategies and trials of ERP, the individual with SAD and/or their family are the ones who will decide which practices will be best to attempt and will be the ones to give feedback on how it went and whether it was effective. At the start of treatment, family members can be thought of as "cheerleaders" on the team to provide support to the individual with SAD. When working with children with SAD, the therapist should be working with the patient's caregivers so that they understand the treatment approaches, and so they can learn to be "coaches" at home. When SAD symptoms affect other settings, such as school attendance, then other individuals may need to be part of the team, such as teachers.

Development of Rating System

To prepare for ERP, the therapist should work with the patient to determine a way to measure distress. For older youth and adults, this may be a numerical scale from zero to ten, where zero indicates no distress and ten is the most possible distress. Younger children may benefit from a color-based scale (red/yellow/green) or word-based scale (hard /medium/easy). During ERP, the goal will be to target situations rated in the mid-range on the scale. Situations rated on the low end of the scale are ones that result in minimal distress, and thus these are situations that do not need to be practiced. Situations rated on the high end of the scale may be too distressing. Starting with a situation rated as "10," "hard," or "red" may be too overwhelming to start. If a patient becomes too overwhelmed, they will likely not learn that they can be successful.

Identification of Goals and Anxiety Triggers

To create the plan for ERP, the therapist will need to determine which situations are being avoided or are only completed with distress or with safety behaviors present. These situations will form the goals for ERP. Elimination of anxiety is not an appropriate goal because anxiety is a normative and helpful emotion to have. It is most helpful to have specific behavioral goals in mind, such as for a child to enter the school building independently and on time each morning. For each of the identified triggers, the therapist should work with the individual and their family to determine the anxious behaviors currently in place, such as avoidance, safety behaviors, or accommodations.

Response Prevention

To set up trials of ERP for success, the therapist must be sure that the individual is not engaging in maladaptive avoidance or safety behaviors. This step involves preventing the anxious response. In young children, this can be thought of as "doing the opposite" as to what anxiety wants. For instance, if anxiety wants the child to watch their parent out the window while they walk outside, "doing the opposite" or "bossing back anxiety" may be for the child to walk into another room or face away from the window. Common safety behaviors in children with SAD include avoidance of separation and seeking reassurance. Ways a child with SAD may avoid separation include the following: accompany caregiver(s) when they leave the home, follow their parent around the home, call out to their parent when in a separate room, stay home rather than attend parties or sleepovers, cling on to a parent at school drop-off, and/or fall asleep or sleep all night with a caregiver present. Common ways that children with SAD seek reassurance may be to text or call their caregiver excessively while at school or while away from them, to ask questions repeatedly about their caregivers' whereabouts or actions while apart, or to confirm repeatedly what time they will be picked up from school or from an activity. Children may also show disruptive behaviors, such as tantrums, to avoid separation or to be sent home when they are separated from attachment figures. Intervention will target and work to change these maladaptive responses during trials of ERP. As ERP progress, the child should agree to goals for decreased safety behaviors. For instance, if a child sends numerous texts to their parent during the school day, they may have a goal to decrease that number by one message every day or every week.

Adults with SAD may also display safety behaviors, such as avoidance of separation from the individual to whom they are attached or frequent calls or texts to that individual. Parents who have separation anxiety from their children may also limit the activities where their children can be away from them because of this anxiety. More information about adult presentations of SAD is discussed in Chapter 10 of this book.

Reducing Accommodation

Accommodation in the context of anxiety disorders are the adjustments caregivers make to reduce or avoid the child's anxiety (Lebowitz, 2013). Family accommodation involves modifying daily routines or behaviors, such as providing reassurance, helping the child avoid anxiety-provoking situations, or completing tasks on the child's behalf (2013). These accommodations, while well intentioned, can unintentionally reinforce the child's anxiety by limiting the opportunity for them to learn they can be successful and independent. In response to the safety behaviors mentioned in the previous section, there are common accommodations that occur for children with SAD. Refer to Table 1 for a list of common safety behaviors and associated family accommodations. Caregivers often accommodate the anxiety by allowing children with SAD to accompany them on errands or around the house or by permitting them to co-sleep when this is not a value of the family. Caregivers also respond to reassurance-seeking questions prior to separation, and/or respond to frequent texts or calls from the child with SAD.

The therapist should work with the family to identify areas of accommodation and work to decrease it systematically. Ceasing all areas of accommodation overnight may be overwhelming for the individual with SAD in addition to their family, so changing these behaviors in a systematic approach is often more effective. In response to reassurance-seeking questions, the therapist can work with the family to find responses in the mid-range of distress that both the parent and child will be able to tolerate.

Table 1. Common Safety Behaviors and Associated Family Accommodation

Safety Behavior	Family Accommodation
Accompany caregiver(s) when they leave the home	Take child with them on all errands and to all events
Follow their parent around the home	Allow child to accompany them to all rooms of the house; leave bathroom door open while parent is using the restroom
Call out to parents when alone in a room	Immediately reply to the child with parent location in the home ("I'm here! I'm in the kitchen!")
Stay home rather than attend parties or sleepovers	Make excuses for child to be picked up early; Permit child to stay home
Cling on to a parent at school drop-off	Spend excessive time at the school before leaving; Hug child multiple times; Reassure child that they are okay and will be safe multiple time
Fall asleep or sleep all night with a caregiver present	Co-sleep with a child; Stay in child's bedroom until they are asleep; Permit child to enter parent's bed during the night
Text or call their caregiver excessively while at school or while away from them	Respond to each text message with messages of reassurance ("You're fine." "I'll be there at the front of the pick-up line."); Pick child up early from school
Ask questions repeatedly about their caregivers' whereabouts or actions while apart	Answer each question immediately; Tell child excessive information that is already known
Ask repeatedly what time they will be picked up from school or from an activity	Answer each question with an immediate response about time of pick-up

For reassurance seeking there are several ways to reduce accommodation. One option to reduce accommodation would be for the family to only answer a question the first time it is asked and then to indicate they cannot respond to repetitions of the question. These follow-up responses could be silence, a statement such as, "I already answered that," or a statement such as, "I already told you the answer. You tell me now." A second idea would be for the parent to delay the response to the question. For example, instead of answering the reassurance-seeking question immediately, at first the parent could wait 5 minutes before answering and then increase that time over a period of days or weeks. A third idea helpful with younger children would be for the family to develop a code word, and this word will be the standard response to any reassurance-seeking question that the child may ask. For instance, if the child asks, "You are going to pick me up right at 3 o'clock, right?" Then the parent would respond only with the word, "Banana," if that were the agreed-upon code word. Similar strategies could be applied to text messages from an individual with SAD. For instance, if the child typically sends their parents ten texts throughout the school day and expects a reply to each one, the parent can reduce accommodation by responding to fewer texts each day or by waiting more time before responding to them. Finally, sometimes caregivers may set goals to reduce the responses that children desire. Sometimes, children wish to hear specific information prior to separation or prior to bedtime, and a plan to decrease accommodation might be to remove one of these sentences at each step of the plan.

While working with a family to decrease accommodation, the rate at which accommodation is reduced should be dependent on the individuals with SAD. Changes should continue to be made that are in the mid-range if difficulty, i.e., not too easy and not too difficult. Once the first step has been achieved several times, it usually is rated as less distressing, and the family will be ready to remove the next piece of accommodation. This process may take several days, or it may take several weeks.

Exposure Practice

It is important that safety behaviors and accommodation be addressed prior to trials of exposure. If exposure practices are completed, but individuals continue to respond with safety behaviors or caregivers continue to respond with accommodation, then new learning is not achieved. Some interventions, such as Eli Lebowtiz's SPACE program (Lebowitz et al., 2014), consists entirely of decreasing accommodation. However, if the individual with SAD is still avoiding or attempting to avoid specific situations, then specific exposure practices will be necessary. Oftentimes, therapists make a hierarchy, or a systematic ordered list, of practices for exposure. For instance, if a goal for the individual with SAD is to stay home with a baby-sitter while the parent leaves the home for three hours, there are various steps to practice. The therapist can work with the individual to rate a variety of situations to create specific trials for ERP, and those rated low- to medium- on the hierarchy could be attempted first. For instance, first, a child may practice staying inside with a baby-sitter while the parent walks outside for 5 minutes. After this step is completed with success, the time could increase to 10 minutes, then to 15 and then to 30, with steps leading up to three hours. Some children will need smaller steps and may only be able initially to tolerate the parent stepping out for 10 seconds or for 1 minute during initial practices. Increasing variability of the parent's return is also typically a target higher on the hierarchy. For instance, at first a child can be told that their parent will return in 5 minutes, and the parent will set a timer to do so. However, parents can work up saying, "I will be back in 20-30 minutes," or "I will be home between 8:00 and 8:30."

Trials of ERP should be completed as regularly as possible, depending on the amount of time for the separation practice. This may mean that an individual with SAD is practicing several trials per day of shorter periods or one trial per day of a longer period of time. Ideally, trials of ERP occur in therapy sessions in addition to outside of sessions. Trials of SAD in a therapy room may involve the parent leaving the room, floor, or building and "traveling" to known or unknown destinations for increasing amounts of time. During these practices, children with SAD can also work up to being in the meeting room alone while the therapist steps out of the room for increasing amounts of time (e.g., first 10 seconds and working up to 5 minutes). During a therapy session, there is a time limit on exposure trials, so some time will need to be spent planning for home-based practices. Eventually, it may be difficult to conduct in-session practices because every possible situation in the therapy environment may be rated as too easy on the hierarchy. When this is the case, sessions will be spent planning and problem-solving home-based exposure trials and reduction of accommodation.

In addition to time, there are other variables to consider when forming a hierarchy. For instance, most children rate that practices are less anxiety provoking when they know their parent's destination or location compared to when the location is unknown. In this case, beginning trials of ERP may involve a child knowing the parent's location, and subsequent trials may involve their parent traveling to an undisclosed location. Time of day is also important to consider, as generally practices during daytime are rated as easier than practices occurring at night.

It should also be noted that learning coping skills was not explicitly mentioned in this or prior sessions. While there are adaptive coping strategies, less adaptive coping strategies can sometimes turn into safety behaviors that are counterproductive to anxiety treatment. For instance, if a child learns they can be away from their parent if they have a special stuffed animal with them, then the child still has not learned that they can handle discomfort, and they will be overly distressed if they forget or misplace the stuffed animal.

Reward System

Some individuals, especially younger children, may not be internally motivated to separate from their caregivers. If this is the case, then a reward system can be established to provide external motivation for ERP tasks. Children could earn an immediate reward after trials of separation. For instance, "If you stay inside the house with your baby-sitter while Mom goes to the store, then you can earn a sweet when I come home." Other times, children can earn points for larger rewards. For instance, "If you can complete 10 practices this week, then we can have a movie night this weekend." These rewards can also be tied to reducing safety behaviors. For instance, a goal can be set with a child to send three texts or less to their caregiver each day from school, and if they are successful, then they can earn a privilege.

Independent Sleep

Co-sleeping is a common safety behavior and aspect of family accommodation that occurs with SAD. However, just because a family reported they co-sleep does not mean that this is an anxiety-driven response. Some families may value co-sleeping, or co-sleeping may be a cultural norm. Other families may not have the options for children and caregivers to sleep in different rooms. However, if the parent is only sleeping with the child due to anxiety concerns, then independent sleep may be a target of treatment. Refer to Chapter 2 of this book for additional cultural considerations related to co-sleeping practices.

Addressing symptoms of SAD during the day is typically rated as easier on the hierarchy. If a child is not able to be alone in a room away from their caregiver during the day, then having that expectation at night when they are tired is unrealistic. Darkness may also be an anxiety-provoking situation interfering with independent sleep. If this is the case, then exposure practice of the child lying in their bed in the dark for increasing amounts of time (and increasing levels of darkness) should be practiced before independent sleep is attempted. It is also usually helpful to establish a specific reward for children to stay in their bed throughout the night. The therapist and the family should put the emphasis on staying in bed rather than on sleeping because sometimes children become distressed when they cannot immediately fall asleep. Sleep is not the goal for SAD treatment, rather the child staying in their room or in their bed quietly for the duration of the night would be the goal.

Table 2. Hierarchy for Independent Sleep

Step	Description
16	Parent says goodnight and leaves room.
15	Parent sits in chair in hallway out of child's view for 30 seconds.
14	Parent sits in chair in hallway out of child's view for 1 minute.
13	Parent sits in chair in hallway out of child's view for 2 minutes.
12	Parent sits in chair in hallway out of child's view for 5 minutes.
11	Parent sits in chair in hallway out of child's view for 10 minutes.
10	Parent sits in chair in hallway out of child's view for 15 minutes.
9	Parent sits in chair in hallway out of child's view until child falls asleep.
8	Parent sits in chair in hallway (still in view of child) until child falls asleep.
7	Parent sits in chair in doorway until child falls asleep.
6	Parent sits in chair close to doorway until child falls asleep.
5	Parent sits in chair halfway to door until child falls asleep.
4	Parent sits in chair 2 feet away from bed without holding hands or touching child until child falls asleep.
3	Parent sits in chair 12 inches away from bed without holding hands or touching child until child falls asleep.
2	Parent sits in chair 6 inches away from bed without holding hands or touching child until child falls asleep.
1	Parent sits in chair right next to bed without holding hands or touching child. Parent stays until child falls asleep.
Current situation:	Parent lies in bed with child until child falls asleep.

There are several approaches to take for independent sleep. For less anxiety-provoking cases, the therapist may be able to help the family set up a reinforcement system, and this will motivate the child to sleep independently. However, the therapist may have to take a more systematic and hierarchical approach with the family. In these cases, the parent may need to work through a hierarchy of reduced accommodation and then reward their child for staying in the room each night. For instance, if a parent is staying in the room until a child falls asleep, they could set time-based goals that decrease each night. For the first night, the parent could stay in the room for 20 minutes, then 19 for the second night, and decrease the time until they are not staying in the room at all. An alternative approach would be for a caregiver to sit in a chair next to the child's bed while they fall asleep rather than lie in bed with them. Once this is achieved, the parent would move the chair closer and closer to the door and eventually outside of the room. A parent may also want to space out "checks" on the child, whereas at first, they will check on the child every 5 minutes until they fall asleep, and this amount of time will increase each night. Refer to Table 2 for a list of steps that could be taken to achieve independent sleep. Note that not all these steps will be necessary for all children, and some children may need alternative steps. In general, a more systematic approach is often needed if a child is transitioning from their parents' bedroom to their own room. If the child leaves their bed in the middle of the night, then the parent should send the child back to their own room. The current level of the hierarchy for the beginning of the night may need to be repeated if the child leaves the bed in the middle of the night (e.g., the parent then sits in the room for 5 minutes before leaving).

Conclusion

Cognitive behavioral therapy (CBT) with exposure and response prevention (ERP) is the first line behavioral intervention for individuals with separation anxiety disorder. This approach involves measurement-based care, psychoeducation, externalization of anxiety, establishing a team-based approach, the development of a rating system, identification of goal and anxiety triggers, response prevention, reducing accommodation, and exposure practice. This intervention is a family-based approach, and therapists would work collaboratively with individuals with SAD and their families to individualize treatment goals and practices. When behavioral intervention is not effective or for moderate to severe cases of anxiety, a combined approach of behavioral intervention and medication management is recommended. More information about medication management of SAD is discussed in the following chapter.

References

American Psychiatric Association. (2022). Anxiety Disorders. In Diagnostic and statistical manual of mental disorders (5th ed., text rev.). https://doi.org/10.1176/appi.books.9780890425787.

Beck, J. S. (2020). *Cognitive Behavior Therapy: Basics and Beyond*. Guilford Publications.

Higa-McMillan, C. K., Francis, S. E., Rith-Najarian, L., & Chorpita, B. F. (2016). Evidence base update: 50 years of research on treatment for child and adolescent anxiety. *Journal of Clinical Child & Adolescent Psychology*, *45*(2), 91-113.

Lebowitz, E. R., Omer, H., Hermes, H., & Scahill, L. (2014). Parent training for childhood anxiety disorders: The SPACE program. *Cognitive and behavioral practice*, *21*(4), 456-469.

Lebowitz, E. R., Woolston, J., Bar-Haim, Y., Calvocoressi, L., Dauser, C., Warnick, E., & Leckman, J. F. (2013). Family accommodation in pediatric anxiety disorders. *Depression and Anxiety*, *30*(1), 47-54.

Scott, K., & Lewis, C. C. (2015). Using measurement-based care to enhance any treatment. *Cognitive and Behavioral Practice*, *22*(1), 49-59.

Walkup, J. T., Albano, A. M., Piacentini, J., Birmaher, B., Compton, S. N., Sherrill, J. T. Kendall, P. C. (2008). Cognitive behavioral therapy, sertraline, or a combination in childhood anxiety. *The New England Journal of Medicine*, *359*(26), 2753–2766.

Chapter 5

Medication Management of Separation Anxiety Disorder

Lauren Koehler Havel*

Department of Pediatrics, Division of Psychiatry, Baylor College of Medicine, Houston, TX, USA

Abstract

This chapter provides an overview of medication management of separation anxiety disorder (SAD). Although there is limited evidence specific to SAD, this chapter provides researched approaches generalized from anxiety disorder treatments in both adults and youth. Pharmacologic treatment is recommended for moderate-to-severe anxiety as part of a combined approach and for mild-to-moderate cases when psychotherapy alone is insufficient. The chapter also discusses the importance of regular monitoring after initiating pharmacotherapy, with weekly assessments for the first month and monthly follow-ups thereafter. Medication treatment should continue for at least 12 months post-remission to reduce relapse risk. Additionally, supportive counseling is critical to manage expectations, address side effects, and ensure that treatment goals are met. Finally, the chapter calls for further research, particularly in youth, to expand the range of therapeutic options and to explore innovative approaches to treating SAD.

Keywords: separation anxiety disorder (SAD), pharmacologic treatment, selective serotonin reuptake inhibitor (SSRI), serotonin-norepinephrine reuptake inhibitor (SNRI), psychopharmacology, medication monitoring

---

* Corresponding Author's Email: Lauren.Havel@bcm.edu.

In: Separation Anxiety: Presentation and Intervention
Editor: Kelly Nicole Banneyer
ISBN: 979-8-89530-386-3

Introduction

In this chapter, I will review the psychopharmacologic treatment of separation anxiety disorder in both youth and adults, with primary goals of outlining a rational, evidence-based approach and providing information to guide counseling and support of medication treatment. While the pharmacologic treatment of anxiety disorders in general has been extensively studied in both youth and adults, rarely is separation anxiety disorder specifically addressed.

Several bodies have provided guidelines for the treatment of anxiety disorders in youth and adults. The American Academy of Child and Adolescent Psychiatry (AACAP) outlines treatment recommendations for youth with a range of anxiety disorders, specifically including separation anxiety disorder (Walter et al., 2020). The American Psychiatric Association (APA) offers guidelines for the treatment of Panic Disorder (Stein et al., 2009) and the UK National Institutes of Health and Care Excellence (NICE) guideline offers recommendations for Generalized Anxiety Disorder (NICE, 2020), both of which recommend pharmacologic treatment of either refractory or severe anxiety disorders. Canadian clinical practice guidelines (Katzman et al., 2014) address a range of anxiety disorders, and detail the evidence base for treatment of separation anxiety disorder in youth, but not adults. Some peer-reviewed articles have additionally laid out rational approaches to pharmacotherapy in anxiety disorders (Melaragno, 2021) based on the available evidence.

Clinically, the psychopharmacologic treatment of separation anxiety disorder is necessary when symptoms do not respond sufficiently to a robust course of psychological intervention or when symptoms are sufficiently severe to warrant combined treatment with both psychotherapy and psychopharmacology. Combined treatment (medication plus psychotherapy concurrently) in youth has been demonstrated to surpass either medication treatment or psychotherapy alone in terms of rates of remission and response (Walkup et al., 2008). It is important to note that medication and psychotherapy tend to perform similarly as independent conditions; in other words, medication may be as effective as CBT (Wang et al., 2017). Given that psychotherapy may not be immediately available or feasible for many patients, medication alone may be considered even for less severe or refractory cases, if it is the most acceptable and practical treatment (Walter et al., 2020).

In addressing the pharmacologic treatment of separation anxiety disorder across the lifespan, there are several important considerations to keep in mind:

- There are no medications specifically approved for separation anxiety disorder.
- In youth, there are only two medications FDA-approved for primary anxiety disorder diagnoses, and the majority of treatment is off-label (Nibras et al., 2023).
- The majority of medication evidence is either generalized from studies of the treatment of other anxiety disorders or inferred from studies that included separation anxiety disorder as part of a larger group of disorders.
- There exists some evidence that separation anxiety may be a negative prognostic factor for treatment in general and may be less responsive to pharmacologic treatment (Minati et al., 2012)

Selective Serotonin Reuptake Inhibitors

The first-line medication treatments for separation anxiety disorder and other non-episodic anxiety disorders (e.g. generalized anxiety disorder, social phobia) are selective serotonin reuptake inhibitors (SSRIs, refer to Table 1). These medications include fluoxetine, sertraline, escitalopram, citalopram, paroxetine, fluvoxamine. Some of these medications have FDA indications for anxiety and related disorders, but there are no specific FDA approvals for separation anxiety disorder. Escitalopram is the only medication in the class with a pediatric anxiety disorder indication, recently given in May 2023 (Strawn, Moldauer, et al., 2023). However, there is no conclusive evidence to suggest that any one agent is superior to the others in the treatment of anxiety in general or separation anxiety disorder in specific. Thus, the use of SSRIs, despite being the first line treatment, may still be off-label, particularly in youth.

Separation anxiety disorder is often approached as part of a larger grouping of anxiety disorders in the study of the efficacy of SSRIs, particularly in youth. Several studies support the use of SSRIs in youth with separation anxiety disorder (Birmaher et al., 2003; Group, 2001; Walkup et al., 2008). Given the recent redefinition of separation anxiety disorder to include adult presentations, one can assume that studies of anxious adults may have captured some with separation anxiety disorder (Silove et al., 2015), but no specific studies of traditional SSRIs have been published with a sample of adults with a primary diagnosis of separation anxiety disorder.

Table 1. Selective Serotonin Reuptake Inhibitors

Drug	FDA Indications for Anxiety (* = in youth)	Starting Dose	Target Dose
Citalopram	none	10 mg	20-40 mg
Escitalopram	*Generalized Anxiety Disorder	5 mg	10-20 mg
Fluoxetine	Panic Disorder	10-20 mg	40-80 mg
Fluvoxamine	none	25 mg	100-300 mg
Paroxetine/ Paroxetine CR	Panic Disorder, Generalized Anxiety Disorder, Social Anxiety Disorder	10/12.5 mg	20-60/ 25-75 mg
Sertraline	Panic Disorder, Social Anxiety Disorder	25 mg	100-200 mg

The primary effect of SSRIs is the blockade of the serotonin transporter, which leads to increased synaptic availability of serotonin. Some SSRIs have affinity and activity at other receptors, for instance, paroxetine's significant anti-cholinergic effects, owing to muscarinic receptor blockade, leading to variability in their side effect profiles. Despite these immediate effects, the therapeutic effect of SSRIs is delayed several weeks (Thase et al., 2001). It is likely that the effective neurochemical changes are related to downstream autoregulatory effects, impacts on expression of genes for cellular signaling proteins, and neurohormonal and neuroinflammatory markers (Tafet & Nemeroff, 2020). Functionally, studies note improvement in connectivity between prefrontal cortex and amygdala, which may explain specific effects of these medications in anxiety disorders (Lu et al., 2021).

SSRI side effects include both early-emerging and late-emerging side effects (Strawn, Mills, et al., 2023). Common early side effects include gastrointestinal distress (including nausea, diarrhea, pain), fatigue, insomnia, and activation. Later side effects may include headache, dry mouth, vivid dreams, weight gain, sexual dysfunction and sweating. Overall, physical symptoms decrease in youth treated with SSRIs; early-appearing side effects may be transient or represent misattributions of existing symptoms of anxiety. Reassurance and watchful waiting are valuable strategies. Suicidal ideation and behavior are reported risks in adolescents and young adults, and SSRIs (as well as all other antidepressants) carry a boxed warning for this concern. In children and young adults with anxiety disorders, the evidence is mixed regarding this possible effect (Bridge et al., 2007; Lagerberg et al., 2021). Given the salient warning, counseling regarding this possible adverse event is crucial when initiating any antidepressant medication, although these warnings should not present a contraindication or reservation regarding medication treatment. In collaboration with the prescribing clinician, all side effects are manageable. Patients and families should be encouraged to discuss any concerns openly, particularly given the discomfort of potential antidepressant discontinuation syndrome.

In summary, when administering SSRIs for separation anxiety disorder, beginning with a low dose of one of the best-tolerated medications is a prudent strategy, keeping in mind potential side effects and interactions with other medications to guide selection of a specific agent. The initial goals are to avoid inducing excessive side effects and to manage the inevitable anxiety associated with starting a new medication. Once a starting dose is tolerated, the dose should be gradually increased to reach a sufficient target dose. The full effects of SSRIs may take up to 6-12 weeks to be evident, though some early benefits may be seen within the first 2-4 weeks of treatment. Consistency in taking medication is important, both to achieving therapeutic benefit and in minimizing side effects. Typically, these medications are taken at the same time each day, with or after food. Missed doses should be taken as soon as they are remembered within the same day. Counseling and support around expectations with these medications, including delayed onset of action, management of side effects, and the fact that medication will not "get rid of anxiety" are crucial in ongoing treatment and meeting the long-term goals of pharmacotherapy.

Serotonin Norepinephrine Reuptake Inhibitors

Closely related to the SSRIs are the serotonin norepinephrine reuptake inhibitors (SNRIs). The medications in this class include duloxetine, venlafaxine, desvenlafaxine, milnacipran and levomilnacipran (see Table 2). Although venalafaxine XR and duloxetine carry official anxiety disorder indications (including duloxetine's indication for pediatric generalized anxiety disorder), these agents are considered later first-line or second-line, owing to the potential for additional side effects compared to SSRIs. This is balanced by the potential for increased response rates, although this comparison has only been thoroughly reviewed in depression studies (de Silva & Hanwella, 2012; Weinmann et al., 2008). The meta-analyses that do examine the SNRIs duloxetine and venalafaxine for anxiety in adults have concluded that both are effective and well-tolerated in short term treatment (Li et al., 2017; Li et al., 2018). In a network meta-analysis of youth treated with various pharmacotherapies for anxiety, SNRIs were effective for pediatric anxiety compared to placebo, but SSRIs were found to be more significantly associated with treatment response (Dobson et al., 2019). In large randomized, placebo-controlled, staged research studies for depression, SNRIs have generally been deployed in later stages or phases, additionally contributing to the recommendation to start with an SSRI prior to an SNRI (Rush et al., 2006).

In addition to serotonin transporter blockade, SNRIs additionally inhibit the reuptake of norepinephrine via the presynaptic norepinephrine transporter. Within the class, these medications vary widely in their receptor affinities. At most therapeutic doses, duloxetine, venlafaxine and desvenlafaxine are predominantly serotonergic; norepinephrine reuptake is dose-dependent. Milnacipran, which has no FDA indications for psychiatric purposes, has a 2:1 ratio of noradrenergic to serotonergic activity. Levomilnacipran has a similar profile and is FDA-approved for Major Depressive Disorder. The additional noradrenergic activity of these medications is attributed to potential side effects such as increased blood pressure, dizziness, and other hemodynamic effects. Otherwise, their side effect profile is quite similar to the SSRIs. On the other hand, these medications have also been demonstrated to reduce neuropathic pain, and many carry FDA indications for fibromyalgia. This may make SNRIs a particularly useful option in patients for whom anxiety is complicated by chronic pain syndromes (Stahl et al., 2005).

Thus, SNRIs are an excellent option when one or two SSRI medications have been ineffective or not well-tolerated for separation anxiety. SNRIs, particularly duloxetine, may be a rational first choice in patients with anxiety comorbid with pain syndromes. The treatment strategy when using SNRIs mirrors the strategy with SSRIs: begin with a low dose, provide counseling about expectations and side effects, and titrate rationally to a goal dose, which should be sustained or further titrated until treatment effect or side effect occurs. SNRIs may be more likely to have an associated discontinuation syndrome; caution is advised when tapering and stopping these medications.

Table 2. Serotonin Norepinephrine Reuptake Inhibitors

Drug	FDA Indications for Anxiety (* = in youth)	Starting Dose	Target Dose
Desvenlafaxine	none	50 mg	50-100 mg
Venlafaxine XR	Panic Disorder, Generalized Anxiety Disorder, Social Anxiety Disorder	37.5 mg	75-225 mg
Duloxetine	*Generalized Anxiety Disorder	20-30 mg	60-120 mg
Milnacipran	none	25 mg twice daily	50 mg twice daily
Levomilnacipran	none	20 mg	40-120 mg

Other Antidepressants

Tricyclic Antidepressants

Tricyclic Antidepressants (TCAs) are a class of medications that primarily inhibit the reuptake of norepinephrine and serotonin. These medications include imipramine, clomipramine, amitriptyline, and desipramine, among others. The TCAs also have a wide variety of other pharmacodynamic properties, including antagonism at alpha-1 adrenergic receptors, muscarinic receptors and histaminic receptors. Though no FDA indications have been granted for any specific anxiety disorder diagnosis within the TCAs, clomipramine is indicated for treatment of Obsessive-Compulsive Disorder, both in youth and adults, either alone or as an adjunct to an SSRI (Piccinelli et al., 1995). A number of randomized controlled trials have evaluated the effectiveness of TCAs vs. placebo in the treatment of adults with anxiety disorders, with positive results (Rickels et al., 1993; Schmitt et al., 2005), and they may be as effective as first-line options (Bakker et al., 2002). Imipramine has been repeatedly studied in youth with school refusal with or without separation anxiety disorder, with mixed results (Berney et al., 1981; Bernstein et al., 2000; Klein et al., 1992). The myriad pharmacodynamic effects of the TCAs means that each is unique in terms of its potential for side effects; as a class, they are not as well-tolerated as SSRIs owing to these "nonselective" profiles (Trindade et al., 1998). In particular, orthostatic hypotension, sedation, dry mouth, urinary retention, weight gain are often problematic and may limit adequate dosing. The utility of TCAs, particularly in vulnerable populations, is also limited by their narrow therapeutic index need for blood level monitoring (Daly & Wilens, 1998; Mitchell, 2001). Therefore, it is reasonable to consider TCAs second- or third-line options, or as adjunctive agents, for older adolescents or young adults who have had sufficient trials of several SSRI and SNRI options in addition to a robust course of psychotherapy and have not experienced sufficient response.

Monoamine Oxidase Inhibitors

Monoamine Oxidase Inhibitors (MAOIs) block the breakdown of serotonin, norepinephrine and dopamine via the enzymes monoamine oxidase A and B. Serotonin is metabolized only by MAO-A, whereas dopamine and norepinephrine are broken down by both. The inhibition of MAOIs may be irreversible or reversible, selective or non-selective. Studies have demonstrated that irreversible MAOIs are superior to placebo in adults with panic disorder (Buigues & Vallejo, 1987) and social anxiety disorder (Nardi et al., 2010). There is also considerable interest in reversible MAOI moclobemide in the treatment of anxiety disorders, panic in particular (Tiller et al., 1997). The choice of an MAOI would be guided by intended treatment target, side effect profile, other medications taken by the patient, and willingness of patients to make significant dietary modifications. Common side effects include orthostatic hypotension, insomnia or sedation, constipation, dry mouth, and headache (Kennedy, 1997). With irreversible inhibitors, which are the only agents available in the United States, the risk of serotonin syndrome and hypertensive crisis is significantly elevated, necessitating caution about foods containing tyramine, sympathomimetic agents, and other serotonergic medications (Lippman & Nash, 1990). As a result of these restrictions and side effect profile, MAOIs would be considered third-line options primarily for adults with treatment-refractory anxiety.

Tetracyclic Antidepressants

Tetracyclic Antidepressants, the available example of which is mirtazapine, have a wide range of receptor activities. Mirtazapine functions as an antihistamine, alpha-2 adrenergic antagonist, and serotonin antagonist, most notably at the 5HT-2 receptors. These activities may all have a role in its anxiolytic properties; it is also quite sedating, and at its lowest doses, may be used as a soporific. Although it has no FDA indications for the treatment of anxiety disorders, mirtazapine has substantial evidence for its use in both adults and youth with anxiety, either independent or comorbid with major depression. In adults, it has been studied and found effective in social anxiety disorder (Muehlbacher et al., 2005; Schutters et al., 2010), panic disorder (Montañés-Rada et al., 2005; Ribeiro et al., 2001), and generalized anxiety disorder (Gambi et al., 2005). In pediatric populations, it has shown efficacy and tolerability for youth with anxiety and ASD (McDougle et al., 2022). Often its other effects (e.g. sedation, appetite stimulation) are helpful in managing the somatic symptoms of anxiety disorders, including chronic gastrointestinal distress (Jamshidfar et al., 2023; Tack et al., 2016). Given its profile, mirtazapine is an appropriate second- or third-line option for the treatment of separation anxiety complicated by significant insomnia or gastrointestinal distress, which are common symptoms in youth.

Other Serotonergic Antidepressants

A variety of other serotonergic antidepressants which may be classified in a variety of ways (such as SARIs, SSRI/5HT-1a, etc.), function, at least in part, via direct modulation of serotonin receptors. These medications are indicated by the FDA for the treatment of Major Depressive Disorder in adults and include vilazodone (SSRI and 5HT-1A partial agonist), vortioxetine (SSRI and 5HT-1A/B agonist, 5HT-3 antagonist) as well as trazodone (5HT-1A partial agonist, among many other activities). As a result of their varying receptor affinities and activities, they also vary in their anxiolytic properties. None is FDA-approved for an anxiety disorder indication, and none has a pediatric indication. Of this group, only vilazodone has been specifically studied in separation anxiety disorder (Schneier et al., 2017). This was a randomized control pilot trial with 24 subjects who were randomized to 12 weeks of placebo or vilazodone. While the results trended towards benefit with vilazodone compared to placebo, the difference in response rates at 12 weeks did not differ significantly between groups. Vilazodone has also been studied in generalized anxiety disorder with positive results, though its utility was limited by the potential for adverse effects (Zareifopoulos & Dylja, 2017). Vortioxetine was not shown to have benefit in generalized anxiety disorder compared to placebo in a double-blind placebo-controlled trial, with an active comparator of duloxetine (Mahableshwarkar et al., 2014). Unique aspects of this group of medications may be reduced incidence of side effects traditionally associated with SSRIs, including a reduced incidence of sexual dysfunction and weight gain. Gastrointestinal side effects and sedation are still possible side effects, among others. While the anxiolytic properties of these medications are promising, the evidence does not clearly support their routine use. These medications thus represent third- or fourth-line options for the treatment of separation anxiety disorder; they may be more appealing options in adults, particularly with comorbidity, given their approval for depression in that age group.

5HT-1a Partial Agonists

5HT-1a partial agonists, or azapirones, approved in the United States, include buspirone and gepirone. Buspirone has additional agonist activity at presynaptic 5HT-1a receptors and is FDA-approved for the treatment of generalized anxiety disorder in adults (Chessick et al., 2006). In youth, its use is off-label, and studies of its effectiveness have been limited by incompleteness, small sample sizes, and lack of blinding (Strawn et al., 2018). Buspirone is, however, generally well-tolerated, with common side effects being lightheadedness, nausea, and sedation (Salazar et al., 2001). Flexible dosing is one advantage of Buspirone that is not offered by SSRIs; owing to its unique mechanism it does have some immediate anxiolytic effects. As such, it may be used adjunctively with SSRIs and other antidepressants, with the exception of MAOIs. On the other hand, its short half-life and the two- or three-times daily dosing schedule may be a limitation for some patients and families. Gepirone has been shown to be more effective than placebo in generalized anxiety disorder (Rickels et al., 1997). Its ER formulation was recently awarded FDA approval for Major Depressive Disorder, with some suggestion that it may be favorable in those with anxious distress. Gepirone demonstrated a favorable side effect profile, particularly regarding weight gain and sexual dysfunction, but may still cause nausea and dizziness (Alpert et al., 2004). Thus, azapirones are potential second-line options for patients with separation anxiety disorder who cannot tolerate SSRIs. Buspirone may be used as adjunctive treatment alongside an SSRI or SNRI when the response to treatment is incomplete.

Other Anxiolytics

There are a number of other medications that possess anxiolytic properties and may be of benefit as adjunctive or third-line options in the treatment of separation anxiety disorder. None of these medications carries FDA approval for the treatment of any anxiety disorder in adults or youth. Propranolol is a beta-adrenergic antagonist ("beta blocker") that reduces heart rate increase and other symptoms of sympathetic nervous system arousal. It is commonly used for performance type social anxiety but may be useful in other situational anxiety conditions (Steenen et al., 2016). Hydroxyzine is an H-1 antihistamine with anxiolytic properties, owing to 5HT receptor activity, which has been studied in GAD and shown to be more effective than placebo (Lader & Scotto, 1998; Llorca et al., 2002). It is often used in lieu of a benzodiazepine for the short-term management of acute anxiety, given its lack of abuse potential. However, it may be sedating and cause other anticholinergic side effects such as dry mouth and cardiac arrythmia at high doses. Gabapentin and pregabalin are both GABA analogues that interact with voltage-gated calcium channels, thereby modulating neurotransmitter release. There have been limited controlled studies of these medications in anxiety disorders, but findings are generally positive (Hong et al., 2022). One advantage of these medications is their complete lack of serotonergic activity, which may make them a good option to treat anxiety in patients with co-occurring bipolar disorder. Neither gabapentin nor pregabalin has been studied in youth with anxiety disorders.

Benzodiazepines

Benzodiazepines act at the GABA-A receptor, which produces their anxiolytic and sedative effects. A number of benzodiazepines are FDA-indicated for the treatment of anxiety disorders, including GAD and panic disorder (Simon et al., 2020). In the United States, the most commonly prescribed benzodiazepines are alprazolam, clonazepam, lorazepam and diazepam. Studies have demonstrated larger effect sizes with benzodiazepines than SSRIs (Gomez et al., 2018). None carries an indication for separation anxiety disorder. In youth, benzodiazepines have not been demonstrated to be superior to placebo for anxiety disorders (Graae et al., 1994; Simeon et al., 1992), including school refusal (Bernstein et al., 1990).

Benzodiazepines do provide rapid, noticeable relief of anxiety and are frequently prescribed in non-psychiatric settings. However, these same properties (potency, rapidity of action) are related to the liability for abuse and dependence with benzodiazepines, a major limitation to their use. Cognitive impairment, sedation, and behavioral disinhibition may occur with the use of benzodiazepines; intoxication resembles alcohol intoxication. There is further evidence that benzodiazepines may impair the extinction learning necessary for the benefit of prolonged exposure therapy and cognitive-behavioral therapy (Hart et al., 2014). Patients using benzodiazepines regularly for anxiety may experience withdrawal effects upon ceasing use. Severe benzodiazepine withdrawal may include seizures, delirium and death. Less serious, rebound anxiety may occur between benzodiazepine doses, particularly with medications with short half-lives, such as alprazolam, and contribute to worsening of anxiety over time. Even given these risks, benzodiazepines can be extremely useful in the management of anxiety, particularly while waiting for other treatments to be effective.

A rational strategy for the use of benzodiazepines in separation anxiety disorder would be to consider their use second-line at minimum in adults, reserved for severe anxiety not yet managed by other means and interfering with functioning. For example, a dose of a benzodiazepine might be used to make necessary travel possible. Practitioners should counsel patients extensively on risks and benefits associated with these medications, including the potential risks for interference with exposure-based treatments. The lowest effective dosage of a longer-acting benzodiazepine, dosed at regular intervals as a bridge, may be useful in minimizing the potential for dose escalation, tolerance, and rebound anxiety.

Antipsychotics

Another category of medications that has been considered for use in anxiety disorders is antipsychotics, specifically second-generation or "atypical" antipsychotics. These medications have varying levels of receptor specificity, which may include Dopamine D2 receptor antagonism (the primary function of the class) as well as serotonin 5HT2 antagonism, among others. It is thought that the 5-HT2 antagonism may exert these medications' primary anxiolytic effects, though antihistaminic and antiadrenergic properties may play a role as well. Their FDA indications are typically for schizophrenia or bipolar disorder. A few have indications for youth for the acute treatment or maintenance of these conditions, including quetiapine, paliperidone, risperidone, aripiprazole and olanzapine.

These medications have not been evaluated in separation anxiety disorder but have been studied in generalized anxiety disorder. A meta-analysis examining the use of Quetiapine XR as a standalone treatment for generalized anxiety disorder found it superior to placebo and similar to SSRIs, both in effectiveness and in discontinuation rates due to side effects (Maneeton et al., 2016). Risperidone used as an adjunctive treatment in patients not experiencing response with an anxiolytic after 4 weeks was found to reduce anxiety symptoms compared to a placebo adjunct, but did not lead to a significant difference in response rate (Brawman-Mintzer et al., 2005).

In terms of short-term side effects, atypical antipsychotics may cause sedation, increased appetite leading to weight gain, effects on pituitary hormones, abnormal movements, and restlessness. Long term side effects include metabolic syndrome and the potential for tardive dyskinesia. The majority of the studies that evaluate these medications for anxiety are short-term studies and as such have not evaluated the prevalence of these side effects in groups of patients using them for anxiety (Gao et al., 2009). Given the seriousness and potential irreversibility of some of these side effects (tardive dyskinesia, in particular), caution should be taken in prescribing these medications for anxiety, even with their potential effectiveness in the short-term management of anxiety.

Thus, second-generation antipsychotics may be considered in specific prescribing situations, such as separation anxiety disorder comorbid with bipolar disorder, or as adjuncts to first- or second-line options, when significant aggression, irritability or mood lability complicate the management of separation anxiety disorder.

Conclusion

While there is limited evidence to support specific pharmacologic strategies in separation anxiety disorder, there is ample support for a rational approach to anxiety disorders in general in both adults and youth, which is likely generalizable to separation anxiety disorder, keeping in mind some of the caveats mentioned at the beginning of this chapter. Following, I have outlined such an approach, including one exemplar of each medication class: In general, pharmacologic treatment should be considered for moderate-to-severe anxiety as part of a combined treatment approach, and for mild-to-moderate anxiety when a course of evidence-based psychotherapy has not led to sufficient response or remission. Pharmacotherapy alone may also be considered as an initial approach for those families for whom psychotherapy is not a feasible option. First-line medication approaches include SSRI (escitalopram) and SNRI (duloxetine) monotherapy; second-line approaches include tricyclic antidepressants (clomipramine), tetracyclic antidepressants (mirtazapine), 5-HT1a partial agonists (buspirone); third- and later-line options include other serotonin modulating antidepressants (vilazodone) and MAOIs (phenelzine). Augmentation or short-term options include benzodiazepines (clonazepam) and other anxiolytics (hydroxyzine); some agents that can be used as monotherapy such as the TCAs and 5-HT1a antagonists can also be used as augmentation of other first-line treatments. Alternative treatments that may be considered in patients with significant or treatment-altering comorbidity may include GABA analogues (gabapentin) and second-generation antipsychotics (quetiapine XR).

After initiation of a medication, monitoring should ideally occur weekly for the first 4 weeks, and monthly thereafter. Once treatment response or remission is achieved, medication treatment should be sustained for 12 months to minimize the risk of relapse. Counseling and supportive management during pharmacotherapy are crucial to manage expectations, side effects, and evaluate whether treatment is meeting both short- and long-term goals. Additional research is needed, particularly in youth, to identify therapeutic alternatives beyond first-line approaches, and to discover novel approaches to the treatment of separation anxiety disorder.

References

Alpert, J. E., Franznick, D. A., Hollander, S. B., & Fava, M. (2004). Gepirone extended-release treatment of anxious depression: evidence from a retrospective subgroup analysis in patients with major depressive disorder. *J Clin Psychiatry*, *65*(8), 1069-1075.

Bakker, A., Van Balkom, A. J. L. M., & Spinhoven, P. (2002). SSRIs vs. TCAs in the treatment of panic disorder: a meta-analysis. *Acta Psychiatrica Scandinavica*, *106*, 163-167.

Berney, T., Kolvin, I., Bhate, S. R., Garside, R. F., Jeans, J., Kay, B., & Scarth, L. (1981). School phobia: a therapeutic trial with clomipramine and short- term outcome. *British Journal of Psychiatry*, *138*, 110-118.

Bernstein, G. A., Borchardt, C. M., Perwien, A. R., Crosby, R. D., Kushner, M. G., Thuras, P. D., & Last, C. G. (2000). Imipramine plus cognitive-behavioral therapy in the treatment of school refusal. *Journal of the American Academy of Child and Adolescent Psychiatry*, *39*, 276-283.

Bernstein, G. A., Garfinkel, B. D., & Borchardt, C. M. (1990). Comparative studies of pharmacotherapy for school refusal. *J Am Acad Child Adolesc Psychiatry*, *29*(5), 773-781. https://doi.org/10.1097/00004583-199009000-00016.

Birmaher, B., Axelson, D., Monk, K., Kalas, C., Clark, D., Ehmann, M., Bridge, J., Heo, J., & Brent, D. (2003). Fluoxetine for the treatment of childhood anxiety disorders. *Journal of the American Academy of Child and Adolescent Psychiatry*, *42*, 415-423.

Brawman-Mintzer, O., Knapp, R. G., & Nietert, P. J. (2005). Adjunctive risperidone in generalized anxiety disorder: a double-blind, placebo-controlled study. *J Clin Psychiatry*, *66*(10), 1321-1325. https://doi.org/10.4088/jcp.v66n1016.

Bridge, J. A., Iyengar, S., Salary, C. B., Barbe, R. P., Birmaher, B., Pincus, H. A., Ren, L., & Brent, D. A. (2007). Clinical Response and Risk for Reported Suicidal Ideation and Suicide Attempts in Pediatric Antidepressant Treatment: A Meta-analysis of

Randomized Controlled Trials. *Journal of the American Medical Association*, *297*(15), 1683-1696.

Buigues, J., & Vallejo, J. (1987). Therapeutic response to phenelzine in patients with panic disorder and agoraphobia with panic attacks. *J Clin Psychiatry*, *48*(2), 55-59.

Chessick, C. A., Allen, M. H., Thase, M., Batista Miralha da Cunha, A. B., Kapczinski, F. F., de Lima, M. S., & dos Santos Souza, J. J. (2006). Azapirones for generalized anxiety disorder. *Cochrane Database Syst Rev*, *2006*(3), Cd006115. https://doi.org/10.1002/14651858.Cd006115.

Daly, J. M., & Wilens, T. (1998). The use of tricyclic antidepressants in children and adolescents. *Pediatric Clinics of North America*, *45*(5), 1123-1135.

de Silva, V. A., & Hanwella, R. (2012). Efficacy and tolerability of venlafaxine versus specific serotonin reuptake inhibitors in treatment of major depressive disorder: a meta-analysis of published studies. . *International Clinical Psychopharmacology*, *27*(1), 8-16.

Dobson, E. T., Bloch, M. H., & Strawn, J. R. (2019). Efficacy and Tolerability of Pharmacotherapy for Pediatric Anxiety Disorders: A Network Meta-Analysis. *Journal of Clinical Psychiatry*, *80*(1), 17r12064.

Gambi, F., De Berardis, D., Campanella, D., Carano, A., Sepede, G., Salini, G., Mezzano, D., Cicconetti, A., Penna, L., Salerno, R. M., & Ferro, F. M. (2005). Mirtazapine treatment of generalized anxiety disorder: a fixed dose, open label study. *J Psychopharmacol*, *19*(5), 483-487. https://doi.org/10.1177/0269881105056527.

Gao, K., Sheehan, D. V., & Calabrese, J. R. (2009). Atypical antipsychotics in primary generalized anxiety disorder or comorbid with mood disorders. *Expert Rev Neurother*, *9*(8), 1147-1158. https://doi.org/10.1586/ern.09.37.

Gomez, A. F., Barthel, A. L., & Hofmann, S. G. (2018). Comparing the efficacy of benzodiazepines and serotonergic anti-depressants for adults with generalized anxiety disorder: a meta-analytic review. *Expert Opin Pharmacother*, *19*(8), 883-894. https://doi.org/10.1080/14656566.2018.1472767.

Graae, F., Milner, J., Rizzotto, L., & Klein, R. G. (1994). Clonazepam in childhood anxiety disorders. *J Am Acad Child Adolesc Psychiatry*, *33*(3), 372-376. https://doi.org/10.1097/00004583-199403000-00011.

Group, T. R. U. o. P. P. A. S. (2001). Fluvoxamine for the treatment of anxiety disorders in children and adolescents. *The New England Journal of Medicine*, *344*, 1279-1285.

Hart, G., Panayi, M. C., Harris, J. A., & Westbrook, R. F. (2014). Benzodiazepine treatment can impair or spare extinction, depending on when it is given. *Behav Res Ther*, *56*, 22-29. https://doi.org/10.1016/j.brat.2014.02.004

Hong, J. S. W., Atkinson, L. Z., Al-Juffali, N., Awad, A., Geddes, J. R., Tunbridge, E. M., Harrison, P. J., & Cipriani, A. (2022). Gabapentin and pregabalin in bipolar disorder, anxiety states, and insomnia: Systematic review, meta-analysis, and rationale. *Mol Psychiatry*, *27*(3), 1339-1349. https://doi.org/10.1038/s41380-021-01386-6.

Jamshidfar, N., Hamdieh, M., Eslami, P., Batebi, S., Sadeghi, A., Rastegar, R., Dooghaie Moghadam, A., & Masjedi Arani, A. (2023). Comparison of the potency of nortriptyline and mirtazapine on gastrointestinal symptoms, the level of anxiety and depression in patients with functional dyspepsia. *Gastroenterol Hepatol Bed Bench*, *16*(1), 468-477. https://doi.org/10.22037/ghfbb.v16i1.2513.

Katzman, M. A., Bleau, P., Blier, P., Chokka, P., Kjernisted, K., Ameringen, M. V., & University, T. C. A. G. I. G. o. b. o. t. A. D. A. o. C. A. C. d. t. a. a. M. (2014). Canadian clinical practice guidelines for the management of anxiety, posttraumatic stress and obsessive-compulsive disorders. *BMC Psychiatry*, *14*(S1).

Kennedy, S. H. (1997). Continuation and maintenance treatments in major depression: the neglected role of monoamine oxidase inhibitors. *J Psychiatry Neurosci*, *22*(2), 127-131.

Klein, R. G., Koplewicz, H. S., & Kanner, A. (1992). Imipramine treatment of children with separation anxiety disorder. *Journal of the American Academy of Child and Adolescent Psychiatry*, *31*, 21-28.

Lader, M., & Scotto, J. C. (1998). A multicentre double-blind comparison of hydroxyzine, buspirone and placebo in patients with generalized anxiety disorder. *Psychopharmacology (Berl)*, *139*(4), 402-406. https://doi.org/10.1007/s002130050731.

Lagerberg, T., Fazel, S., Sjölander, A., Hellner, C., Lichtenstein, P., & Chang, Z. (2021). Selective serotonin reuptake inhibitors and suicidal behaviour: a population-based cohort study. *Neuropsychopharmacology*, *47*, 817-823.

Li, X., Zhu, L., Su, Y., & Fang, S. (2017). Short-term efficacy and tolerability of venlafaxine extended release in adults with generalized anxiety disorder without depression: A meta-analysis. *PLoS ONE*, *12*(10), e0185865.

Li, X., Zhu, L., Zhou, C., Du, H., Wang, C., & Fang, S. (2018). Efficacy and tolerability of short-term duloxetine treatment in adults with generalized anxiety disorder: A meta-analysis. *PLoS ONE*, *13*(3), e0194501.

Lippman, S. B., & Nash, K. (1990). Monoamine oxidase inhibitor update. Potential adverse food and drug interactions. *Drug Saf*, *5*(3), 195-204. https://doi.org/10.2165/00002018-199005030-00004.

Llorca, P. M., Spadone, C., Sol, O., Danniau, A., Bougerol, T., Corruble, E., Faruch, M., Macher, J. P., Sermet, E., & Servant, D. (2002). Efficacy and safety of hydroxyzine in the treatment of generalized anxiety disorder: a 3-month double-blind study. *J Clin Psychiatry*, *63*(11), 1020-1027. https://doi.org/10.4088/jcp.v63n1112.

Lu, L., Mills, J. A., Li, H., Schroeder, H. K., Mossman, S. A., Varney, S. T., Cecil, K. M., Huang, X., Gong, Q., Ramsey, L. B., DelBello, M. P., Sweeney, J. A., & Strawn, J. R. (2021). Acute Neurofunctional Effects of Escitalopram in Pediatric Anxiety: A Double-Blind, Placebo-Controlled Trial. *Journal of the American Academy of Child and Adolescent Psychiatry*, *60*(10), 1309-1318..

Mahableshwarkar, A. R., Jacobsen, P. L., Chen, Y., & Simon, J. S. (2014). A randomised, double-blind, placebo-controlled, duloxetine-referenced study of the efficacy and tolerability of vortioxetine in the acute treatment of adults with generalised anxiety disorder. *Int J Clin Pract*, *68*(1), 49-59. https://doi.org/10.1111/ijcp.12328.

Maneeton, N., Maneeton, B., Woottiluk, P., Likhitsathian, S., Suttajit, S., Boonyanaruthee, V., & Srisurapanont, M. (2016). Quetiapine monotherapy in acute treatment of generalized anxiety disorder: a systematic review and meta-analysis of randomized controlled trials. *Drug Des Devel Ther*, *10*, 259-276. https://doi.org/10.2147/dddt.S89485.

McDougle, C. J., Thom, R. P., Ravichandran, C. T., Palumbo, M. L., Politte, L. C., Mullett, J. E., Keary, C. J., Erickson, C. A., Stigler, K. A., Mathieu-Frasier, L., & Posey, D. J. (2022). A randomized double-blind, placebo-controlled pilot trial of mirtazapine for anxiety in children and adolescents with autism spectrum disorder. *Neuropsychopharmacology*, *47*(6), 1263-1270. https://doi.org/10.1038/s41386-022-01295-4.

Melaragno, A. J. (2021). Pharmacotherapy for Anxiety Disorders: From First-Line Options to Treatment Resistance. *Focus*, *19*(2), 145-160.

Minati, M., Calugi, S., Rucci, P., Shear, M. K., Benvenuti, A., Santoro, D., Mauri, M., & Cassano, G. B. (2012). Predictors of response among patients with panic disorder treated with medications in a naturalistic follow up: The role of adult separation anxiety. . *Journal of Affective Disorders*, *136*, 675-679.

Mitchell, P. B. (2001). Therapeutic drug monitoring of psychotropic medications. *British Journal of Clinical Pharmacology*, *52*, 455-545.

Montañés-Rada, F., De Lucas-Taracena, M. T., & Sánchez-Romero, S. (2005). Mirtazapine versus paroxetine in panic disorder: an open study. *Int J Psychiatry Clin Pract*, *9*(2), 87-93. https://doi.org/10.1080/13651500510018248.

Muehlbacher, M., Nickel, M. K., Nickel, C., Kettler, C., Lahmann, C., Pedrosa Gil, F., Leiberich, P. K., Rother, N., Bachler, E., Fartacek, R., Kaplan, P., Tritt, K., Mitterlehner, F., Anvar, J., Rother, W. K., Loew, T. H., & Egger, C. (2005). Mirtazapine treatment of social phobia in women: a randomized, double-blind, placebo-controlled study. *J Clin Psychopharmacol*, *25*(6), 580-583. https://doi.org/10.1097/01.jcp.0000186871.04984.8d.

Nardi, A. E., Lopes, F. L., Valença, A. M., Freire, R. C., Nascimento, I., Veras, A. B., Mezzasalma, M. A., de-Melo-Neto, V. L., Soares-Filho, G. L., King, A. L., Grivet, L. O., Rassi, A., & Versiani, M. (2010). Double-blind comparison of 30 and 60 mg tranylcypromine daily in patients with panic disorder comorbid with social anxiety disorder. *Psychiatry Res*, *175*(3), 260-265. https://doi.org/10.1016/j.psychres.2008.06.025.

Nibras, S., Truong, A., & Williams, L. L. (2023). Pharmacological Treatment of Anxiety Disorders in Children and Adolescents. In D. McKay & E. A. Storch (Eds.), *Handbook of Child and Adolescent Anxiety Disorders* (pp. 347-355). Springer International Publishing. https://doi.org/10.1007/978-3-031-14080-8_23.

NICE, N. I. f. H. a. C. E. (2020). Generalised anxiety disorder and panic disorder in adults: management. www.nice.org.uk/guidance/cg113.

Piccinelli, M., Pini, S., Bellantuono, C., & Wilkinson, G. (1995). Efficacy of drug treatment in obsessive-compulsive disorder. A meta-analytic review. *The British Journal of Psychiatry*, *166*(4), 424-443.

Ribeiro, L., Busnello, J. V., Kauer-Sant'Anna, M., Madruga, M., Quevedo, J., Busnello, E. A., & Kapczinski, F. (2001). Mirtazapine versus fluoxetine in the treatment of panic disorder. *Braz J Med Biol Res*, *34*(10), 1303-1307. https://doi.org/10.1590/s0100-879x2001001000010.

Rickels, K., Downing, R., Schweizer, E., & Hassman, H. (1993). Antidepressants for the treatment of generalized anxiety disorder. A placebo- controlled comparison of imipramine, trazodone, and diazepam. . *Archives of General Psychiatry*, *50*, 884-895.

Rickels, K., Schweizer, E., DeMartinis, N., Mandos, L., & Mercer, C. (1997). Gepirone and diazepam in generalized anxiety disorder: a placebo-controlled trial. *J Clin Psychopharmacol*, *17*(4), 272-277. https://doi.org/10.1097/00004714-199708000-00006.

Rush, A. J., Trivedi, M. H., Wisniewski, S. R., Stewart, J. W., Neierenberg, A. A., Thase, M. E., Ritz, L., Biggs, M. M., Diane, W., Luther, J. F., Shores-Wilson, K., Niederehe, G., Fava, M., & Team, S. D. S. (2006). Bupropion-SR, Sertraline, or Venlafaxine-XR after Failure of SSRIs for Depression. *The New England Journal of Medicine*, *354*(12), 1231-1242.

Salazar, D. E., Frackiewicz, E. J., Dockens, R., Kollia, G., Fulmor, I. E., Tigel, P. D., Uderman, H. D., Shiovitz, T. M., Sramek, J. J., & Cutler, N. R. (2001). Pharmacokinetics and tolerability of buspirone during oral administration to children and adolescents with anxiety disorder and normal healthy adults. *J Clin Pharmacol*, *41*(12), 1351-1358. https://doi.org/10.1177/00912700122012823.

Schmitt, R., Gazalle, F. K., Lima, M. S., Cunha, A., Souza, J., & Kapczinski, F. (2005). The efficacy of antidepressants for generalized anxiety disorder: a systematic review and meta-analysis. *Brazilian Review of Psychiatry*, *27*(1), 18-24.

Schneier, F. R., Moskow, D. M., Choo, T. H., Galfalvy, H., Campeas, R., & Sanchez-Lacay, A. (2017). A randomized controlled pilot trial of vilazodone for adult separation anxiety disorder. *Depression and Anxiety*, *34*, 1085-1095.

Schutters, S. I., Van Megen, H. J., Van Veen, J. F., Denys, D. A., & Westenberg, H. G. (2010). Mirtazapine in generalized social anxiety disorder: a randomized, double-blind, placebo-controlled study. *Int Clin Psychopharmacol*, *25*(5), 302-304. https://doi.org/10.1097/yic.0b013e32833a4d71

Silove, D., Alonso, J., Bromet, E., Gruber, M., Sampson, N., Scott, K., Andrade, L., Benjet, C., Almeida, J. M. C. d., Girolamo, G. D., Jonge, P. d., Demyttenaere, K., Fiestas, F., Florescu, S., Gureje, O., He, Y., Karam, E., Lepine, J. P., Murphy, S., . . . Kessler, R. C. (2015). Pediatric-Onset and Adult-Onset Separation Anxiety Disorder Accross Countries in the World Mental Health Survey. *American Journal of Psychiatry*, *172*(7), 647-656.

Simeon, J. G., Ferguson, H. B., Knott, V., Roberts, N., Gauthier, B., Dubois, C., & Wiggins, D. (1992). Clinical, cognitive, and neurophysiological effects of alprazolam in children and adolescents with overanxious and avoidant disorders. *J Am Acad Child Adolesc Psychiatry*, *31*(1), 29-33. https://doi.org/10.1097/00004583-199201000-00006.

Simon, N., Hollander, E., Rothbaum, B. O., & Stein, D. J. (Eds.). (2020). *The american psychiatric association publishing textbook of anxiety, trauma, and ocd-related disorders*. American Psychiatric Publishing.

Stahl, S. M., Grady, M. M., Moret, C., & Briley, M. (2005). SNRIs: their pharmacology, clinical efficacy, and tolerability in comparison with other classes of antidepressants. *CNS Spectrums*, *10*(9), 732-747.

Steenen, S. A., van Wijk, A. J., van der Heijden, G. J., van Westrhenen, R., de Lange, J., & de Jongh, A. (2016). Propranolol for the treatment of anxiety disorders: Systematic review and meta-analysis. *J Psychopharmacol*, *30*(2), 128-139. https://doi.org/10.1177/0269881115612236.

Stein, M. B., Goin, M. K., Pollack, M. H., Roy-Byrne, P., Sareen, J., Simon, N. M., & Campbell-Sills L. (2009). *Practice Guideline for the Treatment of Patients with Panic Disorder.* https://psychiatryonline.org/pb/assets/raw/sitewide/practice_guidelines/guidelines/panicdisorder-1410197712490.pdf.

Strawn, J. R., Mills, J. A., Cornwall, G. J., Mossman, S. A., Varney, S. T., Keeshin, B. R., & Croarkin, P. E. (2018). Buspirone in Children and Adolescents with Anxiety: A Review and Bayesian Analysis of Abandoned Randomized Controlled Trials. *J Child Adolesc Psychopharmacol*, *28*(1), 2-9. https://doi.org/10.1089/cap.2017.0060.

Strawn, J. R., Mills, J. A., Poweleit, E. A., Ramsey, L. B., & Croarkin, P. E. (2023). Adverse Effects of Antidepressant Medications and their Managment in Children and Adolescents. *Pharmacotherapy*, *43*, 675-690.

Strawn, J. R., Moldauer, L., Hahn, R. D., Wise, A., Bertzos, K., Eisenberg, B., Greenberg, E., Liu, C., Gopalkrishnan, M., McVoy, M., & Knutson, J. A. (2023). A Multicenter Double-Blind, Placebo-Controlled Trial of Escitalopram in Children and Adolescents with Generalized Anxiety Disorder. *Journal of Child and Adolescent Psychopharmacology*, *33*(3), 91-100.

Tack, J., Ly, H. G., Carbone, F., Vanheel, H., Vanuytsel, T., Holvoet, L., Boeckxstaens, G., Caenepeel, P., Arts, J., & Van Oudenhove, L. (2016). Efficacy of Mirtazapine in Patients With Functional Dyspepsia and Weight Loss. *Clin Gastroenterol Hepatol*, *14*(3), 385-392.e384. https://doi.org/10.1016/j.cgh.2015.09.043.

Tafet, G. E., & Nemeroff, C. B. (2020). Pharmacological Treatment of Anxiety Disorders: The Role of the HPA Axis. *Frontiers in Psychiatry*, *11*, 443.

Thase, M. E., Entsuah, A. R., & Rudolph, R. L. (2001). Remission rates during treatment with venlafaxine or selective serotonin reuptake inhibitors. *British Journal of Psychiatry*, *178*, 234-241.

Tiller, J. W., Bouwer, C., & Behnke, K. (1997). Moclobemide for anxiety disorders: a focus on moclobemide for panic disorder. *Int Clin Psychopharmacol*, *12 Suppl 6*, S27-30.

Trindade, E., Menon, D., Topfer, L. A., & Coloma, C. (1998). Adverse effects associated with selective serotonin reuptake inhibitors and tricyclic antidepressants: a meta-analysis. *Canadian Medical Association Journal*, *159*, 1245-1252.

Walkup, J. T., Albano, A. M., Piacentini, J., Birmaher, B., Compton, S. N., Sherrill, J. T., Ginsburg, G. S., Rynn, M. A., McCracken, J., Waslick, B., Iyengar, S., March, J. S., & Kendall, P. C. (2008). Cognitive Behavioral Therapy, Sertraline, or a Combination in Childhood Anxiety. *The New England Journal of Medicine*, *359*, 2753-2766.

Walter, H. J., Bukstein, O. G., Abright, A. R., Keable, H., Ramtekkar, U., Ripperger-Suhler, J., & Rockhill, C. (2020). Clinical Practice Guildeine for the Assessment and Treatment of Children and Adolescnts with Anxiety Disorders. *Journal of the American Academy of Child and Adolescent Psychiatry*, *59*(10), 1107-1124.

Wang, Z., Whiteside, S. P. H., Sim, L., Farah, W., Morrow, A. S., Alsawas, M., Barrionuevo, P., Tello, M., Asi, N., Beuschel, B., Daraz, L., Almasri, J., Zaiem, F., Larrea-Mantilla, L., Ponce, O. J., LeBlanc, A., Prokop, L. J., & Murad, M. H. (2017). Comparative Effectiveness and Safety of Cognitive Behavioral Therapy and Pharmacotherapy for Childhood Anxiety Disorders: A Systematic Review and Meta-analysis. *JAMA Pediatrics*, *171*(11), 1049-1056.

Weinmann, S., Becker, T., & Koesters, M. (2008). Re-evaluation of the efficacy and tolerability of venlafaxine vs SSRI: meta-analysis. *Psychopharmacology*, *196*(4), 511-522.

Zareifopoulos, N., & Dylja, I. (2017). Efficacy and tolerability of vilazodone for the acute treatment of generalized anxiety disorder: A meta-analysis. *Asian J Psychiatr*, *26*, 115-122. https://doi.org/10.1016/j.ajp.2017.01.016.

Chapter 6

Separation Anxiety and Trauma

Kayleigh N. Watters[1,*]
and Alana Gallagher[2,3]
[1]Psychology Department, Palo Alto University, Palo Alto, CA, USA
[2]VA Ann Arbor Healthcare System, Ann Arbor, MI, USA
[3]Department of Psychiatry, University of Michigan, Ann Arbor, MI, USA

Abstract

Separation anxiety is the profound fear of being separated from someone whom one is deeply attached to. Separation anxiety can occur as a result from changes in one's environment (e.g., moving) and family dynamics (e.g., divorce), insecure attachment to caregivers, and traumatic experiences. Traumatic experiences in both childhood and adulthood are associated with separation anxiety. In trauma survivors, separation anxiety is a response to negative cognitions that develop following a traumatic event that encompasses feelings of helplessness, self-blame, hopelessness, and hypervigilance. Research suggests that prolonged exposure to interpersonal traumas—such as experiences related to war, refugee status, or childhood trauma—may exhibit stronger relationships with separation anxiety compared to non-interpersonal traumas (e.g., natural disasters, car accidents). In the upcoming chapter, we will delve into what separation anxiety is, how one may develop separation anxiety in the aftermath of trauma, background of trauma and its consequences, and explore prospective avenues for researching and addressing separation anxiety as a consequence of trauma within both clinical practice and research.

---

* Corresponding Author's Email:

In: Separation Anxiety: Presentation and Intervention
Editor: Kelly Nicole Banneyer
ISBN: 979-8-89530-386-3

Keywords: separation anxiety, trauma, refugees, childhood trauma

Introduction

Separation anxiety is highly prevelant in both children and adults, and is often triggered by a fear of losing an important emotional connection (Mohammadi et al., 2020; Silove et al, 2010a). This fear may be a result of changes in one's environment and family dynamics, such as moving or divorce (Bowlby, 1969; Ainsworth, 1973). It can also result from insecure attachment related to traumatic experiences. This chapter explores the multifaceted nature of separation anxiety, its development following traumatic events, and the broader spectrum of trauma and its consequences, including a specific focus on refugees.

Separation Anxiety and Attachment

Separation anxiety is the profound fear of being separated from someone whom one is deeply attached to (Bögels et al., 2013). Though most common in childhood, separation anxiety can extend beyond typical (and normative) developmental stages; it can persist or reemerge in adulthood, particularly in response to traumatic events, encompassing feelings of helplessness, self-blame, hopelessness, and hypervigilance (Briere & Scott, 2015). Separation anxiety can result from changes in one's environment (e.g., moving) and family dynamics (e.g., divorce), but can also be a result from experiencing trauma. Research indicates that both childhood and adulthood traumatic experiences are associated with separation anxiety, highlighting the relevance and impact of early attachment on adult psychological functioning post trauma (Bowlby, 1973; Main et al., 1985).

There are several types of attachement styles, one of which most relevant to separation anxiety is insecure attachment. Insecure attachment, characterized by anxiety and avoidance, arises from early experiences with caregivers who are inconsistently responsive or generally neglectful, which disrupts the development of a secure base from which the individual can explore the world (Ainsworth et al., 1978; Baer & Martinez, 2006). Those who are insecurely attached often develop heightened sensitivity to separation and may experience significant distress during transitions or losses later in life

(Sroufe, 2005). This heightened sensitivity to separation and distress during transitions underscores attachment theory's core assertion that early relationships shape out coping mechanisms and responses to stress and separation throughout life.

Attachment theory posits that humans have a fundamental need to establish strong emotional bonds with others (Bowlby, 1969). Disruption to these bonds, whether through loss, separation, or environmental instability, can precipitate feelings of insecurity and anxiety. This concept is further supported by research suggesting that attachment disruptions can lead to increased vulnerability to stress and difficulty in emotional regulation (Sroufe, 2005; Shaver et al., 2016). A type of attachment disruption may be exposure to trauma.

Attachment and Trauma

Exposure to trauma can have devastating effects on psychological well-being. Traumatic events that do not involve intentional harm by others (e.g., motor vehicle accidents, natural disasters, and serious illnesses) can disrupt lives unexpectedly and often lead to feelings of helplessness, vulnerability, severe anxiety, or posttraumatic stress disorder (PTSD; Marganska et al., 2013; Norris et al., 2002; Shalev et al., 1996; Thomas et al., 2021). In the aftermath of such events, survivors may cling to loved ones or become preoccupied with thoughts of potential future separations or losses. Conversely, interpersonal traumas that involve threats or harm perpetrated directly by other people (e.g., physical or sexual abuse, exposure to combat or war-related violence, forced displacement, and fear of persecution) are marked by a deep betrayal of trust that can lead to more complex psychological responses (e.g., complex PTSD) due to the personal nature of the aggression (Cloitre et al., 2009; Courtois, 2008; Herman, 1992; Platt & Freyd, 2015). These experiences can shatter the survivor's sense of safety and security, often leading to a fear of abandonment and an overwhelming desire to maintain physical and emotional proximity to those to whom they feel attached (Bowlby, 1980; Herman, 1992).

Exposure to traumatic events may lead people to revert to earlier states of increased dependency and anxiety when separated from attachment figures (Ainsworth et al., 1978; Cassidy & Mohr, 2001). This is particularly evident in cases where trauma involves a betrayal of trust, such as in abuse by caregivers, which severely impacts a person's ability to form secure attachments and heightens their sensitivity to separation (Herman, 1992).

Trauma theory, which complements attachment theory, offers a lens for understanding the psychological impacts of traumatic experiences, particularly those involving interpersonal trauma, which often involve deep betrayal and powerlessness that disrupts one's sense of self, others, and the world (Herman, 1992; Platt & Freyd, 2015). This betrayal directly challenges the trust and safety central to secure attachment relationships established in early life or deepens the already held belief of insecurity, leading to difficulties in emotional regulation and maintaining secure attachments (Cloitre et al., 2009). Both trauma and attachment theories highlight the detrimental effects of attachment disruption, whether one that occurs at an early age and/or following trauma exposure. Trauma can either exacerbate pre-existing insecurities, compounding the psychological impact, or fundamentally changes the way someone relates to others (Bowlby, 1980; Briere & Scott, 2015). Some examples of how trauma may result in these disruptions and manifest as separation anxiety are childhood trauma and experiences commonly faced by refugees including forced displacement or persecution.

Separation Anxiety and Trauma

Childhood Trauma

Childhood trauma, encompassing abuse and neglect, can fundamentally disrupt a child's sense of security and trust in the world (Dye, 2018). Childhood abuse (physical, emotional, or sexual) and neglect (physical or emotional) can affect a child's developing attachment system (Hocking et al., 2016). Such experiences may lead to a high preoccupation of their relationships or closeness to caregivers (Hoven et al., 2004; Riggs & Kaminski, 2019; Sroufe, 2000). Childhood trauma may also lead to a child feeling they have to be perpetually on guard for threats, often leading to an excessive dependency on any remaining attachment figures (Mikulincer et al., 2009). For example, witnessing domestic violence may cause children to become excessively clingy, fearful of being alone, or overly reliant on one parent for a sense of safety, all hallmarks of separation anxiety (Levendosky et al., 2002). Separation anxiety disorder and PTSD often codevelop in children after trauma, and comorbid rates range from 21% to 63% (Scheeringa et al., 2008, 2015). These early traumas shape children's expectations of relationships, frequently resulting in significant separation anxiety as they grow. Separation anxiety in adults who experienced childhood trauma may look like preoccupation with danger and helplessness (Colak et al., 2023).

Refugees

Refugees encounter a complex interplay of trauma and loss, often rooted in war, violence, and forced displacement, all of which can exacerbate separation anxiety. Indeed, research suggests that 18% of refugees are diagnosed with separation anxiety disorder (Kirmaver et al., 2011; Porter & Haslam, 2005; Silove et al., 2010b; Steel et al., 2009). The trauma experienced by refugees spans pre-migration, during migration, and post-migration phases, involving exposure to violence, loss of loved ones, and the hardships of migration itself (Ali-Naqvi et al., 2023; Betancourt & Khan, 2008; Steel et al., 2009). Furthermore, the intersection of separation anxiety and trauma in refugees creates a cycle of distress where the loss of attachment figures and traumatic experiences mutually reinforce each other, intensifying fears of separation and compounding their psychological impact (Cloitre et al., 2009). Due to the forced separation from their families, communities, and homelands, refugees frequently experience intense separation anxiety, manifesting as nightmares, difficulty concentrating, and a pervasive fear of further loss (Silove et al., 2017). Children may respond with clinginess, tantrums, or hypervigilance, while adults might be preoccupied with the safety of their loved ones or struggle to form new attachments (Alami, 2020). The loss of social networks and cultural connections can intensify these feelings, leading to a sense of isolation and vulnerability (Ager & Strang, 2008).

Clinical Implications and Research Directions

Clinical approaches to treating separation anxiety in the context of trauma must be multifaceted and trauma-informed. For instance, Prolonged Exposure (PE) therapy, which involves repeated, detailed imagining of the trauma and exposure to trauma reminders, has shown effectiveness in reducing trauma-related anxiety by helping survivors confront avoidance (Hembree et al., 2007). In addition, Interpersonal Therapy (IPT), traditionally used to treat depression, can also be adapted to address issues related to interpersonal trauma by focusing on improving interpersonal functioning and resolving conflict within relationships (Bleiberg & Markowitz, 2019). IPT and PE are both effective in the treatment of refugees (Meffert et al., 2014; Paunovic & Öst, 2001; Turrini et al., 2017). In conjunction, mindfulness approaches (including skills taught in dialectical behavioral therapy) may help reduce anxiety by promoting non-judgmental awareness and acceptance of all experiences, including traumatic memories and fears of separation (Gratz et al., 2005). These therapies aim to stabilize emotions and improve coping strategies in individuals experiencing complex reactions stemming from both trauma and separation anxiety. Generally, research suggests that treating PTSD symptoms first is recommended which can decrease the exacerbation of anxiety symptoms (Watkins et al., 2018). This is accurate for trauma-informed treatments such as PE, which decreases PTSD symptoms while also encouraging exposure to anxiety-related stimuli. Clinicians may incorporate additional separation anxiety exposures during PE therapy as exposure therapy is a first-line treatment for separation anxiety disorder (Teunisse et al., 2022).

Despite advances in understanding and treating separation anxiety and trauma, significant gaps remain in the literature. There is a need for more longitudinal studies to explore the long-term effects of different therapeutic interventions on separation anxiety, particularly in refugee populations. Future research may consider exploring specific mechanisms by which various therapies such as PE, IPT, and mindfulness affect not just the symptoms but also the underlying attachment disruptions associated with separation anxiety (Cloitre et al., 2009). Additionally, future research directions may also investigate the cultural applicability and effectiveness of these interventions across diverse populations to ensure that treatment approaches are inclusive and sensitive to the unique contexts and needs of individuals from varied backgrounds.

Conclusion

This chapter highlights the importance of understanding separation anxiety within the context of trauma, while highlighting the role of attachement in developing separation anxiety in the aftermath of trauma. Though this chapter explored research on separation anxiety in different trauma populations, continued research is needed to explore the intersections of separation anxiety and trauma across different populations and trauma types. We also discussed different therpautic aproaches to treating separation anxiety in the context of trauma; however, continued research is also needed to develop interventions tailored to the unique experiences of trauma survivors and bridging the gap between empirical research and therapeutic application.

References

Alami, R. (2020). From war to refuge: A literature review of the psychosocial impact of pre-and post-migration experience on the Syrian child refugee (Doctoral dissertation, Alliant International University).

Ager, A., & Strang, A. (2008). Understanding integration: A conceptual framework. *Journal of Refugee Studies, 21*(2), 166-191.

Ainsworth, M. D. S. (1973). The development of infant-mother attachment. In B. M. Caldwell & H. N. Ricciuti (Eds.), *Review of child development research* (Vol. 3, pp. 1-94). Chicago: University of Chicago Press.

Ali-Naqvi, O., Alburak, T. A., Selvan, K., Abdelmeguid, H., & Malvankar-Mehta, M. S. (2023). Exploring the impact of family separation on refugee mental health: a systematic review and meta-narrative analysis. *Psychiatric Quarterly, 94*(1), 61-77.

Baer, J. C., & Martinez, C. D. (2006). Child maltreatment and insecure attachment: A meta-analysis. *Journal of Reproductive and Infant Psychology, 24*(3), 187-197.

Betancourt, T. S., & Khan, K. T. (2008). The mental health of children affected by armed conflict: Protective processes and pathways to resilience. *International Review of Psychiatry, 20*(3), 317-328.

Bleiberg, K. L., & Markowitz, J. C. (2019). Interpersonal psychotherapy for PTSD: Treating trauma without exposure. *Journal of psychotherapy integration*, *29*(1), 15.

Bögels, S. M., Knappe, S., & Clark, L. A. (2013). Adult separation anxiety disorder in DSM-5. *Clinical Psychology Review, 33*(5), 663-674.

Bowlby, J. (1969). *Attachment and loss: Vol. 1. Attachment*. New York: Basic Books.

Briere, J., & Scott, C. (2015). *Principles of trauma therapy: A guide to symptoms, evaluation, and treatment* (2nd ed.). Thousand Oaks, CA: Sage Publications.

Cassidy, J., & Mohr, J. J. (2001). Unsolvable fear, trauma, and psychopathology: Theory, research, and clinical considerations related to disorganized attachment across the life span. *Clinical Psychology: Science and Practice, 8*(3), 275.

Cloitre, M., Courtois, C. A., Charuvastra, A., Carapezza, R., Stolbach, B. C., & Green, B. L. (2009). Treatment of complex PTSD: Results of the ISTSS expert clinician survey on best practices. *Journal of Traumatic Stress*, 22(6), 615-627.

Cloitre, M., Stolbach, B. C., Herman, J. L., van der Kolk, B., Pynoos, R., Wang, J., & Petkova, E. (2009). A developmental approach to complex PTSD: Childhood and adult cumulative trauma as predictors of symptom complexity. *Journal of Traumatic Stress, 22*(5), 399-408.

Cohen, J. A., & Scheeringa, M. S. (2009). Post-traumatic stress disorder diagnosis in children: challenges and promises. *Dialogues in clinical neuroscience*, 11(1), 91–99.

Colak, M., Sireli, O., & Dayi, A. (2023). Adult Separation Anxiety and Childhood Traumas: The Mediating Role of Cognitive Distortions. *Journal of Child & Adolescent Trauma, 16*(4), 973-980.

Courtois, C. A. (2008). Complex trauma, complex reactions: Assessment and treatment.

Dye, H. (2018). The impact and long-term effects of childhood trauma. *Journal of Human Behavior in the Social Environment*, 28(3), 381-392.

Fernandes, V., & Osório, F. L. (2015). Are there associations between early emotional trauma and anxiety disorders? Evidence from a systematic literature review and meta-analysis. *European Psychiatry, 30*(6), 756-764.

Gratz, K. L., Tull, M. T., & Wagner, A. W. (2005). Applying DBT mindfulness skills to the treatment of clients with anxiety disorders. In *Acceptance and mindfulness-based approaches to anxiety: Conceptualization and treatment* (pp. 147-161). Boston, MA: Springer US.

Herman, J. L. (1992). Complex PTSD: A syndrome in survivors of prolonged and repeated trauma. *Journal of Traumatic Stress, 5*(3), 377-391.

Hembree, E. A., Rauch, S. A., & Foa, E. B. (2003). Beyond the manual: The insider's guide to prolonged exposure therapy for PTSD. *Cognitive and Behavioral Practice, 10*(1), 22-30.

Hocking, E. C., Simons, R. M., & Surette, R. J. (2016). Attachment style as a mediator between childhood maltreatment and the experience of betrayal trauma as an adult. *Child abuse & neglect*, *52*, 94–101.

Hoven, C. W., Duarte, C. S., Wu, P., Erickson, E. A., Musa, G. J., & Mandell, D. J. (2004). Exposure to trauma and separation anxiety in children after the WTC attack. *Applied Developmental Science, 8*(4), 172-183.

Kirmayer, L. J., Narasiah, L., Munoz, M., Rashid, M., Ryder, A. G., Guzder, J., ... & Pottie, K. (2011). Common mental health problems in immigrants and refugees: general approach in primary care. *Canadian Medical Association Journal, 183*(12), E959-E967.

Levendosky, A. A., Huth-Bocks, A. C., Shapiro, D. L., & Semel, M. A. (2002). The impact of domestic violence on the maternal–child relationship and preschool-age children's functioning. *Journal of Family Psychology*, 16(3), 275-287.

Marganska, A., Gallagher, M., & Miranda, R. (2013). Adult attachment, emotion dysregulation, and symptoms of depression and generalized anxiety disorder. *American Journal of Orthopsychiatry, 83*(1), 131.

Meffert, S. M., Abdo, A. O., Alla, O. A. A., Elmakki, Y. O. M., Omer, A. A., Yousif, S., ... & Marmar, C. R. (2014). A pilot randomized controlled trial of interpersonal psychotherapy for Sudanese refugees in Cairo, Egypt. *Psychological Trauma: Theory, Research, Practice, and Policy,* 6(3), 240.

Mikulincer, M., Shaver, P. R., Cassidy, J., & Berant, E. (2009). Attachment-related defensive processes. Attachment theory and research in clinical work with adults, 293-327.

Mohammadi, M. R., Badrfam, R., Khaleghi, A., Hooshyari, Z., Ahmadi, N., & Zandifar, A. (2020). Prevalence, comorbidity and predictor of separation anxiety disorder in children and adolescents. *Psychiatric Quarterly*, *91*, 1415-1429.

Norris, F. H., Friedman, M. J., Watson, P. J., Byrne, C. M., Diaz, E., & Kaniasty, K. (2002). 60,000 disaster victims speak: Part I. An empirical review of the empirical literature, 1981–2001. *Psychiatry: Interpersonal and Biological Processes, 65*(3), 207-239.

Paunovic, N., & Öst, L. G. (2001). Cognitive-behavior therapy vs exposure therapy in the treatment of PTSD in refugees. *Behaviour research and therapy*, 39(10), 1183-1197.

Platt, M. G., & Freyd, J. J. (2015). Betray my trust, shame on me: Shame, dissociation, fear, and betrayal trauma. *Psychological Trauma: Theory, Research, Practice, and Policy*, *7*(4), 398.

Porter, M., & Haslam, N. (2005). Predisplacement and postdisplacement factors associated with mental health of refugees and internally displaced persons: A meta-analysis. *JAMA, 294*(5), 602-612.

Riggs, S. A., & Kaminski, P. (2019). Childhood emotional abuse, adult attachment, and depression as predictors of relational adjustment and psychological aggression. *In The Effect of Childhood Emotional Maltreatment on Later Intimate Relationships* (pp. 75-104). Routledge.

Scheeringa M., Zeanah C. Reconsideration of harm's way: onsets and comorbidity patterns in preschool children and their caregivers following Hurricane Katrina. *J Clin Child Adolesc Psychol*. 2008; 37:508–518.

Scheeringa MS., Zeanah CH., Myers L., Putnam FW. New findings on alternative criteria for PTSD in preschool children. *J Am: Academy Child Adolesc Psychiatry*. 2003; 42:561–570.

Shalev, A. Y., Peri, T., Canetti, L., & Schreiber, S. (1996). Predictors of PTSD in injured trauma survivors: A prospective study. *American Journal of psychiatry*, *153*(2), 219.

Shaver, P. R., Mikulincer, M., Sahdra, B., & Gross, J. (2016). Attachment security as a foundation for kindness toward self and others. *The Oxford handbook of hypo-egoic phenomena*, *10*.

Silove, D. M., Marnane, C. L., Wagner, R., Manicavasagar, V. L., & Rees, S. (2010a). The prevalence and correlates of adult separation anxiety disorder in an anxiety clinic. *BMC psychiatry*, *10*, 1-7.

Silove, D., Momartin, S., Marnane, C., Steel, Z., & Manicavasagar, V. (2010b). Adult separation anxiety disorder among war-affected Bosnian refugees: Comorbidity with PTSD and associations with dimensions of trauma. *Journal of Traumatic Stress: Official Publication of the International Society for Traumatic Stress Studies*, *23*(1), 169-172.

Silove, D., Ventevogel, P., & Rees, S. (2017). The contemporary refugee crisis: an overview of mental health challenges. *World Psychiatry, 16*(2), 130-139.

Sroufe, L. A. (2005). Attachment and development: A prospective, longitudinal study from birth to adulthood. *Attachment & human development*, *7*(4), 349-367.

Steel, Z., Chey, T., Silove, D., Marnane, C., Bryant, R. A., & van Ommeren, M. (2009). Association of torture and other potentially traumatic events with mental health outcomes among populations exposed to mass conflict and displacement: A systematic review and meta-analysis. *JAMA, 302*(5), 537-549.

Teunisse, A. K., Pembroke, L., O'Gradey-Lee, M., Sy, M., Rapee, R. M., Wuthrich, V. M., Creswell, C., & Hudson, J. L. (2022). A scoping review investigating the use of exposure for the treatment and targeted prevention of anxiety and related disorders in young people. *JCPP advances*, *2*(2), e12080.

Thomas, E. A., Owens, G. P., & Keller, E. M. (2021). Relationships among non-interpersonal and interpersonal trauma types, posttraumatic stress, and posttraumatic growth. *Journal of Clinical Psychology, 77*(11), 2592-2608.

Turrini, G., Purgato, M., Ballette, F., Nosè, M., Ostuzzi, G., & Barbui, C. (2017). Common elements of psychological interventions for refugees and asylum seekers resettled in high-income countries: a systematic review. *Epidemiology and Psychiatric Sciences, 26*(2), 176-187.

Watkins, L. E., Sprang, K. R., & Rothbaum, B. O. (2018). Treating PTSD: A Review of Evidence-Based Psychotherapy Interventions. *Frontiers in behavioral neuroscience*, 12, 258.

Chapter 7

Separation Anxiety in Foster Care: Etiology, Assessment, and Intervention

Mackenzie L. Hughes[1,*]
Martha N. Ishiekwene[1]
and Katherine C. Budolfson[2]
[1]Department of Pediatrics, Division of Psychology, Baylor College of Medicine, Texas Children's Hospital, Houston, TX, USA
[2]Department of Pediatrics, Division of Public Health Pediatrics, Baylor College of Medicine, Texas Children's Hospital, Houston, TX, USA

Abstract

Youth in foster care have high rates of abuse and neglect and are significantly more likely to be diagnosed with a mental health concern. Additionally, children in foster care often have experienced sudden and traumatic losses and have complex social situations. The development of separation anxiety disorder (SAD) in children in foster care is likely due to a complex interaction between disrupted attachment relationships, placement instability, and traumatic experiences. This chapter will provide an overview of the importance of comprehensive assessment and diagnosis, considering differential diagnoses to distinguish between SAD, normative anxiety, and trauma-related symptoms. Furthermore, the chapter discusses evidence-based treatments like Trauma-Focused Cognitive Behavioral Therapy (TF-CBT) and Parent-Child Interaction Therapy (PCIT), highlighting modifications for the foster care context. Legal, ethical, and cultural considerations are also addressed,

---

* Corresponding Author's Email: mlhughes@texaschildrens.org,

In: Separation Anxiety: Presentation and Intervention
Editor: Kelly Nicole Banneyer
ISBN: 979-8-89530-386-3

underscoring the need for trauma-informed care and the involvement of child welfare systems in the therapeutic process.

Keywords: foster care, child welfare, separation anxiety

Introduction

Foster care is a general term used in this chapter to refer to a child in a court-ordered out of home placement, which may include non-relative foster homes, kinship care (i.e., placed with a relative), group homes, residential treatment centers (RTC), and temporary placements (e.g., emergency shelters). According to the United States Children's Bureau (2024) report, over 180,000 youth entered foster care in 2022, and over 360,000 children were in foster care on any given day that year. Trends in the number of children entering into foster care have steadily declined since 2016. The most common reason for a child to enter foster care is due to neglect (62%) followed by parental drug abuse (33%), and caregiver inability to cope (13%). Physical or sexual abuse accounted for 13% and 4% of removals, respectively. Child behavior problems (8%), parental incarceration (6%), abandonment (5%), parent death (1%), and relinquishment (1%) are other cited reasons for removal and placement in foster care (Children's Bureau, 2024).

The mean age for a child entering care is 6.9 years (Children's Bureau, 2024). While the distribution of children in foster care is fairly equal as it relates to gender (52% male), there is an over-representation of racial and ethnic minority children in foster care. Black children and American Indian children are overrepresented in foster care compared to the rate in the general population in the United States (Puzzanchera, et al., 2022). The average age of exiting foster care is 8.3 years with the average length of time spent in foster care being 22.6 months. Forty-six percent of youth are reunited with caregivers followed by 27% being adopted (Children's Bureau, 2024).

Etiology of Separation Anxiety in Foster Care

Among youth involved in the child welfare system, approximately a quarter (25.2-27.6%) of the sample was diagnosed with clinically pervasive behavioral and emotional symptoms and the likelihood of being diagnosed with clinically pervasive internalizing behaviors increased with age and when sexual abuse was reported (Garcia et al., 2017). Further, childhood traumatic life experiences (especially sexual abuse and violence exposure) have been implicated in the development of various anxiety symptoms/disorders and both childhood and adult separation anxiety even across countries (Briggs-Gowan et al., 2010; Hogg et al., 2023; Ölmez et al., 2022; Silove et al., 2015).

Disrupted Attachment Relationships for Youth in Foster Care

It is noteworthy that when children are separated from their primary caregivers or parents, the impact of such separation on their mental health or functioning is likely affected by various factors. These factors include but are not limited to pre-separation experiences (e.g., attachment security, violence exposure), circumstances of separation (e.g., removal from abuse, parent incarceration/death), post-separation placement (e.g., high-quality care in a family, group-based care) and developmental stage, as proposed by Humphreys (2019).

When children/youth enter the child welfare system and are removed from their homes of origin, their connections with various individuals and groups, including their biological parent(s), siblings, religious institutions, and many others, are disrupted (Hindt & Leon, 2022). Upon reflecting on their experience in foster care and navigating multiple placements, individuals described a profound sense of loss specifically related to friends and connections to school and siblings (Unrau et al., 2008). Further, youth who were involved in the child welfare system reported difficulty establishing or maintaining relationships and difficulty with trusting others (Unrau et al., 2008). For example, there are high rates of transitions between schools and even school districts while in foster care, reportedly ranging from 57% to 93% (Fawley-King et al., 2017). Such transitions and non-death losses (or ambiguous and symbolic loss) may take a substantial toll on foster children's psychosocial functioning, yet often goes unnoticed or unsupported (Mitchell, 2018). This impact is underscored by longitudinal findings of a relation between internalizing symptoms including anxiety and disruptions in foster children's school and community (Hindt & Leon, 2022). Further, the tight timeframe within which the transition from a foster care home to another home (e.g., for adoption) and the process of this transition can further strain a child's attachment to caregivers and cause distress (Boswell & Cudmore, 2014). In addition to the development of separation anxiety disorder (SAD), frequent and unexpected disruptions in attachments likely play a role in maintaining SAD for youth in foster care.

Finally, siblings are considered an important part of a child's relational network with whom children can and do experience attachment with, thus posing as an important source of continuity and support for foster children (Barnea et al., 2023). This knowledge is reflected in guidelines and policies (e.g., the federal Fostering Connections to Success and Increasing Adoptions Act; Administration for Children and Families, 2010) stressing the importance of prioritizing joint sibling placement when safe. Despite these guidelines, data suggests that 23% to 75% of children experience out-of-home placements without their siblings (Wojciak et al., 2013). Researchers have posited that joint placement with siblings may also have other protective effects such as contributing to placement stability through improved ability to form attachments (Leathers, 2005). Extant research also underscores the mediating role and protective function of positive sibling relationships on the association between trauma and internalizing symptoms like anxiety symptoms (Wojciak et al., 2013). Thus, continued research is required to better understand the protective function of joint placement especially given the multiple barriers that exist to joint placement (Wojciak et al., 2024).

Instability and Unpredictability in Foster Care Placements

Placement instability can be described as the premature ending of a child's stay in a foster care placement for various reasons including moving to residential care, another foster home, or running away. Despite systemic efforts, approximately 22-70% of foster care placements are disrupted each year (Blakey et al., 2012). The likelihood of such instability increases with the presence of risk factors such as older child age, maltreatment history, behavior problems, placement without siblings, low-quality foster parenting, and non-kinship foster care (Konijn et al., 2019). Unsurprisingly, placement instability affects a child's social relationships and bonds (Strijker et al., 2008).

Neurobiological Aspects of Separation Anxiety in Foster Children

The amygdala has often been implicated in the development of anxiety disorders (Davis, 1992; LeDoux & Pine, 2016). Adversity and abuse have been associated with more negative amygdala resting-state functional connectivity and altered amygdala-left precentral gyrus connectivity which has important implications for attentional biases and potential anxiety symptoms (Cheng et al., 2021). Further, research suggests that decreased amygdala reactivity to parent cues (e.g., tactile, olfactory or visual like photographs) can serve a protective function against the development of anxiety symptoms in the long-term (Callaghan et al., 2019). However, children with a history of institutional care are reportedly less likely to display decreased amygdala reactivity to parental stimuli compared to children without such a history. Importantly, attachment security, especially in the context of institutional care can foster resilience given its association with decreased amygdala reactivity (Callaghan et al., 2019).

Assessment and Diagnosis

Assessment of Separation Anxiety Symptoms in Youth in Foster Care

When completing comprehensive assessments for youth in foster care, clinicians should complete clinical interviews with the child and caregivers, administer standardized assessment tools (e.g., Separation Anxiety Assessment Scale, Méndez, X. et al., 2014; Child Behavior Checklist, Achenbach & Rescorla, 2001), and conduct observations of the child when separated from and united with the caregiver as well as the child's balance between exploring and proximity-seeking (Zeanah et al., 2011). In addition to the clinical interview, standardized assessments, and observations, clinicians are encouraged to obtain additional relevant history regarding the child's experiences in foster care.

First, clinicians are encouraged to gain information regarding the age at which the child was placed into foster care and the circumstances surrounding their removal, such as whether there was prior notice and any traumatic experiences associated with the removal. The reason for removal (e.g., neglect, abuse, abandonment) should also be noted. It is important to note that the reason for removal is not a comprehensive list of the child's trauma history and a comprehensive evaluation of the trauma history should also be conducted.

Next, clinicians should obtain information regarding the child's current placement type (e.g., foster home, fictive kinship home, kinship home, group home, etc.), child's perceptions of the placement, and the cultural and familial beliefs of the child's family of origin and current placement. Additionally, information regarding the number of previous placements and the reasons for these changes should be obtained. Clinicians should specifically note the context surrounding any prior placement changes and whether the child was informed ahead of time about these changes.

Clinicians are also encouraged to evaluate the child's contact with their family of origin, including caregivers, parents, andsiblings. The status of the child's contact with their siblings, including whether they are or ever have been in the same home, should be obtained. Visitation plans should be clearly outlined, specifying the parties involved, the frequency and duration, context (e.g., virtual or in-person; supervised or unsupervised), and any disruptions or inconsistencies of visits. It is also important to assess the child's reactions to visits, noting any emotional or behavioral changes that occur prior to or after visits.

Status of the child welfare case should be noted. The status of parental rights should be clarified, indicating whether the rights are intact, relinquished, or terminated. If parental rights have been relinquished or terminated, it's vital to assess the child's understanding of this status. The permanency goal or plan (e.g., family reunification, private or relative adoption) for the child welfare case should be assessed. Additionally, the child's knowledge of this goal is important to consider. The permanency goal can have profound psychological impacts, influencing the child's feelings of security and belonging. If the child's Child Protective Services (CPS) case is still open, they may have concerns about disclosing family-related events, fearing that these disclosures could affect the likelihood of reunification. Further, when children are unaware of the permanency goal, this can lead to uncertainty, anxiety, and distress related to their future and interpersonal relationships.

Informants

Information should be obtained from numerous reporters, including the child, their current caregiver, and the child welfare caseworker. Given the traumatic nature of foster care, it is recommended that foster care related history is obtained outside the presence of the child. Generally, the child's current caregiver (e.g., foster parent) can provide information regarding the child's functioning since the child has been in their home. It is not uncommon for the child's current caregiver to have limited historical information (e.g., family, birth, or developmental history). The child's identified child welfare caseworker (e.g., CPS caseworker) should be contacted to obtain information regarding the child's history related to child welfare (e.g., age of removal, reason for removal, permanency plan) and additional historical information.

Of note, when gaining history and objective data from parties, including children, foster parents, and caseworkers, inconsistencies in reporting is common (De Los Reyes et al., 2015; Oransky et al., 2013; Tarren-Sweeney et al., 2004). As with other populations, internalizing disorders are often overlooked and underreported in youth in foster care. Given the internal nature of the symptoms, it is likely that caseworkers, foster parents, and mental health providers may have difficulty identifying the concern. This issue is amplified by youth in foster care having poor mental health literacy resulting in under reporting of the youth (Munson et al., 2011). Therefore, it is imperative for clinicians to complete a comprehensive assessment of internalizing and externalizing symptoms when working with youth in foster care.

Differential Diagnoses

When children in foster care present with separation anxiety symptoms, it is imperative a comprehensive evaluation be conducted to explore potential differential diagnoses in order to identify the appropriate intervention. Differentiating between contextually appropriate anxiety or worry (e.g., fear of further interpersonal disruptions after removal), separation anxiety, and trauma-related symptoms can be challenging given the overlap of symptoms and behaviors.

Disruptions in attachment, particularly disruptions that may be of sudden and abrupt nature (e.g., removal of a child from their home in the middle of the night), are likely to result in normative anxiety and distress. For children in foster care, these disruptions extend beyond the initial removal from the family of origin and may include changes in placement, separations from siblings, or qualitative or quantitative changes in contact with attachment figures (e.g., changing from in-person to virtual family visits or changing the frequency or duration of visits). Further, children in foster care may be more sensitive to such disruptions due to past experiences of neglect, abandonment and inconsistent caregiving. Differentiating between normative distress related to separations and SAD can be distinguished based on the child's level of distress, functional impairment, persistence of the symptoms, and the child's response to reassurance and support.

Normative distress related to separation from attachment figures can be further complicated when children and youth are not provided with developmentally appropriate information for the separation. Within our clinic practice, many youths have reported they were not given information regarding their removal, reason for removal, or education regarding the child welfare system when initially placed into foster care. Further, state employees and caseworkers often report a lack of training and knowledge regarding how to explain the reason for removal and the child welfare system.

Additionally, symptoms of SAD should be differentiated from Trauma-Related Disorders, including Posttraumatic Stress Disorder (PTSD) and Adjustment Disorders. There is a significant overlap of the symptoms of SAD and PTSD, including increased anxiety, intrusive symptoms, hyperarousal, and avoidance. For instance, excessive worry about the child's or parent's safety and health when separated is a hallmark symptom of SAD but can also be the manifestation of hypervigilance symptoms of PTSD. When assessing these symptoms, it is important for clinicians to gain information regarding the context of symptoms. For instance, if the distress regarding the caregiver's health and safety is primarily present when the child is presented with a real or perceived separation from caregiver, this may indicate SAD. Conversely, if the child is persistently expressing concerns about the health and safety of the caregiver, this may indicate the hyperarousal symptoms of PTSD.

Treatment of Separation Anxiety Symptoms for Youth in Foster Care

When selecting an evidence-based treatment (EBT) option for youth with separation anxiety who are in foster care, clinicians should select the evidence-based treatment option for the presenting concern and incorporate trauma-informed care approaches into the EBT. When a child presents with SAD and no other trauma-related symptoms, clinicians should utilize EBTs for SAD. Detailed descriptions of EBTs for SAD can be found elsewhere in this book (Refer to Chapter 1 for an overview, to Chapter 3 for a detailed description of EBT for separation anxiety in young children, and to Chapter 4 for an overview of EBT with exposure and response prevention). Of note, there are important clinical considerations that clinicians should incorporate when working with youth in foster care.

Addressing SAD within the Context of Trauma Therapy

When the presenting concern is trauma-related symptoms that include symptoms of SAD, providers should select an EBT for trauma. It is recommended that trauma-focused psychotherapies should be considered the first-line treatments for children and adolescents with PTSD; specifically, Trauma-Focused Cognitive Behavioral Therapy (TF-CBT) is recommended because it has the most rigorous empirical support (Cohen, 2010; Morina et al., 2016).

TF-CBT is the most widely used and disseminated treatment for youth who have been exposed to a traumatic event(s) (Cohen et al., 2017). TF-CBT is appropriate for children ages 3-18 years who have experienced a traumatic event (Cohen et al., 2018). TF-CBT is a cognitive behavioral intervention that combines trauma-sensitive interventions with attachment, developmental neurobiology, empowerment, family, and humanistic theories (Cohen et al., 2017).

TF-CBT has been shown to be efficacious for children who have experienced trauma in reducing symptoms of PTSD, depression, anxiety, shame, fear, and behavior problems, and these differences were sustained at 1-year follow-up (Cohen et al., 2004; Cohen et al., 2011; Deblinger et al., 2006; King et al., 2000). Additionally, the effectiveness of TF-CBT has been shown in community settings in diverse clinical settings (Konanur et al., 2015; Webb et al., 2014).

TF-CBT has been shown to be effective for youths with complex trauma and involved in the child welfare system (Cohen et al., 2012). Modifications to TF-CBT have been made to examine the impact on foster parent and youth engagement during treatment. For instance, in a sample of 47 foster care youth and their foster parents, an RCT was conducted to compare TF-CBT with TF-CBT plus evidence-based engagement strategies for retaining foster families in treatment (Dorsey et al., 2014). TF-CBT with enhanced engagement strategies was significantly more likely than standard TF-CBT to retain foster families in treatment through four sessions and prevent premature treatment dropout but no significant differences were found in session cancelations, no-shows, treatment satisfaction, or in clinical outcomes (Dorsey et al., 2014). These findings suggest that evidence-based engagement strategies may enhance foster family's access to evidence-based trauma therapy.

The TF-CBT model is a brief (8-25 sessions) treatment that consists of 3 phases: Phase 1, stabilization and skill building; Phase 2, trauma narration and processing; and Phase 3, integration and consolidation. The nine TF-CBT components, summarized by the acronym PRACTICE, are contained within the three phases (Cohen et al., 2017). The order of the components is based on trauma impact, logic, and the order of skill acquisition (e.g., need for relaxation skills prior to in vivo exposure; Cohen et al., 2017).

Phase 1, stabilization and skill building, consists of psychoeducation, parenting, relaxation, affective expression and modulation, and cognitive processing components (Cohen et al., 2017). When implementing TF-CBT with youth in foster care who also present with symptoms of SAD, providers should incorporate psychoeducation about separation anxiety, contextualize SAD symptoms in the context of the child's experiences for both the child and their caregivers. Additionally, caregivers should gain specific skills related to addressing SAD symptoms, including educating caregivers on the appropriate responses to the child's SAD symptoms. Children should also be provided specific relaxation skills to use when they are distressed related to separation. Finally, children should be encouraged to identify their thoughts, feelings, and behaviors during separation during the cognitive processing component.

Phase 2, trauma narration and processing, consists of the trauma narration and processing component in which the work of gradual exposure that began early in treatment continues in a more concentrated manner. One of the goals of the trauma narrative is to "unlink thoughts, reminders, or discussions of the traumatic event from overwhelming negative emotions such as terror, horror, extreme helplessness, avoidance, anger, anxiety, shame, or rage" (Cohen et al., 2017, p. 172). Processing the child's trauma during the narrative phase can be particularly important for youth who are experiencing trauma-related symptoms and SAD to allow the opportunity to identify the origins of their separation anxiety (e.g., previous disrupted attachments) and process the emotions related to the separation.

Phase 3, integration and consolidation, consists of the in vivo mastery, conjoint child-parent sessions, and enhancing safety components. The in vivo mastery component of TF-CBT can be used to address any ongoing avoidance of nonthreatening situations or cues (e.g., separation from caregivers). Additionally, any remaining safety related concerns pertaining to separation can be addressed during the enhancing safety component.

Addressing SAD within the Context of Parent Training

Parent-Child Interaction Therapy (PCIT) is an evidence-based parent training program designed to reduce externalizing behaviors in children ages 2 – 7

(McNeil & Hembree-Kigin, 2010). PCIT has been adapted to brief and extended formats for foster parents specifically and shown to reduce parenting stress (including parent-child dysfunctional interaction specifically) and enhance parenting behavior compared to the waitlist control/services-as-usual condition (Mersky et al., 2015). Parent-child dysfunctional interaction or parent's dissatisfaction about their interactions with and/or non-acceptance of their child has been found to significantly mediate the relation between stressful live events and child anxiety (Platt et al., 2015). Thus, evidence-based strategies like PCIT which aim to establish warmth and improve parent-child interactions and attachment may be particularly helpful for children in foster care given their unique stressful life experiences and risk factors for anxiety development.

Treatment Considerations

Children in foster care have high rates of mental health concerns and high rates of health care utilization (Bennett et al., 2020). Yet, the extant research suggests that the outpatient mental health interventions provided to children in foster care are not effective in reducing internalizing and externalizing concerns (Bellamy et al., 2010). These poor treatment outcomes are likely due to limited access to evidence-based interventions for children in foster care. Importantly, the research base is lacking for the application of evidence-based therapies to children in foster care with only a small percentage specifically designed for these children or for interventions designed for a general population very few included foster children in the sample (Baker et al., 2013).

Providing clinical care to youth in foster care presents unique considerations, including the need to address frequent placement disruptions, concerns regarding the appropriate caregivers to include in care, and legal and ethical concerns. As previously described, youth in foster care have frequent placement disruptions and may have a change in status at any time (e.g., reunified with their family of origin, adoption, or move to a new placement). The general temporary nature of foster placements is a frequent concern for clinicians, given the risk of attrition. To address this concern, clinicians are encouraged to have frequent contact and communication with the child's child welfare caseworker. Clinicians are encouraged to provide the caseworker with psychoeducation about the child's diagnosis, treatment plan, and specific EBT used (e.g., frequency of sessions, expected duration of the treatment).

Clinicians are also encouraged to request the caseworker keep the provider abreast of any potential changes in the child's placement or status.

Another common concern for clinicians providing psychological intervention for children in foster care is the decision on the appropriate individual to include in the child's course of treatment. For instance, the inclusion of biological parents and/or foster parents are often cited. It is generally recommended that the child's current primary caregiver participate in the EBT with the child to support the child's current functioning. When it is clinically indicated to include caregivers with maltreatment histories, it is also worth prioritizing primary prevention and evidence-based strategies like child maltreatment prevention programs such as SafeCare to reduce the rates at which children are being separated from their biological parents related to abuse or neglect and possibly mitigate SAD (Guastaferro & Lutzker, 2022).

Most evidence-based treatment protocols do not include components to address the unique aspects of children in foster care. When working with children in foster care, clinicians are encouraged to provide the child with general psychoeducation regarding trauma, trauma-related symptoms, and the child welfare system. The goal of this education is to provide children with developmentally appropriate information regarding the reason for removal, separation from caregivers and their families, and placement in foster care. It is also recommended that the clinician collaborate with the patient's child welfare team (e.g., caseworker) to encourage open and developmentally appropriate communication between the child welfare team and patient, particularly related to placement changes or disruptions.

Legal and Ethical Considerations

There are numerous legal and ethical considerations that need to be considered when providing clinical care to youth in foster care. A common concern regarding clinical work with youth in foster care is difficulty discerning the appropriate person to obtain consent for treatment. A comprehensive discussion about discerning the appropriate consenter is beyond this chapter's scope, but providers are encouraged to have a strong working knowledge of the relevant state laws.

Another important ethical consideration is regarding confidentiality. Given the numerous systems (e.g., child welfare, school, legal, medical) youth in foster care are involved with, it is common to have numerous requests for records regarding the child's intervention. While the right to protected health information is based on numerous factors (e.g., state and national laws, individual court orders), it is imperative that providers balance the need for confidentiality with increasing the child's support system. When responding to requests for information (e.g., requests from child welfare team or court orders), providers should limit specifics regarding the child's disclosures and provide general information regarding the child's treatment (e.g., type of intervention, number of sessions).

Pharmacological Intervention for Children in Foster Care

When considering pharmacological interventions for children in foster care experiencing separation anxiety, it is important to understand the broader context of psychotropic medication use in this vulnerable population. Children in foster care are prescribed psychotropic medications at rates 2.5 to 4 times higher than those not in foster care, with almost half of those prescribed psychotropic medications on three or more different classes of medications (Zito et al., 2008). Rates of antipsychotic medication use in children in foster care is up to 26 times higher than those not in foster care, often without an associated psychiatric diagnosis for the antipsychotic prescription (Keefe et al., 2023). These children are at high risk for polypharmacy, with one study showing up to 20% of youth in foster care experiencing questionable psychotropic polypharmacy (Brenner et al, 2014). These medications come with a range of side effects that can cause long-term negative impacts on the physical and mental health of youth in foster care. Thus, in the context of treating separation anxiety in youth in foster care, it is important to evaluate the broader context of their psychotropic medication use to avoid polypharmacy and prioritize nonpharmacological treatment when possible. If psychotropic medication is deemed necessary, it is essential to ensure its cautious and judicious use, taking into account the high risk of polypharmacy in these children. Refer to Chapter 5 of this text for more information about medication management of SAD in youth.

Cultural Contexts of Separation Anxiety in Youth in Foster Care

Cultural norms and expectations regarding parent-child relationships, family dynamics, and caregiver roles may influence the child's presentation of SAD. As stated by one of the pioneers of attachment research, "I think that environmental influences play no significant role in the infant's basic need for an attachment figure who can be trusted. But culture-related differences in ecologies and expectations will certainly affect how some specific aspects of that organization are expressed" (Ainsworth & Marvin, 1995, p. 8). When considering attachment and culture, some worthy questions that have been proposed and are worth considering include: "Who serves as a secure base/safe haven to this child, and in what situations?" "How do racialized experiences e.g., bias-based bullying influence this child's attachment behavior?" and "What are the common and unique forms of caregiving behavior that caregivers of this cultural background have developed to adapt to the ecological context of class- and racism-related threats?" (Stern et al., 2022).

In addition to the aforementioned fact that there is a disproportionately higher representation of children with minoritized racial and ethnic backgrounds in the foster care system, these children also experience disparities in the timeliness of achieving permanence as well as a higher rate of dissolution, and placement disruptions (Sattler & Font, 2021). Age, gender, and behavior/mental health needs have also been implicated as demographic factors that are related to dissolution (Sattler & Font, 2021). Such experiences of dissolution may contribute to and/or maintain symptoms of SAD and require cultural humility in effectively addressing the multi-systemic factors related to these symptoms and their etiology.

Racial and ethnic differences appear to vary or be non-existent in the rates of separation anxiety disorder (Gordon-Hollingsworth et al., 2015; Kendall et al., 2010) and how psychological disorder symptoms like separation anxiety are conceptualized as problematic or pathological. Some studies suggest that parents from certain backgrounds, such as those from an Asian heritage, are more likely to consider such symptoms as problematic (Rothbaum et al., 2007; Weisz et al., 1991). Even when separation anxiety symptoms are deemed problematic by parents, Nguyen and McAloon (2018) found that Caucasian parents report a greater likelihood of seeking support with child SAD symptoms than Asian parents. Further, research suggests that African American youth tend to receive lower ratings on treatment engagement (i.e., attendance, involvement, compliance, content mastery) than Caucasian youth and this subsequently is related to treatment outcomes (Gordon-Hollingsworth et al., 2015). However, other studies have found no such difference suggesting the importance of further research, especially in the context of foster care and/or cross-racial foster parent and child dyads (e.g., Nguyen & McAloon, 2018; Sood et al., 2012). There are multiple factors that could be contributing to the discrepant findings related to treatment outcomes in the context of foster care (e.g., transportation; Dorsey et al., 2014). Thus, it is critical that providers attend to these factors and are proactive about improving treatment engagement and addressing multi-systemic barriers to engagement. For more information about cultural factors impacting separation anxiety disorder, refer to Chapter 2 of this text.

Conclusion

In summary, children in foster care are uniquely at risk for the development of SAD due to their experiences with traumatic loss, disrupted attachment relationships, placement instability, and traumatic experiences. Therefore, it is critical for mental health providers working with youth in foster care to complete comprehensive assessments in order to distinguish between SAD, normative anxiety, and trauma-related symptoms. Once the appropriate diagnosis is determined, providers are encouraged to utilize evidence-based treatments with necessary adaptations for the foster care context. Finally, it is imperative that providers be mindful of the legal, ethical, pharmacological, and cultural considerations when providing services for youth in foster care.

References

Achenbach, T. M., & Rescorla, L. A. (2001). Child Behavior Checklist for Ages 6-18. ASEBA. https://doi.org/10.1037/t47452-000.

Administration for Children and Families (2010). Guidance on Fostering Connections to Success and Increasing Adoptions Act of 2008 (No. ACYF-CB-PI-10-11). Retrieved from Children's Bureau website: https://www.acf.hhs.gov/sites/default/files/documents/cb/pi1011.pdf.

Ainsworth, M. D. S., & Marvin, R. S. (1995). On the shaping of attachment theory and research. In E. Waters, B. E. Vaughn, G. Posada, & K. Kondo-Ikemura (Eds.), Caregiving, cultural, and cognitive perspectives on secure-base behavior and working models. *Monographs of the Society for Research in Child Development, 60*(2–3), 3–21. https://doi.org/https://doi.org/10.1111/j.1540-5834.1995.tb00200.x.

Baker, A. J. L., Borwn, E. J., Schneiderman, M., Sharma-Patel, K., & Berrill, L. M. (2013). Application of evidence-based therapies to children in foster care: A survey of program developers. *APSAC Advisor, 26*(3), 27-34. http://www.apsacny.org/wp-content/uploads/2014/11/APSAC_Advisor_Vol_26_1-pp27-34.pdf.

Barnea, O., Cohen, N., Hindi, I., & Katz, C. (2023). Noticing the unutilized resource of siblinghood: Key conclusions from a scoping review about siblings in out-of-home placements. *Child Abuse & Neglect, 141*. https://doi.org/10.1016/j.chiabu.2023.106192.

Bellamy, J. L., Gopalan, G., & Traube, D. E. (2010). A National Study of the Impact of Outpatient Mental Health Services for Children in Long Term Foster Care. *Clinical Child Psychology and Psychiatry, 15*(4), 467. https://doi.org/10.1177/1359104510377720.

Bennett, C. E., Wood, J. N., & Scribano, P. V. (2020). Health care utilization for children in foster care. *Academic pediatrics*, *20*(3), 341-347. https://doi.org/10.1016/j.acap.2019.10.004.

Blakey, J. M., Leathers, S. J., Lawler, M., Washington, T., Natschke, C., Strand, T., & Walton, Q. (2012). A review of how states are addressing placement stability. *Children and Youth Services Review, 34*(2), 369-378. https://doi.org/10.1016/j.childyouth.2011.11.007.

Boswell, S., & Cudmore, L. (2014). 'The children were fine': acknowledging complex feelings in the move from foster care into adoption. *Adoption & Fostering, 38*(1), 5-21. https://doi.org/10.1177/0308575914522558.

Brenner, S. L., Southerland, D. G., Burns, B. J., Wagner, H. R., & Farmer, E. M. (2014). Use of Psychotropic Medications among Youth in Treatment Foster Care. *Journal of child and family studies*, *23*(4), 666–674. https://doi.org/10.1007/s10826-013-9882-3.

Briggs-Gowan, M.J., Carter, A.S., Clark, R., Augustyn, M., McCarthy, K.J. & Ford, J.D. (2010), Exposure to potentially traumatic events in early childhood: differential links to emergent psychopathology. *Journal of Child Psychology and Psychiatry, 51*, 1132-1140. https://doi.org/10.1111/j.1469-7610.2010.02256.x.

Callaghan, B. L., Gee, D. G., Gabard-Durnam, L., Telzer, E. H., Humphreys, K. L., Goff, B., Flannery, J., Lumian, D. S., Fareri, D. S., Caldera, C., & Tottenham, N. (2019). Decreased amygdala reactivity to parent cues protects against anxiety following early adversity: An examination across 3 years. *Biological Psychiatry: Cognitive Neuroscience and Neuroimaging, 4*(7), 664-671. https://doi.org/10.1016/j.bpsc.2019.02.001.

Cheng, T. W., Mills, K. L., ... & Seghete K. L. M. (2021). Characterizing the impact of adversity, abuse, and neglect on adolescent amygdala resting-state functional connectivity. *Developmental Cognitive Neuroscience, 47*. https://doi.org/10.1016/j.dcn.2020.100894.

Children's Bureau, Administration for Children and Families, Administration on Children Youth and Families, US Department of Health and Human Services (2024). *Preliminary FY[1] 2022 Estimates as of May 9, 2023 - No. 30*. Retrieved from: https://www.acf.hhs.gov/cb/report/afcars-report-30.

Cohen, J. A. (2010). Practice parameter for the assessment and treatment of children and adolescents with Posttraumatic Stress Disorder. *Journal of the American Academy of Child & Adolescent Psychiatry, 49*(4), 414-430. doi:10.1016/j.jaac.2009.12.020.

Cohen, J. A., Deblinger, E., & Mannarino, A. P. (2018). Trauma-focused cognitive behavioral therapy for children and families. *Psychotherapy Research, 28*(1), 47-57. doi:10.1080/10503307.2016.1208375.

Cohen, J. A., Deblinger, E., Mannarino, A. P., & Steer, R. (2004). A multi-site, randomized controlled trial for children with abuse-related PTSD symptoms. *Journal of the*

American Academy of Child and Adolescent Psychiatry, 43(4), 393-402. doi:10.1097/00004583-200404000-00005.

Cohen, J. A., Mannarino, A. P., & Deblinger, E. (2017). *Treating Trauma and Traumatic Grief in Children and Adolescents* (2nd Ed.) (2nd ed.): Routledge.

Cohen, J. A., Mannarino, A. P., & Iyengar, S. (2011). Community treatment of posttraumatic stress disorder for children exposed to intimate partner violence: a randomized controlled trial. *Archives of pediatrics & adolescent medicine, 165*(1), 16-21. doi:10.1001/archpediatrics.2010.247.

Cohen, J. A., Mannarino, A. P., Kliethermes, M., & Murray, L. A. (2012). Trauma-focused CBT for youth with complex trauma. *Child Abuse & Neglect, 36*(6), 528-541. doi: https://doi.org/10.1016/j.chiabu.2012.03.007.

Davis, M. (1992). The role of the amygdala in fear and anxiety. *Annual Review of Neuroscience, 15*, 353–375. https://doi.org/10.1146/annurev.ne.15.030192.002033.

De Los Reyes, A., Augenstein, T. M., Wang, M., Thomas, S. A., Drabick, D. A. G., Burgers, D., & Rabinowitz, J. (2015). The validity of the multi-informant approach to assessing child and adolescent mental health. *Psychological Bulletin.* doi:10.1037/a0038498.

Deblinger, E., Mannarino, A. P., Cohen, J. A., & Steer, R. A. (2006). A follow-up study of a multisite, randomized, controlled trial for children with sexual abuse-related PTSD symptoms. *Journal of the American Academy of Child & Adolescent Psychiatry, 45*(12), 1474-1484. doi:https://doi.org/10.1097/01.chi.0000240839.56114.bb.

Dorsey, S., Pullmann, M. D., Berliner, L., Koschmann, E., McKay, M., & Deblinger, E. (2014). Engaging foster parents in treatment: A randomized trial of supplementing Trauma-focused Cognitive Behavioral Therapy with evidencebased engagement strategies. *Child Abuse & Neglect, 38*(9), 1508-1520. doi:https://doi.org/10.1016/j.chiabu.2014.03.020.

Fawley-King, K., Trask, E. V., Zhang, J., & Aarons, G. A. (2017). The impact of changing neighborhoods, switching schools, and experiencing relationship disruption on children's adjustment to a new placement in foster care. *Child Abuse & Neglect, 63*, 141-150. https://doi.org/10.1016/j.chiabu.2016.11.016.

Garcia, A. R., Gupta, M., Greeson, J. K. P., Thompson, A., & DeNard, C. (2017). Adverse childhood experiences among youth reported to child welfare: Results from the national survey of child & adolescent wellbeing. *Child Abuse & Neglect, 70*, 292-302. doi:https://doi.org/10.1016/j.chiabu.2017.06.019.

Gordon-Hollingsworth, A.T., Becker, E.M., Ginsburg, G.S., Keeton, C., Compton, S. N., Birmaher, B. B., Sakolsky, D. J., Piacentini, J., Albano, A. M., Kendall, P. C., Suveg, C. M., & March, J. S. (2015). Anxiety disorders in Caucasian and African American children: A comparison of clinical characteristics, treatment process variables, and treatment outcomes. *Child Psychiatry & Human Development, 46*, 643–655. https://doi.org/10.1007/s10578-014-0507-x.

Guastaferro, K. & Lutzker, J. R. (2022). The prevention of child maltreatment: Using SafeCare® to highlight successes and needs for improvement in prevention efforts. *International Journal on Child Maltreatment, 5*, 19–29. https://doi.org/10.1007/s42448-021-00090-w.

Hindt, L. A., & Leon, S. C. (2022). Ecological disruptions and well-being among children in foster care. *American Journal of Orthopsychiatry, 92*(1), 39–50. https://doi.org/10.1037/ort0000584.

Hogg, B., Gardoki-Souto, I., Valiente-Gómez, A., Rosa, A. R., Fortea, L., Radua, J., Amann, B. L., & Moreno-Alcázar, A. (2023). Psychological trauma as a transdiagnostic risk factor for mental disorder: an umbrella meta-analysis. *European Archives of Psychiatry and Clinical Neuroscience, 273*(2), 397–410. https://doi.org/10.1007/s00406-022-01495-5.

Humphreys, K. L. (2019). Future directions in the study and treatment of parent–child separation. *Journal of Clinical Child & Adolescent Psychology, 48*(1), 166–178. https://doi.org/10.1080/15374416.2018.1534209.

Keefe, R. J., Cummings, A. D. L., Smith, A. E., Greeley, C. S., & Van Horne, B. S. (2023). Psychotropic Medication Prescribing: Youth in Foster Care Compared with Other Medicaid Enrollees. *Journal of child and adolescent psychopharmacology, 33*(4), 149–155. https://doi.org/10.1089/cap.2022.0092.

Kendall, P. C., Compton, S. N., Walkup, J. T., Birmaher, B., Albano, A. M., Sherrill, J., Ginsburg, G., Rynn, M., McCracken, J., Gosch, E., Keeton, C., Bergman, L., Sakolsky, D., Suveg, C., Iyengar, S., March, J., & Piacentini, J. (2010). Clinical characteristics of anxiety disordered youth. *Journal of Anxiety Disorders, 24*(3), 360-365. https://doi.org/10.1016/j.janxdis.2010.01.009.

King, N. J., Tonge, B. J., Mullen, P., Myerson, N., Heyne, D., Rollings, S., . . . Ollendick, T. H. (2000). Treating sexually abused children with posttraumatic stress symptoms: A randomized clinical trial. *Journal of the American Academy of Child & Adolescent Psychiatry, 39*(11), 1347-1355. doi:10.1097/00004583-200011000-00008.

Konanur, S., Muller, R. T., Cinamon, J. S., Thornback, K., & Zorzella, K. P. M. (2015). Effectiveness of trauma-focused cognitive behavioral therapy in a community-based program. *Child Abuse & Neglect, 50*(Supplement C), 159-170. doi:https://doi.org/10.1016/j.chiabu.2015.07.013.

Konijn, C., Admiraal, S., Baart, J., van Rooik, F., Stams, G., Colonnesi, C., Lindauer, R., & Assink, M. (2019). Foster care placement instability: A meta-analytic review. *Children and Youth Services Review, 96*, 483-499. https://doi.org/10.1016/j.childyouth.2018.12.002.

Leathers, S. J. (2005). Separation from siblings: Associations with placement adaptation and outcomes among adolescents in long-term foster care. *Children and Youth Services Review, 27*(7), 793-819. https://doi.org/10.1016/j.childyouth.2004.12.015.

LeDoux, J. E. & Pine, D. S. (2016). Using neuroscience to help understand fear and anxiety: A two-system framework. *American Journal of Psychiatry, 173*(11), 1083-1093. https://doi.org/10.1176/appi.ajp.2016.16030353.

McNeil, C. B., & Hembree-Kigin, T. L. (2011). *Parent-child interaction therapy* (2nd ed.). Springer.

Méndez, X., Espada, J. P., Orgilés, M., Llavona, L. M., & García-Fernández, J. M. (2014). Children's Separation Anxiety Scale (CSAS): Psychometric Properties. *PLoS ONE, 9*(7). https://doi.org/10.1371/journal.pone.010321.

Mersky, J. P., Topitzes, J., Janczewski, C. E., & McNeil, C. B. (2015). Enhancing foster parent training with Parent-Child Interaction Therapy: Evidence from a randomized field experiment. *Journal of the Society for Social Work and Research, 6*(4), 591–616. https://doi.org/10.1086/684123.

Mitchell, M. B. (2018). "No one acknowledged my loss and hurt": Non-death loss, grief, and trauma in foster care. *Child & Adolescent Social Work Journal, 35*(1), 1–9. https://doi.org/10.1007/s10560-017-0502-8.

Morina, N., Koerssen, R., & Pollet, T. V. (2016). Interventions for children and adolescents with posttraumatic stress disorder: A meta-analysis of comparative outcome studies. *Clinical Psychology Review, 47*(Supplement C), 41-54. doi:https://doi.org/10.1016/j.cpr.2016.05.006.

Munson, M. R., Narendorf, S. C., & McMillen, J. C. (2011). Knowledge of and Attitudes Towards Behavioral Health Services Among Older Youth in the Foster Care System. *Child & adolescent social work journal : C & A, 28*(2), 97–112. https://doi.org/10.1007/s10560-010-0223-8.

Nguyen, S.-A., & McAloon, J. (2018). A cross-cultural comparison of parental perceptions of childhood separation anxiety disorder symptoms and likelihood to seek help. *Journal of Cross-Cultural Psychology, 49*(3), 453-469. https://doi.org/10.1177/0022022118754722.

Ölmez, S. B., Sarıgedik, E., & Ataoğlu, A. (2022). The relationships between separation anxiety disorder, childhood traumas, and anxiety sensitivity in a sample of medical students. *Journal of Affective Disorders Reports, 9*, 100367. https://doi.org/10.1016/j.jadr.2022.100367.

Oransky, M., Hahn, H., & Stover, C. S. (2013). Caregiver and youth agreement regarding youths' trauma histories: Implications for youths' functioning after exposure to trauma. *Journal of Youth and Adolescence, 42*(10), 1528–1542. doi:10.1007/s10964-013-9947-z

Platt, R., Williams, S. R., & Ginsburg, G. S. (2016). Stressful life events and child anxiety: examining parent and child mediators. *Child Psychiatry and Human Development, 47*(1), 23–34. https://doi.org/10.1007/s10578-015-0540-4.

Puzzanchera, C., Taylor, M., Kang, W. and Smith, J. (2022). Disproportionality Rates for Children of Color in Foster Care Dashboard. *National Council of Juvenile and Family Court Judges.*

Rothbaum, F., Kakinuma, M., Nagaoka, R., & Azuma, H. (2007). Attachment and amae: Parent-child closeness in the United States and Japan. *Journal of Cross-Cultural Psychology, 38*(4), 465-486. https://doi.org/10.1177/0022022107302315.

Sattler, K. M. P., & Font, S. A. (2021). Predictors of adoption and guardianship dissolution: The role of race, age, and gender among children in foster care. *Child Maltreatment, 26*(2), 216-227. https://doi.org/10.1177/1077559520952171.

Silove, D., Alonso, J., Bromet, E., Gruber, M., Sampson, N., Scott, K., Andrade, L., Benjet, C., Caldas de Almeida, J. M., De Girolamo, G., de Jonge, P., Demyttenaere, K., Fiestas, F., Florescu, S., Gureje, O., He, Y., Karam, E., Lepine, J. P., Murphy, S., Villa-Posada, J. Kessler, R. C. (2015). Pediatric-onset and adult-onset separation anxiety disorder across countries in the world mental health survey. *American Journal of Psychiatry, 172*(7), 647–656. https://doi.org/10.1176/appi.ajp.2015.14091185.

Sood, E. D., Mendez, J. L., & Kendall, P. C. (2012). Acculturation, religiosity, and ethnicity predict mothers' causal beliefs about separation anxiety disorder and preferences for help-seeking. *Journal of Cross-Cultural Psychology, 43*(3), 393-409. https://doi.org/10.1177/0022022110389492.

Stern, J. A., Barbarin, O., & Cassidy, J. (2022). Working toward anti-racist perspectives in attachment theory, research, and practice. *Attachment & Human Development, 24*(3), 392–422. https://doi.org/10.1080/14616734.2021.1976933.

Strijker, J., Knorth, E. J., & Knot-Dickscheit, J. (2008). Placement History of Foster Children: A Study of Placement History and Outcomes in Long-Term Family Foster Care. *Child Welfare, 87*(5), 107–124. https://www.jstor.org/stable/48623168.

Tarren-Sweeney, M. J., Hazell, P. L., & Carr, V. J. (2004). Are foster parents reliable informants of children's behaviour problems? Child : *Care, Health & Development, 30*(2), 167–175. https://doi.org/10.1111/j.1365-2214.2003.00407.x.

Unrau, Y. A., Seita, J. R., & Putney, K. S. (2008). Former foster youth remember multiple placement moves: A journey of loss and hope. *Children and Youth Services Review, 30*(11), 1256-1266. https://doi.org/10.1016/j.childyouth.2008.03.010.

Webb, C., Hayes, A. M., Grasso, D., Laurenceau, J.-P., & Deblinger, E. (2014). Trauma-focused cognitive behavioral therapy for youth: Effectiveness in a community setting. *Psychological Trauma: Theory, Research, Practice, and Policy, 6*(5),555-562. doi:10.1037/a0037364.

Weisz, J. R., Suwanlert, S., Chaiyasit, W., Weiss, B., & Jackson, E. W. (1991). Adult attitudes toward over-and undercontrolled child problems: Urban and rural parents and teachers from Thailand and the United States. *Journal of Child Psychology and Psychiatry, 32*(4), 645-654. https://doi.org/10.1111/j.1469-7610.1991.tb00341.x.

Wojciak, A. S., McWey, L. M., & Helfrich, C. M. (2013). Sibling relationships and internalizing symptoms of youth in foster care. *Children and Youth Services Review, 35*(97), 1071-1077. https://doi.org/10.1016/j.childyouth.2013.04.021.

Wojciak, A. S., Simpson, J. E., Tomfohrde, O., & Wang, G. (2024). Barriers and facilitators of sibling relationships of youth in foster care from an ecological perspective. *Children and Youth Services Review, 157.* https://doi.org/10.1016/j.childyouth.2023.107408.

Zeanah, C. H., Berlin, L. J., & Boris, N. W. (2011). Practitioner review: Clinical applications of attachment theory and research for infants and young children. *Journal of Child Psychology and Psychiatry, and Allied Disciplines, 52*(8), 819–833. https://doi.org/10.1111/j.1469-7610.2011.02399.x.

Zito, J. M., Safer, D. J., Sai, D., Gardner, J. F., Thomas, D., Coombes, P., Dubowski, M., & Mendez-Lewis, M. (2008). Psychotropic medication patterns among youth in foster care. *Pediatrics, 121*(1), e157–e163. https://doi.org/10.1542/peds.2007-0212.

Chapter 8

Separation Anxiety Behaviors in Children with Chronic Medical Conditions and Extended Hospitalization

Chelsea Tobin*

Department of Pediatrics, Baylor College of Medicine, Houston, TX, USA

Abstract

Children with chronic illness may require prolonged hospital stays which often result in emotional distress and separation anxiety behaviors. Increasing understanding of separation anxiety in pediatric patients, awareness of how this may manifest during prolonged hospitalizations, and interventions to decrease longstanding impact will benefit healthcare workers and caregivers aiming to support this vulnerable population.

Keywords: separation anxiety, pediatric patients, chronic medical conditions, prolonged hospitalization, intensive care, PICU, mental health symptoms in children with critical illness

Introduction

Children with chronic illness who require prolonged hospital stays often endorse heightened feelings of anxiety, particularly when separated from their primary caregivers. This chapter outlines the behavioral manifestations and

* Corresponding Author's Email: CxTobin@TexasChildrens.org.

In: Separation Anxiety: Presentation and Intervention
Editor: Kelly Nicole Banneyer
ISBN: 979-8-89530-386-3

implications of separation anxiety in pediatric patients, utilizing research and clinical observations to bolster understanding and outline relevant interventions.

Understanding Separation Anxiety in Children with Chronic Illness

Separation anxiety, as described by the American Psychiatric Association, is a normative developmental phenomenon characterized by a child's distress when removed from attachment figures such as parents and caregivers (American Psychiatric Association, 2013). However, in pediatric patients with chronic illness who are separated from their parents during hospitalization, this experience is often intensified in the setting of medical procedures, frequent admissions to hospital, and extended periods of time away from familiar routines and the home environment (Kazak et al., 2001).

Manifestations of Separation Anxiety in Pediatric Patients

Separation anxiety often manifests in pediatric patients with chronic illness who require prolonged hospitalization via clinginess, overt distress upon separation from caregivers, sleep disturbance, and developmental regression, as well as resistance to medical procedures, necessary nursing cares, and potentially challenging therapies (Lavigne & Faier-Routman, 1993). Such behaviors, while often disruptive to the patient's medical care, are believed to be coping mechanisms utilized by children experiencing heightened emotional distress and anxiety associated with their hospital stay. Examples of behavioral manifestations of separation anxiety might include a child's refusal to allow providers to complete an examination requiring physical separation from the caregiver, crying out for caregivers and engaging in behavioral outbursts upon caregivers leaving bedside, and as extreme as pulling out necessary lines and tubes to attempt to follow caregivers who may be stepping out to return home for a visit.

Factors Contributing to Separation Anxiety

There are many factors which contribute to separation anxiety in pediatric patients with chronic illness requiring prolonged hospitalization. Such factors include the level of caregiver stress, the child's illness trajectory, prior experiences with medical procedures, and the hospital environment. A parent or caregiver's level of distress about their child's chronic illness has been known to exacerbate separation anxiety behaviors in children, as the child's emotional state is directly influenced by the caregiver's emotional wellbeing (Kazak et al., 2004). Additionally, the severity of the pediatric patient's illness effects their emotional adjustment and influences their level of susceptibility to separation anxiety; patients with worse prognoses or higher burdens of physical symptoms are more likely to experience anxiety with separation from their caregivers (Stuber et al., 2003).

Children with chronic illness who have had previously experienced potentially distressing medical procedures or hospitalizations are at risk of heightened anxiety when separated from caregivers, as they are more likely to have previously undergone painful procedures, traumatic events, and medical trauma (Field et al., 2010). Finally, the hospital environment itself is a significant contributing factor with regard to separation anxiety behaviors in pediatric patients, as the sterile environment, unfamiliar people, invasive procedures, and disruption of routine contribute to heightened anxiety upon separation from caregivers (Vagnoli et al., 2005).

Impact of Separation Anxiety Behaviors on Medical Care

Separation anxiety behaviors can have significant repercussions upon a pediatric patient's well-being and medical course. The impact of separation anxiety on wellbeing can be observed via noncompliance with treatment, as patients with separation anxiety can exhibit uncooperative behaviors such as refusing necessary cares or procedures, possibly contributing to prolonged admission (Cassidy & McConaha, 2006; Cuzzocrea et al., 2014). Pediatric patients with heightened levels of anxiety may also experience increased severity of physical symptom burden as a result of emotional distress, and as such may feel increased suffering during their hospital stay (Kain et al., 2006).

Hospitalization of children with chronic illness often results in disruption of family dynamics in the context of prolonged hospital stays and may place additional strain on parents and family members who may in turn exhibit emotional distress (Carr et al., 2003; Hockenberry et al., 2003). The long-term effects of prolonged hospitalization are not to be overlooked, as without intervention, separation anxiety in children with chronic illness may lead to development of anxiety disorders or other mental health struggles later in life (Carr et al., 2003).

Interventions Targeting Separation Anxiety

There are several interventions which may help to address separation anxiety in children with chronic illness and prolonged hospitalization, such as bolstering caregiver involvement, provision of psychological support, developmentally informed preparation and education, environmental modifications, and the potential use of psychotropic medications. As with most behavioral interventions, targeting the unique role of parents and caregivers is useful when addressing separation anxiety behaviors in children. Encouraging involvement in care and providing direct guidance to caregivers can bolster their confidence; increased levels of caregiver confidence can result in less emotional distress witnessed by the patient, and in turn may result in less distress for the child (Kazak et al., 2001).

Pediatric psychologists and mental health clinicians play an important role in offering interventions and psychological support to children with chronic illness throughout prolonged hospital admissions. Interventions such as play therapy, cognitive behavioral therapy, or behavioral parent training can help children to develop skills to cope with separation anxiety and related emotional distress (Kovacs & Devlin, 1998).

In collaboration with pediatric psychologists, Child Life specialists offer expertise in providing preparation and education to pediatric patients with extended hospitalizations. The combination of therapeutic, developmentally informed activities and age-appropriate information about diagnoses and treatment, as well as preparation and education before and after medical procedures are crucial interventions aimed at bolstering a child's coping and decreasing emotional distress (American Academy of Pediatrics, 2014).

Modification of the child's environment while hospitalized can also have a significant impact upon separation anxiety in pediatric patients. Normalizing activities (e.g., engaging in schoolwork, games), comfort items (e.g., blanket and stuffed toy from home), and allowing caregivers to stay overnight can help to lessen a child's overall anxiety (Knafl et al., 2010). Finally, in cases of severe separation anxiety in which patients are unable to receive necessary medical interventions as a result of behavioral manifestations of separation anxiety, the use of pharmacological interventions may be beneficial in alleviating distress, and may be beneficial in bolstering the child's ability to cope during this challenging time (Simeon at al., 2012).

Conclusion

Separation anxiety behaviors in children with chronic illness and prolonged hospital stays present multifaceted difficulties and require a collaborative and comprehensive treatment approach. Increasing our understanding of separation anxiety may benefit healthcare providers and caregivers in more effectively responding to and managing emotional distress in chronically ill children, while also working to prevent longstanding negative effects of prolonged hospitalization in this vulnerable population.

References

American Academy of Pediatrics. (2014). Child life services. *Pediatrics*, 133(5), e1471-e1481.

American Psychiatric Association. (2013). Diagnostic and statistical manual of mental disorders (5th ed.). Arlington, VA: American Psychiatric Publishing.

Carr, E. G., Horner, R. H., Turnbull, A. P., Marquis, J. G., McLaughlin, D. M., McAtee, M. L., & Smith, C. E. (2003). *Positive behavior support for people with developmental disabilities: A research synthesis*. Washington, DC: American Association on Mental Retardation.

Cassidy, J., & McConaha, B. L. (2006). The development of noncompliance in children: Contributions of early attachment, temperament, and parenting. In R. G. McPherson (Ed.), *Conduct disorders in childhood and adolescence* (2nd ed., pp. 369-391). New York, NY: Guilford Press.

Cuzzocrea, F., Larcan, R., Romeo, C., & Salerno, I. (2014). Anxiety in children with chronic illness who are hospitalized: A review. *Italian Journal of Pediatrics*, 40(1), 102.

Field, T., Hernandez-Reif, M., & Diego, M. (2010). Intrusive and withdrawn depressed mothers and their infants. *Developmental Review*, 30(3), 333-340.

Hockenberry, M. J., Wilson, D., & Winkelstein, M. L. (2003). *Wong's nursing care of infants and children*. St. Louis, MO: Mosby.

Kain, Z. N., Caldwell-Andrews, A. A., Mayes, L. C., & Weinberg, M. E. (2006). Family-centered preparation for surgery improves perioperative outcomes in children: A randomized controlled trial. *Anesthesiology*, 105(5), 1045-1054.

Kazak, A. E., Alderfer, M., Rourke, M. T., Simms, S., Streisand, R., & Grossman, J. R. (2004). Posttraumatic stress disorder (PTSD) and posttraumatic stress symptoms (PTSS) in families of adolescent childhood cancer survivors. *Journal of Pediatric Psychology*, 29(3), 211-219.

Kazak, A. E., Cant, M. C., Jensen, M. M., McSherry, M., Rourke, M. T., Hwang, W. T., ... & Anderson, K. W. (2001). Identifying psychosocial risk indicative of subsequent resource use in families of newly diagnosed pediatric oncology patients. *Journal of Clinical Oncology,* 19(13), 3220-3229.

Knafl, K. A., Deatrick, J. A., Gallo, A. M., Dixon, J., Grey, M., Knafl, G. J., & O'Malley, J. (2010). Assessment of the psychometric properties of the Family Management Measure. *Journal of Pediatric Psychology*, 35(4), 403-419.

Kovacs, M., & Devlin, B. (1998). Internalizing disorders in childhood. *Journal of Child Psychology and Psychiatry*, 39(1), 47-63.

Lavigne, J. V., & Faier-Routman, J. (1993). Psychological adjustment to pediatric physical disorders: A meta-analytic review. *Journal of Pediatric Psychology*, 18(1), 133-157.

Simeon, D., Stein, D. J., Hollander, E., & Cohen, L. J. (2012). Pharmacotherapy of social anxiety disorder. In D. S. Baldwin (Ed.), *Handbook of anxiety and anxiety disorders* (pp. 443-461). Chichester, UK: Wiley-Blackwell.

Stuber, M. L., Meeske, K., Gonzalez, S., Houskamp, B. M., Bartelt, S., Weitzman, C., & Meadows, A. T. (2003). Social, emotional, and behavioral functioning of children with cancer. *Pediatrics,* 112(6), 1158-1168.

Vagnoli, L., Caprilli, S., Robiglio, A., & Messeri, A. (2005). Clown doctors as a treatment for preoperative anxiety in children: A randomized, prospective study. *Pediatrics,* 116(4), e563-e567.

Chapter 9

Separation Anxiety in Children and Adolescents with Autism Spectrum Disorder

Madeline Racine[1,*]
and Natalie Justice[2]

[1]Department of Pediatrics, Division of Psychology, Baylor College of Medicine, Houston, TX, USA
[2]Department of Pediatrics, Division of Behavioral Medicine and Clinical Psychology, University of Cincinnati, Cincinnati, OH, USA

Abstract

Children and adolescents with ASD are at a significant risk for developing anxiety disorders, including separation anxiety disorder. This group may be particularly vulnerable to the negative impact of separation anxiety given that anxiety symptoms can exacerbate social difficulties commonly experienced by children with ASD. Diagnosing separation anxiety disorder in children with ASD can be more challenging than in typically developing children due to difficulties with self-report, lack of well-validated tools, overlap of symptoms, and unique behavioral expression of anxiety in youth with ASD. Nonetheless, emerging research suggests that it is possible and crucial to differentiate anxiety and ASD characteristics. A growing body of research also supports the effectiveness of using cognitive behavioral therapy (CBT) to treat anxiety disorders in children and adolescents with ASD, though various modifications may make these interventions more appropriate and accessible for youth with ASD. This chapter provides a comprehensive

[*] Corresponding Author's Email: madeline.racine@bcm.edu.

In: Separation Anxiety: Presentation and Intervention
Editor: Kelly Nicole Banneyer
ISBN: 979-8-89530-386-3

overview of separation anxiety disorder in the context of ASD, including a general understanding of the diagnostic criteria, prevalence rates, and symptom presentation. Considerations and recommendations for assessment and intervention are also discussed, including treatment modifications to CBT, with a particular emphasis on separation anxiety disorder.

Keywords: autism spectrum disorder, anxiety, separation anxiety, assessment, intervention

Introduction

Autism, or autism spectrum disorder (ASD), is a neurodevelopmental condition characterized by differences in social interaction, communication challenges, and tendency to engage in repetitive behaviors. Prevalence rates of ASD have been steadily increasing in recent years, with recent estimates suggesting 1 in 36 children in the United States meet criteria for ASD (Maenner, 2023). In general, research has found that children with ASD exhibit higher rates of anxiety symptoms compared to their typically developing peers (van Steensel & Heeman, 2017; Vasa et al., 2020) and approximately 40% of children with ASD are diagnosed with at least one anxiety disorder (van Steensel et al., 2011). Among these anxiety disorders, separation anxiety disorder affects an estimated 9% of youth with ASD (van Steensel et al., 2011). Addressing separation anxiety in this population is crucial, as separation anxiety can exacerbate social impairment and cause further challenges for children with ASD. Further, as more children are being diagnosed with ASD than in the past, the demand for interventions and strategies to support children with ASD and co-occurring anxiety disorders also increases. In this chapter, we provide an overview of both autism spectrum disorder and separation anxiety disorder, including general understanding of the diagnostic criteria, prevalence rates, and symptom presentation. We also discuss current literature on the assessment and intervention of anxiety for children with ASD, including challenges and recommendations for clinical practices. It is our hope that this chapter will provide clinicians with essential information to make informed decisions regarding assessment and treatment of youth with ASD and co-occurring anxiety, including separation anxiety disorder, in order to improve quality of care and outcomes for these children.

Understanding Autism Spectrum Disorder

According to the Diagnostic Statistical Manual of Mental Disorders, Fifth Edition (DSM-5), the diagnostic criteria for ASD include both (a) persistent deficits in social communication and social interaction across multiple contexts and (b) the presence of restricted, repetitive patterns of behavior, interests, or activities (2013). Symptoms must be present in early childhood, although they may not become fully apparent until social challenges exceed abilities or may be masked by learned strategies in later life. Additionally, symptoms must cause clinically significant impairment in daily functioning. Current prevalence data suggests that approximately 1 in 36 children in the United States carry a diagnosis of ASD, with boys being about 4 times more likely to receive a diagnosis than girls (Maenner, 2023). This is an increase from previous reports, indicating a rising trend in ASD diagnosis. Increase in prevalence is often attributed to increased awareness of ASD, improved screening and identification, and a better understanding of the ways ASD manifests in individuals (Matson & Kozlowski, 2011).

Autism is considered a spectrum disorder because it affects individuals differently and to varying degrees, resulting in a wide range of experiences, abilities and challenges among individuals with ASD. The core characteristics of ASD include difficulties with social communication and social interaction, as well as repetitive behaviors and restricted interests. However, these traits can occur in a variety of combinations and present with varying degrees of severity. Social communication challenges in individuals with ASD may include difficulty initiating and responding to social initiations, maintaining eye contact, understanding nonverbal cues like facial expressions or gestures, and engaging in reciprocal conversations. Individuals with ASD often find it challenging to make friends or form close, reciprocal relationships and may struggle to fully understand what behaviors are appropriate in different settings. Restricted and repetitive behaviors may manifest as repetitive movements (e.g., hand flapping, rocking, pacing), repetitive use of objects or play (e.g., lining up objects, spinning toys), repetitive or stereotyped patterns of speech (e.g., echolalia, scripting), adherence to routines or ritualized behaviors, and a strong attachment or preoccupation with certain topics or objects. Sensory seeking (e.g., smelling or touching of objects) and sensory avoidant behaviors (e.g., heighted reactions to lights, sounds or textures) are also common in individuals with ASD.

Children and adolescents with ASD experience challenges in daily functioning across various domains. At home, children with ASD may struggle establishing routines and adapting to changes, which can lead to difficulty completing everyday tasks. In school, challenges related to social communication and behavior may impact a child's ability to participate in group activities, follow instructions, and interact with teachers and peers, resulting in academic challenges. In social settings, children with ASD may have difficulty making friends, understanding social norms, and engaging in typical play activities with peers, which can lead to feelings of isolation or peer rejection. In addition to core symptoms, research has found high rates of co-occurrence between ASD and other mental health conditions, such as attention-deficit/hyperactivity disorder (ADHD), anxiety disorders, depressive disorders, and behavioral concerns (Hossain et al., 2020). Co-occurring conditions such as anxiety can exacerbate social impairment and cause further challenges for children with ASD, making it even more difficult to navigate daily life successfully.

Anxiety in Autism Spectrum Disorder

Anxiety disorders are one of the most common co-occurring conditions in youth with ASD. A review of the literature indicates that approximately 40% of children and adolescents with ASD are diagnosed with at least one anxiety disorder (van Steensel et al., 2011); however, rates ranging up to 62% have been reported in some studies (Vasa et al., 2020). This prevalence rate is higher than in typically developing children, where rates of anxiety disorders are reported up to approximately 15-20% (Costello et al., 2005; Kessler et al., 2012; Racine et al., 2021). Additionally, studies comparing anxiety levels of children with ASD to those of typically developing children consistently demonstrate higher rates of anxiety symptoms for children with ASD (van Steensel & Heeman, 2017; Vasa et al., 2020). While most of the research has focused on school-age children, recent comparison studies have included toddlers with ASD suggesting that elevated rates of anxiety are present in the first 3 years of life (Vasa et al., 2020). Some of the most common anxiety disorders seen in children with ASD are specific phobias (30%), obsessive compulsive disorder (17%), social anxiety disorder and agoraphobia (17%), generalized anxiety disorder (15%), separation anxiety disorder (9%), and panic disorder (2%), though prevalence rates vary widely across studies (van Steensel et al., 2011; White et al., 2009).

Kerns and colleagues (2014) explored how anxiety manifests in children with ASD. They found that ASD is generally associated with more varied presentations of anxiety, which may align with or differ from specified anxiety disorders in the DSM. Specifically, children with ASD may experience anxiety in ways that is similar to children without ASD, suggesting co-occurring anxiety that is secondary to ASD and aligns with traditional DSM definitions. Children with ASD may also experience anxiety that differs from DSM definitions and appears to be related to both ASD and an anxiety disorder, which the authors defined as atypical anxiety. This kind of anxiety may include worries around routine novelty and restricted interests (e.g., worry about minor changes in routine, excessive worry about losing access to special interest), compulsive/ritualistic behavior (e.g., mealtime routines, insistence on doors being closed), social fearfulness without accompanying fear of negative evaluation (e.g., frantic efforts to escape or avoid situations where other people are present, increased aggression in social situations), and/or unusual specific phobias (e.g., fear of baby crying, balloons). These symptoms do not appear to be inevitable consequences of ASD, nor do they fit neatly into existing anxiety disorder criteria; however, they do represent an anxiety construct, suggesting that some anxiety symptoms may be unique to ASD populations.

While it is not fully understood why children with ASD experience higher levels of anxiety, several possible explanations have been suggested. Most notably, core symptoms of ASD (e.g., social challenges, communication difficulties, sensory sensitivities, difficulty coping with changes or unexpected transitions) may make children more prone to anxiety (Vasa et al., 2020). Other potential factors contributing to anxiety may include underlying difficulties with sleep, emotional regulation, and behavioral problems (Vasa et al., 2020; White et al., 2014). Negative life events, such as bullying and peer rejection, are also more common in children with ASD and may further contribute to stress and anxiety (Cappadocia et al., 2012). Additional explanations include shared genetic factors underlying both ASD and anxiety disorders (Doherty & Owen, 2014; Hallett et al., 2013b) and diagnostic overlap between the two disorders (van Steensel et al., 2014, Wood & Gadow, 2010). Co-occurring anxiety disorders in children with ASD is associated with impairment above what is attributable to ASD alone, including heighted social skill deficits, family stress, self-injurious behavior, decreased academic performance, and increased health needs (Adams & Emerson, 2020), emphasizing the necessity of addressing anxiety within this population.

Separation Anxiety Disorder and Autism Spectrum Disorder

Diagnostic Criteria and Prevalence

Separation anxiety disorder, as defined by the DSM-5, is characterized by excessive fear or anxiety concerning separation from those to whom the individual is attached, most commonly parents or other family members. This anxiety is developmentally inappropriate and manifests through excessive distress when anticipating or experiencing separation from home or major attachment figures, persistent worry about losing major attachment figures or about possible harm befalling them (e.g., illness, injury, death), excessive worry about experiencing an untoward event (e.g., getting lost, being kidnapped) that causes separation from a major attachment figure, persistent reluctance or refusal to go to school or other settings due to fear of separation, excessive fear or reluctance about being alone at home or in other settings, and/or persistent reluctance or refusal to sleep away from home or to go to sleep without being near a major attachment figure. Additional symptoms may include nightmares about separation and physical complaints (e.g., headaches or stomachaches) when separation occurs or is anticipated. Symptoms must persist for at least 4 weeks in children and adolescents and cause significant impairment in social, academic, occupational, or other important areas of functioning (APA, 2013).

Different epidemiological studies indicate that the prevalence of separation anxiety disorder is about 4 to 5% in children and adolescents (Masi et al., 2001). Separation anxiety is the most prevalent anxiety disorder in children younger than 12 years and decreases in prevalence from childhood through adolescence (APA, 2013). However, some children continue to experience stable and significant symptoms well into adolescence (Kearney et al., 2003). Consistent with other anxiety disorders, separation anxiety is notably higher in youth with ASD, though prevalence rates vary across studies. A meta-analysis analyzing 31 studies involving youth with ASD found that of the 40% of children with at least one anxiety disorder, 9% of these children had separation anxiety disorder (van Steensel et al., 2011). Much higher rates have been found in clinical samples; for instance, a study assessing comorbid anxiety disorders in a large sample (N = 217) of children aged 3-17 with ASD referred to a psychopharmacology clinic found that separation anxiety disorder was present in approximately 37% of these children (Joshi et al., 2010). Consistent with findings from research with typical populations, separation anxiety disorder in children with ASD occurs in both early childhood and adolescence. In a study examining prevalence of anxiety disorders in preschoolers with ASD, separation anxiety disorder and specific phobia were the most prevalent anxiety disorders (Chan et al., 2023). Further, a longitudinal study following youth with ASD from toddlerhood to adolescence found that the most common anxiety type noted in adolescence was separation anxiety at approximately 39% (Ben-Itzchak, et al., 2020). Differences in prevalence rates of separation anxiety disorder in children with ASD are mainly due to sample and methodological heterogeneity, differences in the operationalization of anxiety, and using different assessment methods to assess anxiety in children with ASD (Kerns & Kendall, 2012).

Despite inconsistencies in prevalence rates, it has been well established that co-occurring anxiety, including separation anxiety, is common in children with ASD. Consistent with other anxiety disorders, children and adolescents with ASD may experience high levels of separation anxiety due to challenges associated with core symptoms of ASD. For example, children with ASD often rely on predictable routines and may struggle with changes in caregivers or environments, leading to anxiety when faced with separations. Fear of uncertainty found to be common in children with anxiety and ASD (Keen et al., 2019) may make it challenging to adapt to new or unfamiliar situations and worsen anxiety. Moreover, difficulties with social interaction and understanding social cues may further contribute to anxiety in unfamiliar or unpredictable situations, including separations from caregivers. Sensory sensitivities common in ASD (e.g., sensitivities to noise or touch in unfamiliar environments) may also heighten anxiety when separated from familiar caregivers who typically help manage these needs.

Symptom Presentation and Implications

Existing literature suggests that the presentation of separation anxiety disorder in children with ASD is generally similar to that of children without ASD (Wood & Gadow, 2010; Hayashida et al., 2010). However, because some anxiety symptoms may be unique to ASD populations, children with ASD and co-occurring separation anxiety disorder may display varied presentations or exaggerated symptoms compared to children without ASD. For example, symptoms such as restlessness or edginess, social discomfort, fear of uncertainty, and general fearfulness may be heighted for children with ASD compared to typically developing children (Hallett et al., 2013a; Keen et al.,

2019). Due to challenges with communication, children with ASD may struggle to express their worries verbally and symptoms may be more likely to manifest behaviorally through increased clinginess, tantrums, and/or repetitive behaviors. Increased severity of repetitive and/or ritualistic behaviors has been consistently associated with increased anxiety in ASD (Ben-Itzchak et al., 2020) and in some cases has predicted specific types of anxiety, including separation anxiety (Magiati et al., 2016). Several studies have hypothesized that repetitive and ritualistic behaviors in ASD may serve as a coping strategy for lowering high levels of anxiety (Ben-Itzchak et al., 2020; Spiker et al., 2012). Moreover, caregivers and clinicians often anecdotally report unusual attachments to objects in children with ASD and high levels of separation anxiety (Magiati et al., 2016). Irritability also frequently accompanies the manifestation of anxiety disorders in children with ASD (Mayes et al., 2011) and higher levels of anxiety has been associated with more oppositional behavior and social withdrawal in young children with ASD (Sukhodolsky et al., 2020).

Separation anxiety in childhood causes significant impairment in a child's daily functioning, as symptoms can disrupt normal daily routines, impair social interactions, and hinder school performance. Children with ASD may be particularly vulnerable to the negative impact of separation anxiety because anxiety symptoms can exacerbate challenges related to core symptoms of ASD and cause further impairment. For example, separation anxiety in children with ASD may limit opportunities for social engagement and peer interaction, leading to increased social difficulties and social isolation. Separation anxiety may also contribute to behavioral difficulties in children with ASD, including tantrums, irritability, and increased rigidity, making it difficult to complete everyday tasks and activities. For adolescents particularly, adolescents with ASD often exhibit lower adaptive behavior and daily living skills compared to their typically developing peers. Separation anxiety can hinder the development of these skills by limiting independent activities and social interactions essential for skill development. Moreover, children with ASD already prone to sleep difficulties (Mannion & Leader, 2014) may experience worsened symptoms due to separation anxiety including refusal or reluctance to sleep alone or increased nightmares. Given the high prevalence of separation anxiety disorder in children with ASD and the associated potential for exacerbated impairment, it is critical that clinicians identify and address separation anxiety in children and adolescents with ASD.

Assessment Considerations

Accurate assessment of anxiety disorders among children with ASD is challenging due to difficulties with self-report, lack of well-validated tools, overlap of ASD features with anxiety symptoms, and unique behavioral expression of anxiety in youth with ASD. Clinicians must take into account various factors when assessing separation anxiety in children with ASD (Vasa et al., 2016; Zaboski & Storch, 2018). Vasa and colleagues (2016) provide specific clinical recommendations for assessment of anxiety in youth with ASD developed by The Autism Speaks Autism Treatment Network (ATN)/Autism Intervention Research on Physical Health Anxiety Workgroup, a multidisciplinary team of clinicians and researchers with expertise in ASD. Similarly, Kerns and colleagues (2016) provide a clinical framework for diagnosing anxiety disorders in youth with ASD with a focus on differentiating anxiety and ASD symptoms. Below are various considerations and recommendations for assessing anxiety disorders among youth with ASD based on the literature, with particular emphasis on separation anxiety disorder.

Conduct a Multi-Informant and Multi-Method Assessment

Similar to diagnosing anxiety in children without ASD, assessment should include multiple methods and multiple informants, including data from clinical interviews, rating scales gathered from multiple informants (e.g., child, parent, teacher), and behavioral observations. Children with ASD may have difficulty self-reporting anxiety due to cognitive and language deficits. Additionally, children with ASD may struggle with emotional insight and have difficulty describing their internal experiences, making it difficult for them to accurately describe their feelings of anxiety (Matson & Shoemaker, 2009). There is also limited data on psychometric properties for self-report measures in ASD samples (Kerns et al., 2015) and it has been suggested that children with ASD tend to underreport overall levels of anxiety on measures of self-report compared to parent report (Kalvin et al., 2020). Taken together, clinicians should determine when self-report is appropriate and interpret results cautiously, especially when emotional insight is compromised. Vasa and colleagues (2016) recommend assessing a child's ability to understand and express emotions (e.g., "Do you know what it means to be scared or worried?", "Tell me about something you worry about?") and providing developmentally appropriate descriptions of these terms. Additionally, they recommend using forced choice questions (i.e., those requiring yes or no) rather than open ended questions and using a visual analog scale rather than verbal responses for children with ASD who have difficulty reporting their anxiety.

Given limitations with self-report methods, assessment should rely on accurate reporting by parents and other caregivers through clinical interview and parent report measures. Because there may be differences between child and parent perceptions of anxiety, clinicians should also gather information from teachers and school staff to supplement parent report and provide insight into the child's behavior across settings and situations. Assessment should also include behavioral observations, especially when child self-report is limited. When possible, clinicians should observe the parent-child interaction and the child's behavior when faced with separation. Specific behaviors to observe may include fearful affect, excessive clinginess, crying, and increased repetitive behaviors when anticipating or experiencing separation. Irritability, tantrums, aggression, and self-injurious behavior may also reflect increased anxiety in children with ASD (Magiati et al., 2016; Mayes et al., 2011). Further, clinicians should observe or inquire about worsening sleep problems and regression in skills, as these behaviors may suggest the presence of anxiety in children with ASD.

Clinicians assessing separation anxiety in children with ASD should recognize the limitations in available assessment measures for this population. At present, there is no gold standard for assessing anxiety, including separation anxiety, in youth with ASD. Further, most anxiety measures have been designed and validated for typically developing populations (Rudy et al., 2013). While measurements such as the Screen for Child Anxiety Related Emotional Disorders (SCARED; Muris et al., 1999) and Spence Children's Anxiety Scale (SCAS; Spence, 1997), demonstrate excellent psychometric properties for typically developing children, there is less research on their effectiveness in assessing anxiety symptoms in children with ASD. Overall, standard parent report anxiety scales have been found to have moderate to poor sensitivity in detecting clinical anxiety in ASD, particularly in children with intellectual impairment (Kerns et al., 2020). However, one study to date found that the psychometric properties of the SCARED for children with ASD and anxiety disorders were comparable to children with anxiety disorders without ASD (van Steensel et al., 2013), suggesting that this may be an effective tool for assessing anxiety in children with ASD. Preliminary data on the SCAS indicate that it may also serve as an effective anxiety-screening tool in youth with ASD (Magiati et al., 2014). Additionally, the Multidimensional Anxiety Scale for Children (MASC; March, 1997) has been shown to be useful and sensitive to treatment outcomes in children with ASD and co-occurring anxiety symptoms (Reaven et al., 2012), though this measure may fail to effectively assess clinical anxiety in children who are not seeking treatment. Data from two systematic reviews also provide some support for the use of the Revised Child Anxiety and Depression Scale (RCADS; Chorpita et al., 2000), the Child and Adolescent Symptom Inventory, Fourth Edition (CASI-4R; Gadow & Sprafkin, 2002), and the Pediatric Anxiety Rating Scale (PARS; Research Units on Pediatric Psychopharmacology Anxiety Study Group, 2002), though both reviews noted various measurement limitations across these scales (Lecavalier et al., 2014; Wigham & McConachie, 2014).

Standard anxiety measures may also fail to detect atypical fears and ambiguous, ASD-related anxiety symptoms. The Anxiety Disorders Interview Schedule—Child/Parent, Parent Version (Silverman & Albano, 1996) with the Autism Specific Addendum (ADIS/ASA; Kerns et al., 2017) assesses differential diagnosis of comorbid anxiety disorders (e.g., social phobia, separation anxiety, generalized anxiety, specific phobia) and is the only tool to probe for more varied presentations and ambiguous symptoms of anxiety in ASD (e.g., fears of change, unusual sensory stimuli, social unpredictability), though further psychometric examination is needed. Taken together, clinicians should interpret data cautiously when using anxiety measures designed for typically developing children.

Assess for Separation Anxiety Disorder and Anxiety Symptoms Related to ASD

Many youths with ASD experience anxiety in ways that is similar to children without ASD and meet criteria for separation anxiety disorder according to the DSM-5. However, youth with ASD may also exhibit atypical anxiety symptoms that are connected to core symptoms of ASD and do not align neatly with the DSM-5 categories. These symptoms include anxiety about transitions or changes in routine, compulsive/ritualistic behavior, social fearfulness without accompanying fear of negative evaluation, and unusual specific phobias (Kerns et al., 2016). Thus, assessment of anxiety in children with ASD should focus on both typical symptoms of separation anxiety disorder, as well as atypical symptoms common in children with ASD.

The overlap of ASD features with anxiety symptoms makes it difficult to differentiate anxiety and ASD. For example, whereas reluctance to separate from a caregiver may reflect excessive distress and worry about losing their caregiver in children with separation anxiety, in youth with ASD, reluctance to separate may reflect fear of uncertainty and difficulty with changes in routine. Confusion about social situations and sensory over-sensitivity, common in children with ASD, may lead to social avoidance and contribute to difficulties separating from caregivers, mirroring symptoms of separation anxiety. Ritualistic and repetitive behaviors are core symptoms of ASD but can also present in separation anxiety disorder. Physical symptoms, such as stomachaches or headaches, could be interpreted as physical symptoms of anxiety or sensory sensitivities.

Given overlapping symptoms, clinicians must carefully assess symptoms and potential contributing factors to determine whether overlapping symptoms are explained solely by ASD or are consistent with a diagnosis of separation anxiety disorder. To help differentiate these symptoms, Vasa and colleagues (2016) recommend asking questions to help determine the function of the behavior and/or referring to a behavioral psychologist who can conduct a functional behavioral analysis to help differentiate these etiologies. Specifically, clinicians should determine whether anxiety is triggered by fear surrounding separating from a caregiver or more related to ASD challenges (e.g., being left with someone who will not maintain routines, leaving to go somewhere where there are social challenges, experiencing sensory over-sensitivity in the moment). A child who willingly participates in otherwise avoided activities (e.g., extracurriculars, playdates) as long as caregiver is present, may indicate avoidance of separation is related to anxiety rather than social indifference or disinterest characteristic of ASD. Clinicians should also ask questions about behavioral signs of anxiety when a child is faced with separation (e.g., is separation or anticipation of separation associated with fearful affect, increased repetitive or ritualistic behavior, increased disruptive behaviors, and/or physical complaints) to further tease out overlapping symptoms. Further, it is important to assess baseline ASD symptoms to differentiate between ASD characteristics and newly developed anxiety symptoms (e.g., When did difficulty separating begin? Has there been an increase in repetitive behaviors?).

Assess for Other Factors That May Be Contributing to Anxiety

After determining the presence of anxiety, Vasa and colleagues (2016) recommend assessing other factors that may trigger or exacerbate anxiety. Children with ASD may present with other psychiatric symptoms, including inattention, hyperactivity, aggression, irritability, and self-injury that can exacerbate anxiety and hinder progress in treatment (Hossain et al., 2020). Co-occurring medical conditions, such as gastrointestinal and sleep problems, are also common in children with ASD and may further contribute to anxiety. Certain medications can also impact anxiety. Therefore, addressing these conditions should be an integral part of treatment and may need to be prioritized before directly treating separation anxiety. Collaboration with family and medical professionals may be warranted in order to develop interventions (e.g., establishing a healthy sleep routine, dietary adjustments, parent training to address behavior problems) and help alleviate these concerns.

In addition to considering co-occurring conditions, clinicians should also evaluate and consider psychosocial factors that may be contributing to anxiety. Given preference for routines and sameness, children with ASD may experience significant distress and anxiety when there are changes in their environment (e.g., new school, change in teacher, change in parent's job schedule, change in therapy services or supports). Children with ASD are also more likely to experience bullying and peer rejection than typically developing peers (Cappadocia et al., 2012) and may experience increased academic stress due to lack of appropriate educational supports (Ashburner et al., 2010), which may lead to anxiety, including school avoidance and/or separation difficulties. Parental anxiety and parental responses to anxiety should also be evaluated, as modeling anxiety during separations and overprotective parenting behaviors (e.g., overly attending to distress, excessive reassurance, permitting child to avoid anxiety-provoking situations) may contribute to increased anxiety in children. Once psychosocial factors are identified, clinicians should work with families to alleviate stressors. Vasa and colleagues (2016) specifically recommend clinicians provide strategies to increase structure and predictability throughout the child's day, help with educational advocacy (e.g., talking to school staff or providing letters indicating need for increased services), provide resources (e.g., behavioral intervention, social skills groups, respite care), and promote parental self-care (e.g., seeking personal mental health treatment, taking breaks, parent support groups).

Assess the Degree of Anxiety-Related Impairment

Once all the data has been gathered, clinicians should assess if anxiety is causing impairment in daily functioning (e.g., family life, social, academic, physical health, general well-being) and should specifically consider whether anxiety symptoms cause significant impairment above and beyond what may be related to ASD challenges alone. When DSM-5 criteria for separation anxiety are met, this diagnosis should be given. When criteria are not met, but impairing anxiety is apparent, clinicians should consider a diagnosis of unspecified anxiety disorder (Kerns et al., 2016). Children with ASD who are demonstrating anxiety related to separation from caregiver but do not meet full criteria for the diagnosis may still benefit from intervention strategies and supports aimed at addressing separation anxiety disorder. When symptoms are primarily related to ASD challenges (e.g., reluctance to separate due to insistence on sameness, avoidance of school or other social situations due to social indifference or social difficulty), treatment should prioritize addressing core symptoms of ASD (e.g., increasing flexibility and ability to tolerate changes in routine, enhancing social skills, teaching strategies to manage sensory sensitivities). In conclusion, determining how anxiety symptoms contribute to overall impairment and functioning of the child with ASD will help prioritize treatment goals.

Intervention Considerations

Overview of Cognitive Behavioral Therapy (CBT)

Separation anxiety disorder in children can be effectively treated using evidence-based strategies that focus on reducing anxiety symptoms and improving a child's ability to cope with separation from their caregivers. One of the most widely recognized and empirically supported forms of treatment for anxiety disorders in children and adolescents is Cognitive Behavior Therapy (CBT). CBT is a structured therapy that emphasizes the connection between an individual's thoughts, feelings and behaviors and aims to help individuals identify and modify negative thought patterns and behaviors to reduce psychological distress. To address anxiety in children, CBT involves several core components, including psychoeducation on anxiety (i.e., teaching child and family about anxiety and recognizing anxiety triggers), cognitive restructuring (i.e., teaching child to challenge and modify anxious or irrational thoughts), and exposure to feared stimuli (i.e., gradually exposing child to anxiety-provoking stimuli). Relaxation techniques and coping skills may also be taught to help a child regulate emotions and manage physiological symptoms of anxiety.

When treating separation anxiety disorder, CBT is tailored to address the specific fears and behaviors associated with the child's anxiety about separation from attachment figures. This includes developing a hierarchy of feared separation situations (i.e., list of the child's specific feared situations ranked in order from least anxiety provoking to most anxiety provoking) and engaging in gradual exposure exercises. For example, a child may start with brief separations from their parent (e.g., child plays alone in their room with their parent in another room) and then gradually increase the duration of time and distance from their parent as their anxiety diminishes (e.g., child stays in the home while parent goes outside to check the mail). As a child's confidence grows, exposure exercises become more difficult (e.g., change in caregiver during school drop-off or pick-up, participating in extra-curricular activities without caregiver present, visiting relatives, sleeping over at a friend's house). Children may also be taught cognitive strategies to help them reframe from catastrophic thoughts about separation, as well as relaxation techniques or coping skills to help manage physiological symptoms of anxiety during separations. Caregiver involvement is critical in using CBT to address separation anxiety in children, as parents can help implement exposure exercises in daily life, reduce avoidance behaviors, and reinforce brave behaviors. Involving caregivers also helps them understand the nature of their child's anxiety and how to respond in a way that reduces rather than exacerbates anxiety symptoms (Creswell et al., 2014). Please refer to earlier chapters in this book for further details on treatment of separation anxiety disorder in typically developing youth.

CBT for Children with ASD

While much of the research on CBT involves typically developing children, a growing body of evidence demonstrates positive outcomes for children with ASD. Two large meta-analyses examining the efficacy of CBT for anxiety among youth with ASD found that CBT significantly reduced anxiety symptoms in children with ASD (Sukhodolsky et al., 2013; Ung et al., 2015). Consistent with these findings, a more recent meta-analysis conducted by

Perihan and colleagues (2020) found that CBT produced moderate reductions in anxiety for children with ASD and children benefited the most from CBT when their parents were involved in the intervention. Although the literature initially consisted of case studies and small group studies, several manualized CBTs have been developed or modified for children with ASD and studied for their effectiveness. A review by Kester and Lucyshyn (2018) found moderate effect sizes in anxiety change for several manualized CBTs developed for school-age children with ASD, including: Facing Your Fears (Reaven et al., 2012), Behavioral Interventions for Anxiety in Children with Autism (BIACA; Wood et al., 2015), Cool Kids Anxiety Program: Autism Spectrum Disorder Adaptation (Cool Kids ASD; Chalfant et al., 2007), Exploring Feelings (Clarke et al., 2017), and Multimodal Anxiety and Social Skills Intervention (MASSI; White et al., 2013). A modified version of the Coping Cat program (Kendall, 1994) has also been found to be effective in reducing levels of anxiety in children with ASD (McNally Keehn et al., 2013).

Despite the growing evidence for using CBT to treat anxiety in children with ASD, the research on using CBT to address separation anxiety in children with ASD is extremely limited. No intervention study to date, to the authors' knowledge, has focused solely on separation anxiety disorder in children with ASD. However, various studies have demonstrated the effectiveness of CBT in reducing anxiety symptoms in children with ASD, including symptoms related to separation anxiety disorder. For instance, Bischof and colleagues (2018) explored the effectiveness of a parent training CBT curriculum (Cool Little Kids) to address anxiety problems in preschoolers with ASD and found lower rates of separation anxiety symptoms at 1- and 2-year follow-up compared to the control group. Driscoll and colleagues (2020) also evaluated a family-centered CBT protocol (Being Brave Intervention) in preschool and elementary aged children with ASD and co-occurring anxiety disorders and found significant decreases in parent and clinician rated anxiety symptoms and increased ability to cope with feared situations following treatment. Notably, 25% of this sample had a diagnosis of separation anxiety disorder with most feared situations including sleeping in own room, drop offs at school, social activities, and being apart from mother in the home. Additionally, McNally Keehn and colleagues (2013) evaluated whether a modified version of the Coping Cat program could be effective in reducing anxiety in children with ASD. Their sample included 22 school-aged children diagnosed with ASD, of which 8 of these children had a diagnosis of separation anxiety disorder. Children in the CBT condition evidenced significantly larger reeducations in anxiety than those on the waiting list. A randomized control trial by Storch and colleagues (2013) also included school-age children with ASD and anxiety disorder, including separation anxiety disorder, and found that adapted CBT for youth with ASD demonstrated large effects in reducing anxiety symptoms.

Taken together, the literature supports the effectiveness of using CBT to treat anxiety in youth with ASD, including those experiencing separation anxiety disorder. Unfortunately, most studies have been conducted with children with ASD who have average or above average cognitive functioning and adequate verbal skills. Thus, it is unclear whether CBT is appropriate for individuals with ASD who demonstrate cognitive deficits or have minimal verbal skills. Positively, most studies using CBT programs for youth with ASD, including the ones noted above, have made various modifications or adaptations that may help address these challenges in youth with ASD.

Modifications to CBT

Existing studies of CBT for anxiety in youth with ASD tend to incorporate core treatment components that are similar to treatment of anxiety in typically developing youth. This includes psychoeducation about the nature of anxiety, cognitive restructuring, relaxation techniques, and exposure exercises, as well as parent psychoeducation and intervention. However, most CBT programs for youth with ASD have included various modifications or adaptations to make these interventions more appropriate for children with ASD. Because children with ASD often present with unique challenges, clinicians should consider a child's cognitive ability, language level, and ASD symptom severity when determining the appropriateness of CBT and potential modifications. While some children with ASD may not require modifications, other children may need modifications to facilitate and understand cognitive and emotional concepts. Although not investigated empirically, various modifications to CBT programs have been proposed and discussed in the literature and these modifications appear to make CBT programs more appropriate and accessible for youth with ASD (McNally Keehn et al., 2013; Moree & Davis, 2010; Ung et al., 2015). These modifications are briefly elaborated upon in the following section, with particular focus on treating separation anxiety disorder symptoms.

Simplify Cognitive Aspects of Treatment

Children with ASD often have difficulty identifying and articulating their thoughts and feelings (Matson & Shoemaker, 2009), making traditional cognitive restructuring techniques less effective. Thus, CBT for children with ASD may emphasize behavioral components (e.g., exposure exercises, role-plays) and deemphasize cognitive components (e.g., cognitive restructuring), especially when a child has lower cognitive abilities or limited verbal language. For example, Chalfant and colleagues (2007) simplified cognitive components of a manualized CBT intervention delivered to children with ASD by providing children with a worksheet of a large list of helpful and unhelpful thoughts to identify rather than having them come up with their own thoughts. Clinicians working with children with ASD and separation anxiety disorder may take a similar approach by presenting them with a list of different fears or worry thoughts or providing them with a list of helpful coping thoughts that they can select from. For children with lower cognitive or verbal abilities, cognitive components may be omitted, with more focus on behavioral strategies (e.g., exposure practice) and higher use of parent-management strategies (e.g., coaching parents on use of behavior management skills during separations).

Use Visual Supports

Children with ASD often benefit from visual supports due to challenges with verbal communication and abstract concepts (Moree & Davis, 2010). The use of visual supports in treatment can promote comprehension, increase engagement, and reduce anxiety. While visual supports are often recommended for children with ASD who have difficulties with verbal communication, children with ASD and advanced language concepts can also benefit from visual supports. Thus, adding visual supports is frequently recommended in CBT and can be easily incorporated into treatment to address separation anxiety symptoms.

A common approach in using visual supports for children with ASD is the use of visual schedules. These schedules outline a child's daily activities and routines to help them understand what to expect and when, which can help children feel more secure and less anxious about transitions and separations. For example, a visual schedule for a child with separation anxiety might include pictures or icons representing arrival at school, class activities, break time, and the time when the parent will return. Visual timers can also be helpful in managing transitions and reducing anxiety. A visual timer can show a child how much time is left before a transition occurs, such as the end of a therapy session or time until the parent returns. Another effective visual support for children with ASD is the use of social narratives and social stories. Social stories are short, personalized stories that describe various social situations, expectations, and appropriate responses. For a child experiencing separation anxiety, a social story might detail the process of saying goodbye to a parent, what the child will do while the parent is away, and the reassurance that the parent will return.

Visual checklists can also be used throughout therapy to remind a child of session activities and provide step-by-step guidance for exposure exercises. A visual checklist for an exposure exercise aimed at reducing separation anxiety might include visual pictures/icons to represent the following steps: separate from parent (e.g., picture of parent and child), engage in activity during separation (e.g., picture of a puzzle or toy), use a coping strategy or relaxation technique (e.g., picture of deep breathing or sensory/calm down toy), check visual timer (e.g., picture of timer), rate current emotion (e.g., picture of different faces to check anxiety level), and reunite with parent (e.g., picture of parent returning). Clinicians should use visual checklists by guiding a child through each step and providing reinforcement (e.g., praise or small reward) after completing each step. Using checklists consistently will likely help the child know what to expect, reducing their anxiety and gradually building confidence in handling separations.

Incorporating visual supports into psychoeducation and cognitive components of CBT can also help enhance a child's engagement and understanding. Because many children with ASD have difficulties with abstract language, visuals can help accommodate a child's more literal thinking style and help them better understand their emotions. For instance, clinicians could have children draw a visual depiction of their anxiety and symptoms. When assessing anxiety levels throughout treatment, it is recommended that clinicians use a visual analog scale rather than verbal responses to help children with ASD identify their current emotions (Vasa et al, 2016). While the use of a "fear thermometer" is commonly used in CBT interventions for typically developing children, youth with ASD may benefit from simplifying this thermometer to include less anchors (e.g., 3 rather than 5 anchors to represent fear levels) or adding pictures (e.g., emotion faces or characters) to visually depict each emotion or fear level rather than simply using traditional Likert scale numbers. Studies have also found that children with ASD benefit from using visuals to teach emotional identification and cognitive restructuring, such as using thought bubbles and cartoons (Sze & Wood, 2007; Sze & Wood, 2008).

Incorporate Child's Specific Interests

Children with ASD often have focused or specialized interests. While these interests can sometimes dominate conversations or free time, clinicians can utilize these interests strategically to build rapport, increase understanding of therapy material, and motivate and reinforce participation. For example, if a child is particularly interested in dinosaurs, the clinician may have dinosaur toys available for the child to play with during warm-up periods each session or may engage in conversation with the child about dinosaurs. When teaching anxiety concepts, the clinician could create a social narrative where a young dinosaur has to leave its parent but learns to be brave in the new environment. The clinician could also use a dinosaur stuffed animal or figurine to model and role-play separation scenarios. Dinosaurs could also be incorporated into visual materials, including using different dinosaurs to represent different levels of emotions on a fear thermometer or using dinosaur stickers to reward brave behavior.

Teach Relaxation or Calming Strategies

While relaxation components are sometimes omitted from CBT programs aimed at addressing anxiety, these skills are often included in CBT protocols for youth with ASD. Utilization of relaxation skills is suggested to be particularly helpful given heightened sensory and physiological arousal that is often linked to exaggerated emotional reactions (e.g., tantrums, anger) in children with ASD; thus, teaching relaxation strategies can help facilitate emotional regulation (Konstantareas & Steward, 2006). Children with ASD may also be less likely to engage in cognitive restructuring and have difficulty utilizing positive thoughts, especially during anxiety-provoking situations. Thus, relaxation strategies can be taught and prompted during exposure exercises to help reduce anxiety and engage more fully in exposures (Chalfant et al., 2007). For example, a clinician may teach deep breathing before beginning exposures related to separation anxiety or allow a child to have a preferred item or sensory toy to aid in distraction during separation practices.

Tailor Reinforcement to Meet Individual Needs

Positive reinforcement and rewards are often a key component of treatment in the context of ASD and can be used to enhance motivation, increase engagement in therapy, and promote desired behaviors. Studies show that immediate and tangible rewards tailored to a child's specific interests are critical in promoting desired behaviors and may be more effective than more abstract forms of reinforcement, like social recognition and praise, in children with ASD (Koegel & Koegel, 2012). For example, a child may earn a snack or access to a preferred toy after completing brief separation from their caregiver. Some children may also benefit from a token system where they earn stickers or points that they can trade in later for a larger reward. If a family is unsure of what rewards will be most effective for a child with ASD, the clinician can consider conducting a preference assessment, which involves systematically identifying items or activities a child finds most motivating and rewarding. This can be done through direct observation, presenting a child with different potential rewards to see what they choose, or using a structured questionnaire to gather information from the child or caregiver. Clinicians should also ensure that a child cannot freely access reinforcement throughout the day and that reinforcement is reserved for brave behaviors in order to maintain the value and effectiveness of the reinforcement throughout treatment.

Increase Caregiver Involvement

Many CBT programs for children with ASD incorporate higher caregiver involvement and studies have found improved outcomes when caregivers are more involved in treatment (Perihan et al., 2020). For example, some CBT modifications for children with ASD have included more check-in time with parents at the end of session to review content and skills and discuss homework to ensure homework compliance and skill generalization (McNally Keehn et al., 2013). When a child presents with cognitive or verbal impairment, CBT may include more focus on parent training and teaching parent-management strategies, as opposed to teaching self-directed cognitive strategies with the child.

Caregiver involvement is a key component in the treatment of separation anxiety given the nature of the child's anxiety. Psychoeducation should be conducted with caregivers to help them understand the nature of their child's anxiety, recognize how their own behaviors or parenting styles can impact their child's anxiety (e.g., inadvertently reinforcing separation anxiety by allowing child to avoid or providing excessive reassurance), and learn how to respond in a way that reduces anxiety rather than exacerbates it. Caregivers are often seen as "coaches" throughout therapy and play a key role in conducting exposure exercises in real life to ensure generalization of skills outside of session. For children with ASD, caregivers can also implement consistent and predictable routines and utilize visual supports discussed above to help reduce uncertainty and anxiety around separations.

Caregivers may be further involved in treatment when a child presents with behavior problems (e.g., aggression, noncompliance, tantrums) that can exacerbate anxiety and hinder progress in treatment. To address these issues, clinicians can incorporate behavioral management strategies and parent training prior to addressing separation anxiety symptoms. This may include teaching child-directed interaction (i.e., Special Time), differential attention (i.e., using positive attention and planned ignoring), compliance training, and functional communication training. Parent implementation of these strategies will not only be important in improving a child's behavior prior to addressing anxiety but will also help parents feel more confident in managing their child's behavior during anxiety-provoking situations.

Medication Considerations

While CBT is the first line of intervention for children with separation anxiety disorder, pharmacological interventions may also be considered in some cases, particularly when separation anxiety is severe or co-occurring with other disorders such as depression or generalized anxiety disorder. Selective serotonin reuptake inhibitors (SSRIs) are commonly prescribed and have been shown to be effective in reducing anxiety symptoms of separation anxiety disorder in typically developing children (Mohatt et al., 2013). While SSRIs are frequently prescribed in children and adolescents with ASD (Hsia et al., 2014), research supporting the efficacy of SSRIs in this population is limited. Given the lack of efficacy and potential negative side effects, medication for anxiety is not recommended as the first line of intervention for children with ASD and should be used in conjunction with therapy rather than as a standalone treatment. If pharmacological medications are warranted in addressing separation anxiety disorder in a child with ASD, it is recommended that the child start at a low dose and titrate slowly with close monitoring of benefits and adverse effects (Vasa et al., 2014). Refer to Chapter 5 of this text for more information about medication management of anxiety symptoms.

Conclusion

Given the increasing prevalence of ASD and high prevalence of anxiety disorders within this population, clinicians are likely to encounter children with ASD and co-occurring anxiety in their practice. Unfortunately, assessment of anxiety disorders in this population is often challenging due to difficulties with self-report and emotional insight, as well as a lack of well-validated tools. Overlapping symptoms of ASD and anxiety disorders also present challenges to differential diagnoses. Thus, clinicians must take into account various factors when assessing separation anxiety in children with ASD and use caution when interpreting assessment measures.

Clinicians should also be familiar with evidence-based interventions for children with ASD and co-occurring anxiety disorders. While the research on separation anxiety disorder in this population is limited, a growing body of research supports the effectiveness of using CBT to treat anxiety disorders in children and adolescents with ASD. Various modifications have been proposed in the literature to make these interventions more effective and appropriate for children with ASD, including simplifying cognitive aspects, using visual supports, incorporating specific interests, teaching relaxation skills, tailoring reinforcement, and increasing caregiver involvement.

Future directions for research on ASD and anxiety should focus on developing and validating assessment measures and interventions specifically tailored to this population. Specifically, there is a need to develop reliable and valid measures to assess anxiety in youth with ASD in order to better understand anxiety in this population and differentiate between anxiety and ASD characteristics. While CBT has been shown to be generally effective in this population, most studies have been conducted with children who are considered "high-functioning", and more work is needed to understand if interventions are effective for youth with lower cognitive and verbal skills. Future studies should also aim to include samples that are racially, ethnically and socioeconomically diverse in order to strengthen generalizability of these treatments. Treatment research should also evaluate modifications to CBT protocols in order to determine effectiveness and help broaden the reach of these interventions to children with ASD. Finally, future treatment studies should focus on specific anxiety types, including separation anxiety disorder, in order to increase understanding among clinicians and improve outcomes for children with ASD and co-occurring anxiety disorders.

References

Adams, D., & Emerson, L. M. (2021). The impact of anxiety in children on the autism spectrum. *Journal of Autism and Developmental Disorders,* 51, 1909-1920.

American Psychiatric Association. (2013). *Diagnostic and statistical manual of mental disorders: DSM-5* (5th ed.). Washington, DC: American psychiatric association.

Ashburner, J., Ziviani, J., & Rodger, S. (2010). Surviving in the mainstream: Capacity of children with autism spectrum disorders to perform academically and regulate their emotions and behavior at school. *Research in Autism Spectrum Disorders*, *4*(1), 18-27.

Ben-Itzchak, E., Koller, J., & Zachor, D. A. (2020). Characterization and prediction of anxiety in adolescents with autism spectrum disorder: A longitudinal study. *Journal of abnormal child psychology*, *48*(9), 1239-1249.

Bischof, N. L., Rapee, R. M., Hudry, K., & Bayer, J. K. (2018). Acceptability and caregiver-reported outcomes for young children with autism spectrum disorder whose parents attended a preventative population-based intervention for anxiety: A pilot study. *Autism Research*, *11*(8), 1166-1174.

Cappadocia, M. C., Weiss, J. A., & Pepler, D. (2012). Bullying experiences among children and youth with autism spectrum disorders. *Journal of autism and developmental disorders*, *42*, 266-277.

Chalfant A., Rapee R., & Carroll L. (2007). Treating anxiety disorders in children with high functioning autism spectrum disorders: A controlled trial. *Journal of Autism and Developmental Disorders, 37*(10):1842–1857.

Chan, N., Fenning, R. M., & Neece, C. L. (2023). Prevalence and phenomenology of anxiety in preschool-aged children with autism spectrum disorder. *Research on Child and Adolescent Psychopathology*, *51*(1), 33-45.

Chorpita, B. F., Yim, L., Moffitt, C., Umemoto, L. A., & Francis, S. E. (2000). Assessment of symptoms of DSM-IV anxiety and depression in children: A revised child anxiety and depression scale. *Behaviour Research and Therapy, 38*(8), 835-855.

Clarke, C., Hill, V., & Charman, T. (2017). School based cognitive behavioural therapy targeting anxiety in children with autistic spectrum disorder: a quasi-experimental randomised controlled trail incorporating a mixed methods approach. *Journal of autism and developmental disorders*, *47*, 3883-3895.

Costello, E. J., Egger, H. L., & Angold, A. (2005). The developmental epidemiology of anxiety disorders: phenomenology, prevalence, and comorbidity. *Child and Adolescent Psychiatric Clinics*, *14*(4), 631-648.

Creswell, C., Murray, L., & Cooper, P. (2014). Parent involvement in cognitive behavioral therapy for anxiety disorders in children and adolescents. *Current Psychiatry Reports, 16*(10), 443.

Doherty, J. L., & Owen, M. J. (2014). Genomic insights into the overlap between psychiatric disorders: implications for research and clinical practice. *Genome medicine*, *6*, 1-13.

Driscoll, K., Schonberg, M., Stark, M. F., Carter, A. S., & Hirshfeld-Becker, D. (2020). Family-centered cognitive behavioral therapy for anxiety in very young children with autism spectrum disorder. *Journal of Autism and Developmental Disorders*, *50*(11), 3905–3920.

Gadow, K. D., & Sprafkin, J. (2002). *Child and Adolescent Symptom Inventory-4R*. Stony Brook, NY: Checkmate Plus.

Hallett, V., Lecavalier, L., Sukhodolsky, D. G., Cipriano, N., Aman, M. G., McCracken, J. T., ... & Scahill, L. (2013a). Exploring the manifestations of anxiety in children with autism spectrum disorders. *Journal of autism and developmental disorders*, *43*, 2341-2352.

Hallett, V., Ronald, A., Colvert, E., Ames, C., Woodhouse, E., Lietz, S., ... & Happé, F. (2013b). Exploring anxiety symptoms in a large-scale twin study of children with autism spectrum disorders, their co-twins and controls. *Journal of Child Psychology and Psychiatry*, *54*(11), 1176-1185.

Hayashida, K., Anderson, B., Paparella, T., Freeman, S. F., & Forness, S. R. (2010). Comorbid psychiatric diagnoses in preschoolers with autism spectrum disorders. *Behavioral Disorders*, *35*(3), 243-254.

Hossain, M. M., Khan, N., Sultana, A., Ma, P., McKyer, E. L. J., Ahmed, H. U., & Purohit, N. (2020). Prevalence of comorbid psychiatric disorders among people with autism spectrum disorder: An umbrella review of systematic reviews and meta-analyses. *Psychiatry research*, *287,* 112922.

Hsia, Y., Wong, A. Y., Murphy, D. G., Simonoff, E., Buitelaar, J. K., & Wong, I. C. (2014). Psychopharmacological prescriptions for people with autism spectrum disorder (ASD): a multinational study. *Psychopharmacology*, *231*, 999-1009.

Joshi, G., Petty, C., Wozniak, J., Henin, A., Fried, R., Galdo, M., ... & Biederman, J. (2010). The heavy burden of psychiatric comorbidity in youth with autism spectrum disorders: A large comparative study of a psychiatrically referred population. *Journal of autism and developmental disorders*, *40*, 1361-1370.

Kalvin, C. B., Marsh, C. L., Ibrahim, K., Gladstone, T. R., Woodward, D., Grantz, H., ... & Sukhodolsky, D. G. (2020). Discrepancies between parent and child ratings of anxiety in children with autism spectrum disorder. *Autism Research*, *13*(1), 93-103.

Kearney, C. A., Sims, K. E., Pursell, C. R., & Tillotson, C. A. (2003). Separation anxiety disorder in young children: A longitudinal and family analysis. *Journal of Clinical Child and Adolescent Psychology*, *32*(4), 593-598.

Keen, D., Adams, D., Simpson, K., Den Houting, J., & Roberts, J. (2019). Anxiety-related symptomatology in young children on the autism spectrum. *Autism*, *23*(2), 350-358.

Kendall, P. C. (1994). Treating anxiety disorders in children: results of a randomized clinical trial. *Journal of consulting and clinical psychology*, *62*(1), 100.

Kerns, C. M., & Kendall, P. C. (2012). The presentation and classification of anxiety in autism spectrum disorder. *Clinical Psychology: Science and Practice*, *19*(4), 323.

Kerns, C. M., Kendall, P. C., Berry, L., Souders, M. C., Franklin, M. E., Schultz, R. T., ... & Herrington, J. (2014). Traditional and atypical presentations of anxiety in youth with autism spectrum disorder. *Journal of autism and developmental disorders*, *44*, 2851-2861.

Kerns, C. M., Maddox, B. B., Kendall, P. C., Rump, K., Berry, L., Schultz, R. T., ... & Miller, J. (2015). Brief measures of anxiety in non-treatment-seeking youth with autism spectrum disorder. *Autism*, *19*(8), 969-979.

Kerns, C. M., Renno, P., Kendall, P. C., Wood, J. J., & Storch, E. A. (2017). Anxiety disorders interview schedule–autism addendum: Reliability and validity in children with autism spectrum disorder. *Journal of Clinical Child & Adolescent Psychology*, *46*(1), 88-100.

Kerns, C. M., Rump, K., Worley, J., Kratz, H., McVey, A., Herrington, J., & Miller, J. (2016). The differential diagnosis of anxiety disorders in cognitively-able youth with autism. *Cognitive and Behavioral Practice*, *23*(4), 530-547.

Kerns, C. M., Winder-Patel, B., Iosif, A. M., Nordahl, C. W., Heath, B. Solomon, M. & Amaral, D. G. (2020). Clinically significant anxiety in children with autism spectrum disorder and varied intellectual functioning. *Journal of Clinical Child & Adolescent Psychology*, *50*(6), 780-795.

Kessler, R. C., Petukhova, M., Sampson, N. A., Zaslavsky, A. M., & Wittchen, H. U. (2012). Twelve-month and lifetime prevalence and lifetime morbid risk of anxiety and mood disorders in the United States. *International journal of methods in psychiatric research*, *21*(3), 169-184.

Kester, K. R., & Lucyshyn, J. M. (2018). Cognitive behavior therapy to treat anxiety among children with autism spectrum disorders: A systematic review. *Research in Autism Spectrum Disorders*, *52*, 37-50.

Koegel, R. L. & Koegel, L. K. (2019). *Pivotal response treatment for autism spectrum disorders.* Paul H. Brookes Publishing Company.

Konstantareas M. M. & Stewart, K. (2006). Affect regulation and temperament in children with autism spectrum disorder. *Journal of Autism and Developmental Disorders,* *36*(2), 143–154.

Lecavalier, L., Wood, J. J., Halladay, A. K., Jones, N. E., Aman, M. G., Cook, E. H., ... & Scahill, L. (2014). Measuring anxiety as a treatment endpoint in youth with autism spectrum disorder. *Journal of autism and developmental disorders*, *44*, 1128-1143.

Maenner, M. J. (2023). Prevalence and characteristics of autism spectrum disorder among children aged 8 years—Autism and Developmental Disabilities Monitoring Network, 11 sites, United States, 2020. *MMWR. Surveillance Summaries*, *72.*

Magiati, I., Chan, J. Y., Tan, W. L. J., & Poon, K. K. (2014). Do non-referred young people with Autism Spectrum Disorders and their caregivers agree when reporting anxiety symptoms? A preliminary investigation using the Spence Children's Anxiety Scale. *Research in Autism Spectrum Disorders*, 8(5), 546-558.

Magiati, I., Ong, C., Lim, X. Y., Tan, J. W. L., Ong, A. Y. L., Patrycia, F., ... & Howlin, P. (2016). Anxiety symptoms in young people with autism spectrum disorder attending special schools: Associations with gender, adaptive functioning and autism symptomatology. *Autism*, *20*(3), 306-320.

Mannion, A., & Leader, G. (2014). Sleep problems in autism spectrum disorder: A literature review. *Review Journal of Autism and Developmental Disorders*, *1*, 101-109.

March J. S. *Multidimensional Anxiety Scale for Children: Technical manual.* Multi-Health Systems, Inc; North Tonawanda, New York: 1997.

Masi, G., Mucci, M., & Millepiedi, S. (2001). Separation anxiety disorder in children and adolescents: epidemiology, diagnosis and management. *CNS drugs*, *15*, 93-104.

Matson, J. L., & Kozlowski, A. M. (2011). The increasing prevalence of autism spectrum disorders. *Research in autism spectrum disorders*, *5*(1), 418-425.

Matson, J. L., & Shoemaker, M. (2009). Intellectual disability and its relationship to autism spectrum disorders. *Research in developmental disabilities*, *30*(6), 1107-1114.

Mayes, S. D., Calhoun, S. L., Murray, M. J., Ahuja, M., & Smith, L. A. (2011). Anxiety, depression, and irritability in children with autism relative to other neuropsychiatric disorders and typical development. *Research in Autism Spectrum Disorders*, *5*(1), 474-485.

McNally Keehn, R. H., Lincoln, A. J., Brown, M. Z., & Chavira, D. A. (2013). The Coping Cat program for children with anxiety and autism spectrum disorder: A pilot randomized controlled trial. *Journal of autism and developmental disorders*, *43*, 57-67.

Mohatt J. W., Keller A. E., Walkup J. T. (2013). Psychopharmacology of pediatric anxiety disorders. In: Vasa R. A. & Roy A. K. (Eds.), *Pediatric Anxiety Disorders, A Clinical Guide* (pp. 289-316). New York, NY: Springer Publishing.

Moree, B. N., & Davis, T. E. (2010). Cognitive-behavioral therapy for anxiety in children diagnosed with autism spectrum disorders: Modification trends. *Research in Autism Spectrum Disorders*, *4*(3), 346-354.

Muris, P., Merckelbach, H., Schmidt, H., & Mayer, B. (1999). The revised version of the Screen for Child Anxiety Related Emotional Disorders (SCARED-R): Factor structure in normal children. *Personality and Individual Differences, 26*, 99–112.

Perihan, C., Burke, M., Bowman-Perrott, L., Bicer, A., Gallup, J., Thompson, J., & Sallese, M. (2020). Effects of cognitive behavioral therapy for reducing anxiety in children with high functioning ASD: A systematic review and meta-analysis. *Journal of Autism and Developmental Disorders*, *50*(6), 1958–1972.

Racine, N., McArthur, B. A., Cooke, J. E., Eirich, R., Zhu, J., & Madigan, S. (2021). Global prevalence of depressive and anxiety symptoms in children and adolescents during COVID-19: a meta-analysis. *JAMA pediatrics*, *175*(11), 1142-1150.

Reaven, J., Blakeley-Smith, A., Culhane-Shelburne, K., & Hepburn, S. (2012). Group cognitive behavior therapy for children with high-functioning autism spectrum disorders and anxiety: A randomized trial. *Journal of Child Psychology and Psychiatry*, *53*(4), 410-419.

Research Units on Pediatric Psychopharmacology Anxiety Study Group. (2002). The Pediatric Anxiety Rating Scale (PARS): Development and psychometric properties. *Journal of the American Academy of Child & Adolescent Psychiatry, 41*, 1061–1069.

Rudy, B. M., Lewin, A. B., & Storch, E. A. (2013). Managing anxiety comorbidity in youth with autism spectrum disorders. *Neuropsychiatry*, *3*(4), 411.

Silverman, W. K., & Albano, A. M. (1996). The anxiety disorders interview schedule for children (ADIS-C/P). *San Antonio, TX: Psychological Corporation.*

Spence, S. H. (1997). Structure of anxiety symptoms among children: a confirmatory factor-analytic stupody. *Journal of Abnormal Psychology, 106,* 280–297.

Spiker, M. A., Lin, C. E., Van Dyke, M., & Wood, J. J. (2012). Restricted interests and anxiety in children with autism. *Autism*, *16*(3), 306-320.

Storch, E. A., Arnold, E. B., Lewin, A. B., Nadeau, J. M., Jones, A. M., De Nadai, A. S., ... & Murphy, T. K. (2013). The effect of cognitive-behavioral therapy versus treatment as usual for anxiety in children with autism spectrum disorders: A randomized, controlled trial. *Journal of the American Academy of Child & Adolescent Psychiatry*, *52*(2), 132-142.

Sukhodolsky, D. G., Bloch, M. H., Panza, K. E., & Reichow, B. (2013). Cognitive-behavioral therapy for anxiety in children with high-functioning autism: A meta-analysis. *Pediatrics, 132*(5), e1341-e1350.

Sukhodolsky, D. G., Lecavalier, L., Johnson, C., Smith, T., Swiezy, N., Bearss, K., ... & Scahill, L. (2020). Anxiety in 3-to 7-year-old children with autism spectrum disorder seeking treatment for disruptive behavior. *Autism*, *24*(2), 400-410.

Sze, K. M., & Wood, J. J. (2007). Cognitive behavioral treatment of comorbid anxiety disorders and social difficulties in children with high-functioning autism: A case report. *Journal of contemporary Psychotherapy*, *37*, 133-143.

Sze, K. M., & Wood, J. J. (2008). Enhancing CBT for the treatment of autism spectrum disorders and concurrent anxiety. *Behavioural and Cognitive Psychotherapy*, *36*(4), 403-409.

Ung, D., Selles, R. R., Small, B. J., & Storch, E. A. (2015). A systematic review and meta-analysis of cognitive-behavioral therapy for anxiety in youth with high-functioning autism spectrum disorders. *Child Psychiatry & Human Development*, *46*(4), 533-547.

van Steensel, F. J. A., Bögels, S. M., Magiati, I., & Perrin, S. (2014). Anxiety in individuals with ASD: Prevalence, phenomenology, etiology, assessment, and interventions. *Comprehensive guide to autism*, *581*.

van Steensel, F. J., & Heeman, E. J. (2017). Anxiety levels in children with autism spectrum disorder: A meta-analysis. *Journal of child and family studies*, *26*(7), 1753-1767.

van Steensel, F. J., Bögels, S. M., & Perrin, S. (2011). Anxiety disorders in children and adolescents with autistic spectrum disorders: a meta-analysis. *Clinical child and family psychology review*, *14*, 302-317.

van Steensel, F. J., Deutschman, A. A., & Bögels, S. M. (2013). Examining the screen for child anxiety-related emotional disorder as an assessment tool for anxiety in children with high-functioning autism spectrum disorders. *Autism*, *17*(6), 681-692.

Vasa, R. A., Carroll, L. M., Nozzolillo, A. A., Mahajan, R., Mazurek, M. O., Bennett, A. E., ... & Bernal, M. P. (2014). A systematic review of treatments for anxiety in youth with autism spectrum disorders. *Journal of Autism and Developmental Disorders*, *44*, 3215-3229.

Vasa, R. A., Keefer, A., McDonald, R. G., Hunsche, M. C., & Kerns, C. M. (2020). A scoping review of anxiety in young children with autism spectrum disorder. *Autism Research*, *13*(12), 2038-2057.

Vasa, R. A., Mazurek, M. O., Mahajan, R., Bennett, A. E., Bernal, M. P., Nozzolillo, A. A., ... & Coury, D. L. (2016). Assessment and treatment of anxiety in youth with autism spectrum disorders. *Pediatrics*, *137*(Supplement_2), S115-S123.

White, S. W., Mazefsky, C. A., Dichter, G. S., Chiu, P. H., Richey, J. A., & Ollendick, T. H. (2014). Social-cognitive, physiological, and neural mechanisms underlying emotion regulation impairments: Understanding anxiety in autism spectrum disorder. *International Journal of Developmental Neuroscience*, 39, 22-36.

White, S. W., Ollendick, T., Albano, A. M., Oswald, D., Johnson, C., Southam-Gerow, M. A., ... & Scahill, L. (2013). Randomized controlled trial: Multimodal anxiety and social skill intervention for adolescents with autism spectrum disorder. *Journal of autism and developmental disorders*, *43*, 382-394.

White, S. W., Oswald, D., Ollendick, T., & Scahill, L. (2009). Anxiety in children and adolescents with autism spectrum disorders. *Clinical psychology review*, *29*(3), 216-229.

Wigham, S., & McConachie, H. (2014). Systematic review of the properties of tools used to measure outcomes in anxiety intervention studies for children with autism spectrum disorders. *PloS one*, *9*(1), e85268.

Wood, J. J., & Gadow, K. D. (2010). Exploring the nature and function of anxiety in youth with autism spectrum disorders. *Clinical Psychology: Science and Practice*, *17*(4), 281.

Wood, J. J., Ehrenreich-May, J., Alessandri, M., Fujii, C., Renno, P., Laugeson, E., ... & Storch, E. A. (2015). Cognitive behavioral therapy for early adolescents with autism spectrum disorders and clinical anxiety: A randomized, controlled trial. *Behavior therapy*, *46*(1), 7-19.

Zaboski, B. A., & Storch, E. A. (2018). Comorbid autism spectrum disorder and anxiety disorders: a brief review. *Future neurology*, *13*(1), 31-37.

Chapter 10

Separation Anxiety Disorder in Adults

Yenvy Bui*
Alysia M. Palomo
and Gabriela Quintero
Rice University, Houston, TX, USA

Abstract

This chapter describes Separation Anxiety Disorder (SAD) in adults, a condition historically associated with childhood but now recognized and diagnosed in adult populations. The chapter begins by describing the diagnostic criteria of SAD for adults, in addition to prevalence, symptom presentation, and developmental models. Key risk factors, including genetic predispositions, familial environmental influences, and traumatic or adverse experiences, are explored to provide a comprehensive understanding of the development of SAD in adulthood. Common co-occurring anxiety and mood disorder conditions are described in addition to appropriate measures for assessment. Finally, treatment approaches, both psychological and pharmacological, along with appropriate adaptions, are discussed.

Keywords: adult separation anxiety disorder, adult separation anxiety treatment, adult separation anxiety intervention

---

* Corresponding Author's Email: yenvybui@yahoo.com.

In: Separation Anxiety: Presentation and Intervention
Editor: Kelly Nicole Banneyer
ISBN: 979-8-89530-386-3

How Does Separation Anxiety Present in Adults?

Separation anxiety disorder (SAD) is a class of anxiety disorders characterized by "developmentally inappropriate and excessive fear or anxiety concerning separation from those to whom the individual is attached" (National Library of Medicine, 2016). Previously considered a concern that primarily affects children, separation anxiety disorder has been shown to be present in adults. To understand the adult presentation of this disorder, one must first understand the symptomatology and diagnosis of separation anxiety in children. According to the fifth edition of the Diagnostic and Statistical Manual of Mental Disorders (DSM-5), separation anxiety disorder is characterized by developmentally inappropriate and excessive fear or anxiety concerning separation from those to whom the individual is attached (APA, 2013). A key feature is the temporal persistence of the fear, anxiety, or avoidance, lasting at least four weeks in children and adolescents and typically six months or more in adults (2013). The severity of the symptoms ranges from anticipatory uneasiness to high levels of anxiety about separation, all of which could significantly negatively affect everyday life (Center for Behavioral Health Statistics and Quality, 2016). These adverse consequences can permeate into social and emotional functioning, affecting family and friend relationships, physical health, and academic performance. Adult separation anxiety disorder is classified as childhood-onset or adult-onset.

Separation anxiety disorder was previously categorized under "Disorders Usually Diagnosed in Infancy, Childhood, and Adolescence," in the 4th edition of the Diagnostic Statistical Manual (DSM-IV; APA, 1994). This change is one of several modifications made to the DSM that have impacted the inclusion of adults. For example, the DSM-5 has been revised to remove the requirement that the age of onset be before the age of 18 years. Moreover, the criteria for making a diagnosis have been adjusted to be more inclusive of symptoms in adults. In the DSM-5, for an individual to be diagnosed with separation anxiety disorder, they must display "developmentally inappropriate and excessive fear or anxiety concerning separation," that is evidenced by meeting at least three of eight given criteria (2013). DSM-IV criteria are more closely aligned with behaviors considered developmentally inappropriate for children and adolescents. For instance, criterion 4 describes "Persistent reluctance or refusal to go to school or elsewhere because of fear of separation" (1994) as a symptom of separation anxiety whereas criterion 4 in the DSM-5 now includes home and work in addition to school, creating a more age-inclusive description of the symptom (2013). Similarly, criterion 6 in the

DSM-IV describes experiencing excessive fear over being "alone or without major attachment figures...or without significant adults" (1994). This criterion now excludes "significant adults," in its description, maintaining the more general term "major attachment figures," in the DSM-5 (2013). Furthermore, the DSM-5 now differentiates between children and adults in the duration requirement, specifying that the "fear, anxiety, or avoidance is persistent, lasting at least four weeks in children and adolescents and typically six months or more in adults" (2013). The final major change from the DSM-IV is the removal of the early onset specifier (onset before the age of 6) in the DSM-5. These changes have "signaled a major shift in the conceptualization of [separation anxiety disorder] from a disorder of childhood to one that can occur throughout the lifespan" (Manicavasagar & Silove, 2020, p. 26).

Prevalence

Clinical data suggest that 4.1% of children will exhibit clinical-level separation anxiety disorder, and one-third of these will have symptoms that persist into adulthood without identification and treatment (Ehrenreich et al., 2008). Over the past two decades, research has shifted to explore the development and identification of separation anxiety disorder in adults, with a growing number of individuals receiving diagnoses (Silove & Rees, 2014). In the first epidemiological study of adult separation anxiety disorder, data collected from the National Comorbidity Survey Replication (NCS-R) were used to estimate the prevalence rates of SAD in adults and children (Shear et al., 2006). It was found that the lifetime and 12-month prevalence rates of adult separation anxiety disorder were estimated to be 6.6% and 1.9%, respectively (2006). Lifetime prevalence estimates for adult separation anxiety disorder exceeded lifetime estimates for childhood separation anxiety disorder, which were estimated at 4.1% (2006). Childhood separation anxiety estimates from this study were found to be similar to previously published estimates, which are generally around 5% and range from 2-13% (Costello & Angold, 1995).

In a study examining prevalence rates across 18 countries using data from the World Health Organization (WHO) World Mental Health Survey, it was found that lifetime separation anxiety disorder prevalence estimates averaged 4.8% across countries, with estimates ranging from 0.2%-9.8% (Silove et al., 2015). Notably, "43.1% of respondents with lifetime separation anxiety disorder had onsets in adulthood" (2015, p. 650). Rates of adult-onset separation anxiety differed between countries, with higher lifetime prevalence rates in low- or lower middle-income countries in comparison to upper-middle and high-income countries (2015). However, it should be noted that this study shares limitations with the NCS-R study in that diagnoses made from interviews were not confirmed by clinicians, and retrospective reports from respondents introduce potential recall bias (2015).

Symptoms

Separation anxiety in both adults and children manifests as "an excessive and inappropriate fear for the safety, health and accessibility of one or more persons to whom the individual has a strong attachment" (Manicavasagar & Silove, 2020, p. 19). Additionally, separation from an attachment figure can result in similar fears concerning the individual's own health and safety. These fears can result in both physical and psychological symptoms that influence the daily life of the individual, such as being unwilling to leave places of "perceived safety," or "interpersonal difficulties arising from excessive need to remain in close proximity to or be in contact with attachments" (Manicavasagar & Silove, 2020, p. 19). A key difference between adult separation anxiety disorder and childhood separation anxiety disorder is the attachment figure; children are more likely to be attached to adults, specifically parents, while adult separation anxiety disorder might include a wider range of attachment figures, such as their children or spouses (Feriante et al., 2024).

The conceptualization of anxiety disorders generally includes three components: physiological responses, subjective cognitive distress, and behavioral responses (Beidel & Alfano, 2011). Manicavasagar and Silove (2020) categorize the features of adult separation anxiety into three domains based on clinical interviews: behavioral, emotional, and cognitive. In the behavioral domain, excessive reassurance seeking, being reluctant to leave the home, and maintaining contact with attachment figures were common features. Additionally, Manicavasagar and Silove (2020) note a distinction in seeking out key attachment figures. Adults may maintain contact with attachment figures by talking in person or over the phone, which can "represent a substitute for the clinging and shadowing behavior shown by young children" (2020, p.21). Finally, adults may insist on knowing the "precise timing and condition of reunions," with attachment figures or engage in "'sleep rituals,' such as sleeping with the lights on," to ensure that attachment figures are nearby (2020, p.21).

In the emotional domain, features included anxiety, panic attacks, and physical symptoms such as gastric upset stemming from actual or anticipated separation from attachment figures. Other common features included an "inability to tolerate changes in routines" as well as "recurrent nightmares with themes of separation," (2020, p.22).

Common cognitive features identified by Manicavasagar and Silove (2020) included rumination and excessive worry surrounding being separated from attachment figures or attachment figures being harmed. As previously mentioned, the individual may also experience catastrophic thoughts regarding their own health and safety when separated from attachment figures (2020). For adults, the common separation events may differ from children. For example, common separation events in children may be going to school, while adults may worry about their jobs causing the separation (2020). Finally, an adult may worry that "the intensity of their attachment may affect their relationship with key attachment figures," (2020, p.22).

Clinicians describe that children may display other unique symptoms of separation anxiety disorder that are not present in adults, such as bedwetting or throwing temper tantrums whenever a caregiver leaves (Cleveland Clinic, n.d.). The cause of these symptoms may also differ between children and adults. For example, a change in schools or parents' divorce may be more common triggers in children (Cleveland Clinic, n.d.).

Developmental Models

Manicavasagar and Silove (2020) note that for several decades, the dominant developmental model has been that separation anxiety disorder is a childhood disorder that "tends to manifest as panic disorder-agoraphobia" in adulthood if symptoms persist (p. 76). This model, the SA-PD/AG hypothesis, proposes that over time, "one cluster of symptoms... transforms into another, each arising from the same underlying diathesis" (p. 76). Manicavasagar and Silove (2020) note that the most common research strategy used to test this hypothesis was to "assess whether adults with panic disorder and/or agoraphobia differed from those with other anxiety disorders or normal controls" (p. 79) in reporting a history of childhood separation anxiety or school refusal. In their meta-analysis of studies that examined this hypothesis, Manicavasagar and Silove (2020) found that these studies generally support this hypothesis. However, methodological limitations, small sample sizes, and other experimental design issues may impact the validity of these findings (2020).

A second common model developed more recently is the generic vulnerability model, which proposes that heightened separation anxiety or separation anxiety disorder is a "childhood marker of general vulnerability to a wide range of common mental disorders...in adulthood." (2020, p.76). In other words, separation anxiety itself is not the cause of adult psychological disorders, but rather another "underlying vulnerability" (2020, p.76) that persists throughout life. Manicavasagar and Silove (2020) found that several studies support the generic developmental model, however, these studies faced similar limitations such as small sample sizes, issues with case control matching, and unclear diagnostic criteria that may have impacted results (2020, pp. 85-88).

Risk Factors and Co-Occurring Conditions

This section aims to synthesize and analyze existing research on adult separation anxiety disorder, with a focus on risk factors and co-occurring conditions. Exploring the characteristics of this disorder in the context of adult patients can provide valuable insights, leading to more accurate diagnoses and effective treatment.

Risk Factors in Childhood

Psychological research has routinely investigated the question of nature versus nurture, pitting genetic influence against environmental factors. To gain a comprehensive picture of risk factors, one must consider all components together, taking a holistic view. Hereditary variation, environmental factors, and traumatic experiences are just a few examples of the many elements that can be risk factors for anxiety disorders (Blanco et al., 2014).

Genetic Predisposition

Genetic research related to anxiety disorders is of growing interest, with many fascinating studies. Yet, the detection of genetic variants and genes associated with anxiety disorders has made slow progress, limited by small sample sizes and biological technicalities (Purves et al., 2020). Within genome-wide association studies like the one conducted by Purves and colleagues (2020), researchers hope to conduct larger-scale investigations of what genetic markers relate to anxiety disorders. By combining tested symptomatology with self-reported measures, researchers identified five novel genome-wide significant loci that potentially interact with the risk of anxiety disorders (2020). It is worth noting that this genetic connection has been recorded in various studies and is not limited to this analysis. As such, it is likely genetics plays a role in an underlying liability distribution, with variation in a range of anxiety-related traits, including anxiety disorders, depression, and neuroticism, occurring to different degrees across the population (Waszczuk et al., 2014).

Familial Environment and Attachment Style

When dealing with separation anxiety in children, it is imperative to consider family environment and relationships. Utilizing this perspective requires understanding epigenetics, which is how environmental factors and behaviors can cause changes that affect gene expression (CDC, 2022). The familial atmosphere is a crucial detail that could influence epigenetics, with a specific part being attachment styles. Attachment is a vital aspect of the relationship between a child and a parent, focusing on making a child feel safe, secure, and protected (Benoit, 2004). There are two main categories of attachment: secure attachment and insecure attachment. Secure attachment is characterized by sensitive and loving caregiving, which results in organized stress management (2004). Insecure attachment is characterized by insensitive, avoidant, or atypical care that results in organized maladaptive stress management or even disorganized management (2004). Current research in developmental psychopathology conceptualizes insecure attachment as part of a complex network that interacts to result in either risk or resilience to the development of stress-related psychopathology such as anxiety disorders (Fonagy & Luyten, 2009).

According to current research, stressful experiences, physiological stress regulation, and attachment relationships are inherently linked (Murgatroyd & Spengler, 2011). The activation of the attachment invariably follows the early stages of detecting and processing fear-related cues, stress responses, and states of anxiety (2011). From human behavioral studies, researchers have determined that a history of insecure-anxious infant-caregiver attachment is a risk factor for developing anxiety disorders in middle childhood and adolescence (Nolte et al., 2011). This result is rooted in the dysfunctional stress regulation and fear appraisal strategies that occur within an insecure attachment relationship, linking coping, environment, and psychopathology. Overall, an attachment-based framework integrates isolated strands of research that successfully characterize processes inherent to anxiety disorders (2011).

Traumatic Experiences

Traumatic experiences have significant consequences on mental health, demonstrating clear connections to epigenetics and the development of anxiety disorders. Early-life hardships can leave long-lasting biochemical markers on an individual's genetic composition, potentially influencing the emergence of anxiety disorders (Arce & Serrano, 2023). An interesting case study that explores this concept is a psychological investigation of children who experienced the terrorist attack at the World Trade Center on September 11, 2001. Of a representative sample of New York City public school students (N = 8,236), probable separation anxiety disorder was present in 12.3% of the sample just six months after the attack (Hoven et al., 2004). Separation anxiety disorder has only rarely been studied as a post-disaster reaction, yet there are various reasons researchers could use to explain anxiety following exposure to a traumatic event. One such explanation predicts trauma triggers the attachment system, inhibiting exploration and activating affectional bonds (2004). Simply put, we seek immediate comfort from our attachments, placing a heavy burden on those relationships. In summary, an investigation of traumatic experiences provides insight into the neurobiology and behavioral patterns that influence the development of separation anxiety disorder. For additional information about the relation between traumatic experiences and SAD, refer to Chapter 6 of this book.

Risk Factors in Adulthood

Many of the aforementioned risk factors lay the groundwork for potential factors contributing to the development of separation anxiety in adulthood. Instead of new factors emerging, there is a progression of these fundamental ideas and the integration of additional features. A primary example is the continuity of diagnosis, which builds upon genetic and environmental factors and maladaptive coping mechanisms stemming from attachment styles and comfort.

As stated earlier, various factors can serve as the foundation for separation anxiety disorder to persist from childhood into adulthood. This notion has been reinforced by the recent decision of the APA to remove the age-at-onset criterion for separation anxiety disorder in DSM-5, eliciting an opportunity to examine the epidemiology of separation anxiety disorder as a condition with onsets spanning the lifespan (Silove et al., 2015). Silove and colleagues (2015) used data from the World Health Organization to evaluate an expanded definition of separation anxiety disorder in a sample of 38,993 adults across 18 countries using a composite diagnostic interview, which allowed for onsets in adulthood (2015). The findings were remarkable, with a lifetime prevalence of separation anxiety disorder averaging 4.8% across all countries and 41.3% of lifetime onsets occurring after the age of 18 (2015). Furthermore, childhood predictors of SAD such as childhood adversity and traumatic events mirrored and were comparable predictors for the development of SAD in adulthood (2015), underscoring continuity as a risk factor.

Co-Occurring Conditions

Research on co-occurring conditions serves a valuable purpose: to explore the classification, interaction, and treatment of disorders in patients. In the past, SAD has been linked to a higher likelihood of developing various other disorders, including internalizing disorders like depression, anxiety disorders, and externalizing disorders (2015).

Anxiety and Mood Disorders

Mood disorders are a group of mental health conditions that are marked by significant changes in emotion (Sekhon & Gupta, 2023). These disorders are broadly categorized into depressive and bipolar disorders that often occur concurrently and are studied with separation anxiety disorder. For example, clinical interviews based on the latest diagnostic criteria for separation anxiety were used to assess 508 adult patients who were diagnosed with anxiety and mood disorders, including bipolar I, bipolar II, major depression, panic disorder, obsessive-compulsive disorder, and social phobia (Pini et al., 2010). The study revealed that 20.7% of the patients were diagnosed with adult separation anxiety disorder without any history of childhood separation anxiety, while 21.7% had adult separation anxiety disorder with a history of childhood separation anxiety (2010). This result is not surprising; most research shows that anxiety disorders are intricately linked and highly co-occurring with themselves and other mental disorders (Goldstein-Piekarski et al., 2016).

Hence, this result indicates not only that adult separation anxiety is much more common than previously thought but also how comorbidity can relate to its prevalence. Lifetime comorbid risk is considerably higher than lifetime prevalence for most anxiety and mood disorders (Kessler et al., 2012). However, the magnitude of the difference is much higher for disorders with later ages of onset (2012). Current research is challenging the traditional understanding of separation anxiety, altering the common perception of the disorder's age of onset and prevalence.

Assessment Measures

Diagnosing SAD in adults requires a systematic, multi-tiered approach due to its overlapping symptoms with other anxiety disorders, such as panic disorder and generalized anxiety disorder. Initial screenings often utilize the Separation Anxiety Symptoms Inventory (SASI) and/or the Adult Separation Anxiety-27 (ASA-27) Self-Assessment Questionnaire, which identifies individuals with potential SAD based on their symptom severity. Those scoring above a predetermined threshold are then evaluated further through structured clinical interviews, such as the Structured Clinical Interview for Separation Anxiety Symptoms (SCI-SAS) and/or Mini International Neuropsychiatric Interview (MINI), providing a robust framework for a confirmatory diagnosis. The assessment process is complemented by psychological evaluations that delve into personality, attachment styles, and life quality impacts, facilitating a nuanced understanding of the disorder. More information on each of these measures follows.

Separation Anxiety Symptoms Inventory

The Separation Anxiety Symptoms Inventory (SASI; Silove et al., 1993) is an important tool in the diagnosis and assessment of SAD in adults. The SASI is a 15-item self-report questionnaire that offers a comprehensive list of symptoms to evaluate the severity and presence of separation anxiety traits based on memories of symptoms prior to 18 years of age. These symptoms include excessive worry about losing significant others, distress when anticipating or experiencing separation, and physical symptoms of anxiety when separation is imminent. The inventory is structured to reflect the multidimensional nature of SAD, capturing both emotional and behavioral responses to perceived or actual separations from attachment figures. The utility of the SASI lies in its ability to provide a detailed symptom profile that is essential for formulating treatment plans and monitoring treatment progress over time.

Adult Separation Anxiety-27 Self-Assessment Questionnaire

The Adult Separation Anxiety-27 (ASA-27; Manicavasagar et al., 2003) self-assessment questionnaire serves as a preliminary screening tool for separation anxiety in adults. It consists of 27 items that respondents rate based on their recent experiences related to separation anxiety symptoms. The questionnaire is designed to identify individuals who may require further psychological evaluation for SAD. A score of 22 or higher typically indicates the presence of significant separation anxiety symptoms, warranting additional diagnostic assessments. The ASA-27 is particularly useful in outpatient settings, helping to streamline the identification process of potential SAD among adults presenting with anxiety-related complaints.

Structured Clinical Interview for Separation Anxiety Symptoms

Following initial screenings, the Structured Clinical Interview for Separation Anxiety Symptoms (SCI-SAS; Cyranowski et al., 2002) is employed to confirm SAD diagnoses through a detailed exploration of the individual's anxiety related to separation. The SCI-SAS provides a reliable and valid clinical assessment, ensuring that the diagnosis of SAD is based on standardized criteria. This method helps in distinguishing SAD from other anxiety disorders, which may share symptoms, thereby guiding appropriate treatment approaches.

Mini International Neuropsychiatric Interview

The Mini International Neuropsychiatric Interview (MINI; Lecrubier et al., 1997) is a short, structured diagnostic interview used for the assessment of psychiatric disorders, including SAD. It is well-regarded for its efficiency and comprehensiveness in clinical settings. The MINI facilitates the differential diagnosis of various mental health conditions and confirms the diagnosis of SAD by evaluating symptoms against the criteria established in major diagnostic manuals such as the DSM-5 and ICD-11. The use of the MINI helps in ensuring a holistic assessment, considering co-occurring conditions, thus supporting a more tailored and effective therapeutic intervention strategy.

Treatment: Behavioral Intervention

In managing adult SAD, behavioral therapies are essential due to the complex interplay of personal and social dynamics that define this condition. Despite limited randomized controlled trials specifically testing psychological interventions for adult SAD, considerable anecdotal evidence and clinical experience suggest the efficacy of certain therapeutic approaches. This section describes the practical aspects of psychological treatments for adult SAD, focusing on actionable strategies and methods that clinicians can use to enhance treatment efficacy.

Cognitive Behavioral Therapy (CBT)

Cognitive Behavioral Therapy (CBT) stands as a foundational approach in treating many anxiety disorders, including SAD, because of its structured, goal-oriented method that challenges dysfunctional thoughts and behaviors. However, traditional CBT protocols often necessitate adaptations to address the specific characteristics of SAD more effectively.

Core Components

- *Psychoeducation.* Typically the initial phase of CBT for SAD, psychoeducation helps patients understand the nature and impact of their condition. It clarifies symptoms and sets realistic expectations for the treatment trajectory. It includes understanding the specific triggers and stressors that exacerbate SAD symptoms, making extreme emotional responses more predictable and controllable, and helping patients anticipate and plan for potentially stressful situations (Horowitz, 2015). This approach has been researched and applied specifically to adults with SAD.

- *Cognitive Restructuring*. This technique involves identifying and challenging the irrational beliefs and catastrophic thoughts that often accompany SAD. By reframing these thoughts, patients can reduce undue anxiety about separation and begin to see situations more realistically. Cognitive therapy helps address dysfunctional thoughts about separations from key attachments and doubts about the ability to cope with anxiety, using thought challenging and cognitive restructuring to correct core beliefs about the danger associated with separations (Telch et al., 1989).
- *Exposure Therapy*. Gradual, controlled exposure to feared situations is a critical component. For SAD, this may involve practicing separations from attachment figures in a stepwise manner, starting with less challenging separations and progressively tackling ones that are more difficult. The process typically involves developing a list of fear-evoking situations, ranking them from least to most feared, and systematically overcoming anxiety through repeated exposure (Mattick et al., 1990).
- *Group and Individual Formats*. CBT can be effective in both formats, but individual therapy may be particularly beneficial for tailoring the exposure scenarios and cognitive interventions to the unique anxieties of a person with SAD (Manicavasagar & Silove, 1997).

Other Behavioral Therapies

While CBT is the most studied and utilized approach, other behavioral therapies also offer potential benefits for individuals with SAD.

Mindfulness-Based Cognitive Therapy

Combining mindfulness practices with traditional CBT techniques, Mindfulness-Based Cognitive Therapy (MBCT) helps patients develop an awareness of the present moment and a nonjudgmental acceptance of their emotional state (Alsubaie et al., 2017). This approach can be particularly helpful in managing the intense emotions that surface during separations and in reducing overall anxiety levels. Anxiety management techniques, such as mindfulness meditation and relaxation exercises, help patients regulate arousal and develop adaptive coping strategies, providing a sense of control over distressing symptoms.

Dialectical Behavior Therapy

Originally developed to treat borderline personality disorder, Dialectical Behavior Therapy (DBT)'s emphasis on distress tolerance and emotional regulation can be adapted for SAD, particularly in cases where intense emotional swings are prominent (Panos et al., 2013). DBT for SAD might involve skills training in areas such as emotional regulation and interpersonal effectiveness, which can help patients manage the fears of abandonment and instability in relationships. Structured problem-solving approaches can assist in overcoming obstacles to completing exposure tasks and addressing hesitancy in therapy.

Acceptance and Commitment Therapy

Acceptance and Commitment Therapy (ACT) promotes psychological flexibility through mindfulness, acceptance strategies, commitment, and behavior change techniques. ACT helps individuals with SAD engage in life more fully by accepting their feelings of anxiety during separations rather than avoiding them, thus decreasing the impact of anxiety on their actions and decisions. Techniques in ACT emphasize the importance of accepting emotions and committing to actions aligned with personal values, despite anxiety.

Challenges and Considerations

Effective treatment of SAD must consider other co-occurring disorders, the severity of symptoms, and individual patient differences. Customizing treatment to fit the patient's specific needs is essential for successful outcomes. The involvement of family and close attachments is often crucial, as they can play a significant role in either facilitating or inhibiting change. Engaging close attachments in psychoeducation and therapy can enhance treatment efficacy and support patients in overcoming separation anxiety (Kins et al., 2013).

Treatment: Pharmacological Intervention

The exploration of pharmacological treatments for adult SAD is still in its emerging stages, primarily due to the recent acknowledgment of SAD in adults within diagnostic systems. Traditional approaches for anxiety disorders, including selective serotonin reuptake inhibitors (SSRIs) and other common medications, have been tested with mixed results. Studies examining the efficacy of SSRIs and other antidepressants for adult SAD have shown varying outcomes. In a notable trial involving vilazodone, an SSRI with additional partial agonist activity at the 5HT1a receptor, the medication did not significantly outperform placebo in response rates at 12 weeks (Schneier et al., 2017). However, there were trends toward improvement in separation anxiety symptoms, suggesting a potential, albeit limited, role for SSRIs in treating adult SAD. These findings imply that while SSRIs can be effective for a range of anxiety disorders, their efficacy in adult SAD may require further investigation due to the unique aspects of this condition. The limited effectiveness of conventional anxiety disorder medications on adult SAD could be attributed to the distinct nature of separation anxiety, which may not be adequately addressed by general anti-anxiety pharmacological strategies. This specificity suggests a need for targeted medications to be developed specifically to address the core symptoms of adult SAD.

Conclusion

Assessing the impact of adult SAD on the outcomes of treatments for other conditions is a complex issue, primarily because SAD in adults is often overlooked and underdiagnosed (Cyranowski et al., 2002; Shear et al., 2006). The reasons for this include the relatively recent recognition of the adult form of the disorder in diagnostic systems, a traditional focus on childhood occurrences, and a general lack of clinical expertise in treating adult SAD. Furthermore, individuals with SAD may either normalize their symptoms or feel embarrassed by them, leading to underreporting and concealment, which complicates accurate diagnosis and treatment.

Adult SAD significantly challenges the treatment of co-occurring mental health conditions. The unique symptoms of SAD, such as intense fear of separation and excessive need for reassurance, are not typically addressed by standard treatment protocols for adults with anxiety disorders. This mismatch can lead to poorer overall treatment outcomes. Studies indicate that individuals with SAD who receive general treatment for anxiety conditions tend to show less improvement compared to those without SAD (Aaronson et al., 2008; Dudaee-Faass et al., 2009; Rochester & Baldwin, 2015).

Moreover, pharmacological approaches commonly used to manage anxiety symptoms, such as SSRIs and benzodiazepines, also show reduced efficacy in individuals with adult SAD. This is likely due to the specific and profound nature of separation anxiety, which differs significantly from general anxiety mechanisms targeted by these medications (Milrod et al., 2014).

Given these challenges, there is an increasing recognition of the need for specialized, tailored interventions that specifically address the root causes and manifestations of adult SAD. Innovative treatment approaches might include the integration of family or attachment figures into therapy, strengthening the therapeutic relationship to build trust and security, and directly targeting maladaptive thoughts and behaviors related to separation anxiety. These focused strategies are essential to improve treatment responsiveness and overall mental health outcomes for individuals with adult SAD.

References

Aaronson, C. J., Shear, M. K., Goetz, R. R., Allen, L. B., Barlow, D. H., White, K. S., Ray, S., Money, R., Saksa, J. R., Woods, S. W., & Gorman, J. M. (2008). Predictors and time course of response among panic disorder patients treated with cognitive-behavioral therapy. *The Journal of Clinical Psychiatry*, *69*(3), 418–424. https://doi.org/10.4088/jcp.v69n0312.

Alsubaie, M., Abbott, R., Dunn, B., Dickens, C., Keil, T. F., Henley, W., & Kuyken, W. (2017). Mechanisms of action in mindfulness-based cognitive therapy (MBCT) and mindfulness-based stress reduction (MBSR) in people with physical and/or psychological conditions: A systematic review. *Clinical Psychology Review*, *55*, 74–91. https://doi.org/10.1016/j.cpr.2017.04.008.

American Psychiatric Association. (1994). *Diagnostic and statistical manual of mental disorders* (4th ed.).

American Psychiatric Association. (2013). *Diagnostic and Statistical Manual of Mental Disorders* (5th ed.).

Arce, L., & Serrano, I. (2023). Impact of childhood trauma on the epigenetics of anxiety disorder. *Archives of Clinical Psychiatry, 50*(6), 205.

Baldwin, D. S., Gordon, R., Abelli, M., & Pini, S. (2016). The separation of adult separation anxiety disorder. *CNS Spectrums, 21*(4), 289-294. https://doi.org/10.1017/S1092852916000080.

Beidel, D. C., & Alfano, C. A. (2011). *In Child Anxiety Disorders*. Routledge. https://doi.org/10.4324/9780203864258-6.

Benoit, D. (2004). Infant-parent attachment: Definition, types, antecedents, measurement and outcome. *Pediatrics & Child Health, 9*(8), 541–545. https://doi.org/10.1093/pch/9.8.541.

Blanco, C., Rubio, J., Wall, M., Wang, S., Jiu, C. J., & Kendler, K. S. (2014). Risk factors for anxiety disorders: common and specific effects in a national sample. *Depression and Anxiety, 31*(9), 756–764. https://doi.org/10.1002/da.22247.

Centers for Disease Control and Prevention (CDC). (2022, August 15). *What is epigenetics?* https://www.cdc.gov/genomics/disease/epigenetics.htm#:~:text=Epigenetics%20is%20the%20study%20of.

Center for Behavioral Health Statistics and Quality. (2016). 2014 National Survey on Drug Use *and Health: DSM-5 Changes: Implications for Child Serious Emotional Disturbance (unpublished internal documentation).* Substance Abuse and Mental Health Services Administration, Rockville, MD.

Cleveland Clinic. *Separation Anxiety Disorder in Children & Adults*. (n.d.). Retrieved April 19, 2024, from https://my.clevelandclinic.org/health/diseases/23142-separation-anxiety.

Costello, E. J. & Angold, A. (1995) Developmental epidemiology, In: *Manual of Developmental Psychopathology*, Cicchetti, D. & Cohen, D. (Eds.), Vol. I, pp. 23-56, Wiley, New York.

Cyranowski, J. M., Shear, M. K., Rucci, P., Fagiolini, A., Frank, E., Grochocinski, V. J., Kupfer, D. J., Banti, S., Armani, A., & Cassano, G. (2002). Adult separation anxiety: psychometric properties of a new structured clinical interview. *Journal of Psychiatric Research*, *36*(2), 77–86. https://doi.org/10.1016/s0022-3956(01)00051-6.

Dudaee-Faass, S., Marnane, C., & Wagner, R. (2009). Ambiguity in the manifestation of adult separation anxiety disorder occurring in complex anxiety presentations: two clinical case reports. *Clinical Psychologist*, *13*(3), 111–115. https://doi.org/10.1080/13284200903283774.

Ehrenreich, J. T., Santucci, L. C., & Weiner, C. L. (2008). Separation Anxiety Disorder In Youth: Phenomenology, Assessment, And Treatment. *Psicologia Conductual, 16*(3), 389–412. https://doi.org/10.1901/jaba.2008.16-389.

Feriante, J., Torrico, T. J., & Bernstein, B. (2024). Separation anxiety disorder. In *StatPearls*. StatPearls Publishing. http://www.ncbi.nlm.nih.gov/books/NBK560793/.

Florescu, S., Gureje, O., He, Y., Karam, E., Lepine, J.-P., Murphy, S., Kessler, R. C. (2015). World Mental Health Survey. *The American Journal of Psychiatry, 172(7*), 647-656. https://doi.org/10.1176/appi.ajp.2015.14091185,

Fonagy, P., & Luyten, P. (2009). A developmental, mentalization-based approach to the understanding and treatment of borderline personality disorder. *Developmental Psychopathology, 21*(1), 355–1381.

Goldstein-Piekarski, A. N., Williams, L. M., & Humphreys, K. (2016). A trans-diagnostic review of anxiety disorder comorbidity and the impact of multiple exclusion criteria on studying clinical outcomes in anxiety disorders. *Translational Psychiatry, 6*(6), e847. https://doi.org/10.1038/tp.2016.108,

Horowitz, M. J. (2015). Explanatory understanding in a single case of Separation Anxiety Syndrome. *Journal of the American Psychoanalytic Association*, *63*(5), 921–927. https://doi.org/10.1177/0003065115607492,

Hoven, C. W., Duarte, C. S., Wu, P., Erickson, E. A., Musa, G. J., & Mandell, D. J. (2004). Exposure to Trauma and Separation Anxiety in Children After the WTC attack.

Applied Developmental Science, 8(4), 172-183. https://doi.org/10.1207/s1532480xads0804_1,

Kessler, R. C., Petukhova, M., Sampson, N. A., Zaslavsky, A. M., & Wittchen, H.-U. (2012). Twelve-month and lifetime prevalence and lifetime morbid risk of anxiety and mood disorders in the United States. *International Journal of Methods in Psychiatric Research, 21*(3), 169-184. https://doi.org/10.1002/mpr.1359,

Kins, E., Soenens, B., & Beyers, W. (2013). Separation anxiety in families with emerging adults. *Journal of Family Psychology, 27*(3), 495–505. https://doi.org/10.1037/a0032869,

Lecrubier, Y., Sheehan, D., Weiller, E., Amorim, P., Bonora, I., Sheehan, K. H., Janavs, J., & Dunbar, G. (1997). The Mini International Neuropsychiatric Interview (mini). A short diagnostic structured interview: Reliability and validity according to the Cidi. *European Psychiatry, 12*(5), 224–231. https://doi.org/10.1016/s0924-9338(97)83296-8,

Manicavasagar, V., Silove, D., Wagner, R., & Drobny, J. (2003). A self-report questionnaire for measuring separation anxiety in adulthood. *Comprehensive Psychiatry, 44*(2), 146–153. https://doi.org/10.1053/comp.2003.50024,

Manicavasagar, V., & Silove, D. (2020). *Separation anxiety disorder in adults: Clinical features, diagnostic dilemmas and treatment guidelines*. Academic Press.

Manicavasagar, Vijaya, & Silove, D. (1997). Is there an adult form of separation anxiety disorder? A brief clinical report. *Australian & New Zealand Journal of Psychiatry, 31*(2), 299–303. https://doi.org/10.3109/00048679709073835,

Mattick, R. P., Andrews, G., Hadzi-Pavlovic, D., & Christensen, H. (1990). Treatment of panic and agoraphobia. *The Journal of Nervous and Mental Disease, 178*(9), 567–576. https://doi.org/10.1097/00005053-199009000-00003,

Milrod, B., Markowitz, J. C., Gerber, A. J., Cyranowski, J., Altemus, M., Shapiro, T., Hofer, M., & Glatt, C. (2014). Childhood separation anxiety and the pathogenesis and treatment of adult anxiety. *American Journal of Psychiatry, 171*(1), 34–43. https://doi.org/10.1176/appi.ajp.2013.13060781.

Murgatroyd, C., & Spengler, D. (2011). Epigenetics of early child development. *Frontiers in Psychiatry, 2*, 16. https://doi.org/10.3389/fpsyt.2011.00016,

National Library of Medicine (2016). *Table 15, DSM-IV to DSM-5 Separation anxiety disorder comparison*. Substance Abuse and Mental Health Services Administration (US). https://www.ncbi.nlm.nih.gov/books/NBK519712/table/ch3.t11/,

Nolte, T., Guiney, J., Fonagy, P., Mayes, L. C., & Luyten, P. (2011). Interpersonal stress regulation and the development of anxiety disorders: An attachment-based developmental framework. *Frontiers in Behavioral Neuroscience, 5*, 55. https://doi.org/10.3389/fnbeh.2011.00055,

Panos, P. T., Jackson, J. W., Hasan, O., & Panos, A. (2013). Meta-analysis and systematic review assessing the efficacy of dialectical behavior therapy (DBT). *Research on Social Work Practice, 24*(2), 213–223. https://doi.org/10.1177/1049731513503047,

Pini, S., Abelli, M., Shear, K. M., Cardini, A., Lari, L., Gesi, C., Muti, M., Calugi, S., Galderisi, S., Troisi, A., Bertolino, A., & Cassano, G. B. (2010). Frequency and clinical correlates of adult separation anxiety in a sample of 508 outpatients with mood and anxiety disorders. *Acta Psychiatrica Scandinavica, 122*(1), 40-46. https://doi.org/10.1111/j.1600-0447.2009.01480.x.

Purves, K. L., Coleman, J. R. I., Meier, S. M., Rayner, C., Davis, K. A. S., Cheesman, R., Bakvad-Hansen, M., Barglum, A. D., Wan Cho, S., Jargen Deckert, J., Gaspar, H. A., Bybjerg-Grauholm, J., Hettema, J. M., Hotopf, M., Hougaard, D., Habel, C., Kan, C., McIntosh, A. M., Mors, O., Eley, T. C. (2020). A major role for common genetic variation in anxiety disorders. *Molecular Psychiatry, 25*(12), 3292-3303. https://doi.org/10.1038/s41380-019-0559-1.

Rochester, J., & Baldwin, D. S. (2015). Adult separation anxiety disorder: accepted but little understood. *Human Psychopharmacology: Clinical and Experimental, 30*(1), 1–3. https://doi.org/10.1002/hup.2452.

Schneier, F. R., Moskow, D. M., Choo, T.-H., Galfalvy, H., Campeas, R., & Sanchez-Lacay, A. (2017). A randomized controlled pilot trial of Vilazodone for Adult Separation Anxiety Disorder. *Depression and Anxiety, 34*(12), 1085–1095. https://doi.org/10.1002/da.22693.

Sekhon, S., & Gupta, V. (2023). *Mood Disorder*. In *StatPearls*. StatPearls Publishing.

Shear, K. (2006). Prevalence and correlates of estimated DSM-IV child and adult separation anxiety disorder in the national comorbidity survey replication. *American Journal of Psychiatry, 163*(6), 1074. https://doi.org/10.1176/appi.ajp.163.6.1074.

Shear, K., Jin, R., Ruscio, A. M., Walters, E. E., & Kessler, R. C. (2006). Prevalence and correlates of estimated DSM-IV child and adult separation anxiety disorder in the National Comorbidity Survey Replication. *The American Journal of Psychiatry, 163*(6), 1074-1083. https://doi.org/10.1176/appi.ajp.163.6.1074.

Silove, D., & Rees, S. (2014). Separation anxiety disorder across the lifespan: DSM-5 lifts age restriction on diagnosis. *Asian Journal of Psychiatry, 11*, 98–101. https://doi.org/10.1016/j.ajp.2014.06.021.

Silove, D., Alonso, J., Bromet, E., Gruber, M., Sampson, N., Scott, K., Andrade, L., Benjet, C., Caldas de Almeida, J. M., De Girolamo, G., de Jonge, P., Demyttenaere, K., Fiestas, F., Florescu, S., Gureje, O., He, Y., Karam, E., Lepine, J. P., Murphy, S., Villa-Posada, J., Kessler, R. C. (2015). Pediatric-Onset and Adult-Onset Separation Anxiety Disorder Across Countries in the World Mental Health Survey. *The American Journal of Psychiatry, 172*(7), 647–656. https://doi.org/10.1176/appi.ajp.2015.14091185.

Silove, D., Manicavasagar, V., O'Connell, D., Blaszczynski, A., Wagner, R., & Henry, J. (1993). The Development of the Separation Anxiety Symptom Inventory (SASI). *Australian & New Zealand Journal of Psychiatry, 27*(3), 477–488. https://doi.org/10.3109/00048679309075806.

Telch, M. J., Brouillard, M., Telch, C. F., Agras, W. S., & Taylor, C. B. (1989). Role of cognitive appraisal in panic-related avoidance. *Behaviour Research and Therapy, 27*(4), 373–383. https://doi.org/10.1016/0005-7967(89)90007-7.

Waszczuk, M. A., Zavos, H. M., Gregory, A. M., & Eley, T. C. (2014). The phenotypic and genetic structure of depression and anxiety disorder symptoms in childhood, adolescence, and young adulthood. *JAMA Psychiatry, 71*(8), 905–916. https://doi.org/10.1001/jamapsychiatry.2014.655.

Index

B

C

D

E

F

G

H

I

M

T

V

W

Y